Pit Bulls For Dummies®

D0571992

Five-Minute Health Check

Keep an eye out for any of the following problems:

- **Mouth:** Red, bleeding, swollen, or discolored gums; loose or dirty teeth; ulcers of tongue or gums; bad breath
- **Eyes:** Squinting, discharge, cloudiness, discolored whites, unequal or unresponsive pupils
- **Ears:** Bad odor, redness, debris, crusted tips, head shaking or tilting, ear scratching
- **Nose:** Thick or colored discharge; crusted top
- **Feet:** Abrasions, split nails, swollen or misaligned toes
- **Anal region:** Redness, swelling, discharge; also scooting or licking the area
- **Skin:** Parasites, hair loss, crusts, red spots, lumps, sores
- **General:** Lameness, incoordination, asymmetry of muscles, weight change, swellings, mammary or testicular changes, discharge from penis or vulva, swollen abdomen, coughing, gagging, lethargy, increased aggression, black or bloody stool; changes in urine or urination, appetite, or water consumption

Normal Values

Respiration: 10-30 breaths per minute at rest

Pulse: 60-120 beats per minute at rest

Temperature: 101.5 to 102.5 degrees F

Capillary refill time: Less than 2 seconds

Gum color: Pink (not white, red, bluish, yellowish, or with tiny red spots)

Hydration: Skin should pop back into position within 3 seconds of being lifted.

Veterinarian's phone number: _____

After-hours or emergency-clinic phone number: _____

Pit Bulls For Dummies®

Emergency First Aid

Artificial Respiration:

1. Open and clear dog's mouth and pull the tongue forward.
2. Seal your mouth over the dog's mouth and nose and blow for two seconds. Repeat every four seconds.

CPR:

1. Place one hand on top of the other on the dog's left chest two inches up from and behind the elbow.
2. Press and release quickly about 100 times per minute.
3. Give two breaths into the nose every 15 compressions.

Obstructions: Wrap your hands around the abdomen behind the rib cage and compress briskly. If the dog is unconscious, pull its tongue forward and explore the throat.

Drowning: Hold the dog upside down so that water can run out; then give artificial respiration.

Bleeding: Cover the wound with clean dressing and apply pressure. Elevate the wound site and apply a cold pack.

Heat stroke: Wet the dog and place it in front of a fan. (Do not plunge the dog into ice water.) Offer water for drinking.

Bloat: Go to an emergency veterinarian immediately. No home treatment available.

Antifreeze ingestion: Go to an emergency veterinarian immediately. No home treatment available.

Rodent poisoning: Go to an emergency veterinarian immediately. No home treatment available.

For Dummies: Bestselling Book Series for Beginners

Pit Bulls

FOR

DUMMIES®

by D. Caroline Coile, Ph.D.

Wiley Publishing, Inc.

Pit Bulls For Dummies®

Published by
Wiley Publishing, Inc.
909 Third Avenue
New York, NY 10022
www.wiley.com

For general information on our other products and services or to obtain technical support, please contact our Customer Care Department within the U.S. at 800-762-2974, outside the U.S. at 317-572-3993, or fax 317-572-4002.

Wiley also publishes its books in a variety of electronic formats. Some content that appears in print may not be available in electronic books.

Library of Congress Cataloging-in-Publication Data:

Library of Congress Control Number: 00-110832

ISBN: 0-7645-5291-0

Manufactured in the United States of America

15 14 13 12 11 10 9

1B/RR/RQ/QS/IN

About the Author

D. Caroline Coile, Ph.D. has long been fascinated by dog breeds and their unique histories, functions, and capabilities. Her scientific research interests have focused on the physiology and sensory systems of dogs. She has shared her findings in over 100 scientific journal and dog magazine articles, and in 18 books about dogs. Her dog writing awards include the Dog Writer's Association of America Maxwell Award, Denlinger Award, and the Eukanuba Canine Health Award. Her own dogs include nationally ranked #1 dogs in obedience and conformation, and Best in Show, Best in Specialty Show, and Pedigree Award winners. They teach her something new about dogs every day.

Publisher's Acknowledgments

We're proud of this book; please send us your comments through our online registration form located at www.dummies.com/register.

Some of the people who helped bring this book to market include the following:

Acquisitions, Editorial, and Media Development

Senior Project Editor: Tim Gallan

Acquisitions Editor: Scott Prentzas

Copy Editors: Ben Nussbaum, Suzanna R. Thompson

Technical Editor: Lora Bauer

Editorial Manager: Pam Mourouzis

Media Development Manager: Laura Carpenter

Editorial Assistant: Carol Strickland

Cover Photos: Cydney Conger, Corbis Images

Illustrator: Barbara Frake

Photographer: Except where noted, all photos courtesy of Winter/Churchill@DOGPHOTO.COM.

Production

Project Coordinator: Nancee Reeves

Layout and Graphics: Jackie Nicholas, Jill Piscitelli, Julie Trippetti, Jeremey Unger

Proofreaders: John Bitter, Andy Hollandbeck, Susan Moritz, Angel Perez, York Production Services, Inc.

Indexer: York Production Services, Inc.

Publishing and Editorial for Consumer Dummies

Diane Graves Steele, Vice President and Publisher, Consumer Dummies

Joyce Pepple, Acquisitions Director, Consumer Dummies

Kristin A. Cocks, Product Development Director, Consumer Dummies

Michael Spring, Vice President and Publisher, Travel

Brice Gosnell, Publishing Director, Travel

Suzanne Jannetta, Editorial Director, Travel

Publishing for Technology Dummies

Richard Swadley, Vice President and Executive Group Publisher

Andy Cummings, Vice President and Publisher

Composition Services

Gerry Fahey, Vice President of Production Services

Debbie Stailey, Director of Composition Services

Contents at a Glance

Introduction 1

Part I: Tough Love 5
Chapter 1: Pitting and Petting: The Pit Bull's Past 7
Chapter 2: Sizing Up the Pit Bull 17
Chapter 3: Deciding If It's Bully for You 33
Chapter 4: Shopping the Bull Market 41

Part II: Your Pet Bull 51
Chapter 5: Pit Projects 53
Chapter 6: Living with Your Pit Bull 67

Part III: Good Bull! 85
Chapter 7: Coping with a Pit Bull Terrorist 87
Chapter 8: Training the Teacher's Pit 99
Chapter 9: Going Out to the Bull Games 115

Part IV: The Fit Pit 125
Chapter 10: Feeding a Bottomless Pit Bull 127
Chapter 11: Primping Your Pit Bull 135
Chapter 12: A Clean Bull of Health 149
Chapter 13: Sick as a Dog 165
Chapter 14: Pit Bull First Aid 179
Chapter 15: Staying Well Up in Years 189

Part V: The Part of Tens 195
Chapter 16: More Than Ten Pit Bull Resources 197
Chapter 17: Ten Ways to Help the Pit Bull's Reputation 201

Index 207

Cartoons at a Glance

By Rich Tennant

page 5

page 51

page 195

page 125

page 85

Cartoon Information:
Fax: 978-546-7747
E-Mail: richtennant@the5thwave.com
World Wide Web: www.the5thwave.com

Table of Contents

Introduction **1**

   Why You Need This Book 1

   How to Use This Book 2

   How This Book Is Organized 2

      Part I: Tough Love 2

      Part II: Your Pet Bull 3

      Part III: Good Bull! 3

      Part IV: The Fit Pit 3

      Part V: The Part of Tens 3

   Icons Used in This Book 4

   Where to Go from Here 4

Part 1: Tough Love **5**

Chapter 1: Pitting and Petting: The Pit Bull's Past **7**

   Creating Canine Gladiators 7

   Showing Off 10

   Becoming America's Sweetheart 13

   Overcoming Pride and Prejudice 14

Chapter 2: Sizing Up the Pit Bull **17**

   Toughing It Out 17

   Building a Better Bulldog 18

      The American Dog Breeder's

      Association standard 19

      The United Kennel Club standard 23

      The American Kennel Club standard for the American

      Staffordshire Terrier 25

   Strutting His Stuff 27

      UKC conformation shows 28

      AKC conformation shows 30

Chapter 3: Deciding If It's Bully for You **33**

   Making a Commitment 33

   Making the Match 35

   Getting to the Heart of the

      Matter (or Your Pit Bull) 37

   Brushing Up on the Law 39

Chapter 4: Shopping the Bull Market 41

Avoiding Bad Blood 41
Searching High and Low 42
    Classified information 42
    Kennel review 43
    To the rescue 45
Checking the Bona Fidos 45
    ADBA registration 46
    UKC registration 46
    AKC registration 47
Picking Your Pit 48

Part II: Your Pet Bull 51

Chapter 5: Pit Projects 53

Avoiding Dangerous Pitfalls 53
Fencing In Your Pit Bull 54
Providing a Cozy Doghouse 56
Lying Down with Dogs 56
    Bull dozers 57
    Crates can be great 57
    The bull pen 59
Making Bull Buys 59
    Pit Bulls, balls, and other toys 59
    Chewies for choosy Pit Bulls 61
    Bull bowls 62
    Collars for your Pit Bull 62
    A leash on life 64
    Brush up on grooming supplies 65
    The scoop on poop 65

Chapter 6: Living with Your Pit Bull 67

Acting Like a Pit Bull in a China Shop: House Rules 67
Taking the Pit Stop Outside 68
When the Plumbing's Broken 69
Trying Your Patience 70
Understanding Pit Talk 70
Becoming a Social Animal 73
Going to Kindergarten 75
Meeting the Children 75
Going for a Bull Run 77
Making a Splash 79
Hitting the Road 80
Finding a Pit-Sitter 82
Finding a Lost Love 83

Part III: Good Bull! *85*

Chapter 7: Coping with a Pit Bull Terrorist 87

Fighting Like Cats and Dogs 87
    Cats 87
    And dogs 88
Saving Your Home 91
Calming the Raging Bull 92
    All in good fun? 92
    Biting the hand that feeds 93
    Beware of dog 95
Plucking up Courage 96
Corralling the Escape Artist 97
Digging Up Some Dirt 98
Tales from the Bark Side 98

Chapter 8: Training the Teacher's Pit 99

Training Your Pit to Wag Her Tail 99
    Working for food 100
    Making ideas click quick 101
Getting the Timing Right 101
Following the Ten Commandments 102
    1. Thou shalt not live in the past 102
    2. Thou shalt not train your dog to be bad 102
    3. Thou shalt not confuse 103
    4. Thou shalt not speak in tongues 103
    5. Thou shalt not use force 103
    6. Thou shalt not hurt thy friend 103
    7. Thou shalt not beat a dead horse 103
    8. Thou shalt not end on a low note 104
    9. Thou shalt not go crazy 104
    10. Thou shalt not lose your patience 104
Going to School 104
Getting the Right Stuff 105
Starting Basic Training 106
    Coming to terms 106
    Sitting bull 108
    Staying power 109
    Learning ups and downs 111
    Walking well-heeled 111
Trying Every Trick in the Book 113

Chapter 9: Going Out to the Bull Games 115

Pulling His Weight . . . and More 115
    Training to pull 116
    ADBA weight pulling competition 117
    IWPA weight pulling competition 118

Staying in Step with Obedience 119
    Novice (U-CD) exercises 120
    Open (U-CDX) exercises 120
    Utility (U-UD) exercises 121
Overcoming Obstacles 121
Staying on Track 123
Getting a Grip on Schutzhund 123
Rounding Up a Herding Title 124

Part IV: The Fit Pit 125

Chapter 10: Feeding a Bottomless Pit Bull 127
Food For Thought 127
What about BARF? 130
Boning Up on Nutrition 131
    Eschewing the fat 132
    Skin and bones 133
Feeding Time 133
Terrier Perrier: Water for Your Dog 134

Chapter 11: Primping Your Pit Bull 135
Taking Your Pit to the Cleaners 135
Smelling Like a Rose 137
Debugging Your Dog 137
    Making fleas flee 137
    Ticking off ticks 139
    Managing mange 139
    Losing those lousy lice 140
Saving Your Dog's Skin 141
    Scratching the surface of allergic itching 141
    Pyoderma and impetigo 142
    Cooling down hot spots 142
Nailing Down Nail Care 142
Going in One Ear and Cleaning Out the Other 143
Keeping an Eye on the Bull's Eye 145
Keeping Your Dog Armed to the Teeth 147

Chapter 12: A Clean Bull of Health 149
Examining Your Pit Bull 149
    In the pink: Checking gums 151
    Checking body temperature 151
    Checking pulse, heartbeat, and breathing rate 152
The Good Doctor 152
Blood Tests 153
Medicine at Home 154

A Shot in the Bark: Vaccinations 156
    Puppy vaccinations 156
    Rabies 157
    Distemper 157
    Hepatitis 157
    Leptospirosis 158
    Parvovirus 158
    Coronavirus 158
    Tracheobronchitis (kennel cough) 158
    Lyme disease 159
Global Worming 159
    Ascarids 160
    Hookworms 161
    Whipworms 161
    Tapeworms 161
    More worms 162
Gut Feelings 163
    Coccidia 163
    Giardia 163
Heartworming Relationships 163

Chapter 13: Sick as a Dog **165**
Just Not Himself 165
Diarrhea 166
Vomiting 167
Coughing 168
Urinary Problems 169
Endocrine Disorders 170
    Hypothyroidism 170
    Cushing's syndrome 170
Immunological Problems 170
Blood Parasites 171
    Erlichiosis 171
    Babesia 171
Cancers 172
Lame but Game 172
    An arm and a leg 173
    From the hip 174
Doctoring Your Dog 175
    Holistic medicine 176
    Homeopathic medicine 176
    Herbology 176
    Chiropractic medicine 176
    Acupuncture 177
Home Remedies 177

Chapter 14 : Pit Bull First Aid **179**

ABCs of First Aid 181
Artificial respiration 182
CPR 182
Specific Emergencies 183
Poisoning 183
Seizures 185
Heat stroke 185
Hypothermia 186
Bleeding 186
Limb fractures 187
Bloat (gastric torsion, gastric dilatation-volvulus) 187
Insect stings and allergic reactions 187
Snakebite 188
Burns 188
Electrical shock 188

Chapter 15: Staying Well Up in Years **189**

Eat and Run 189
Act Your Age 191
When You've Done Everything 193
Eternally in Your Heart 194

Part V: The Part of Tens *195*

Chapter 16: More Than Ten Pit Bull Resources **197**

Chapter 17: Ten Ways to Help the Pit Bull's Reputation **201**

Putting Temperament to the Test 201
Earning a Citizenship 202
Heeling and Healing 202
Coming to the Rescue 202
Sniffing Out Trouble 203
Competing with the Best of Them 203
Organizing a Local Pit Bull Group 203
Setting an Example 203
Spreading the Word 204
Supporting the Cause 204

Index *207*

Introduction

●●●

*P*ull up a chair and spend some time with one of the most amazing, yet controversial, breeds to ever wag a tail. A breed of satin and steel, Pit Bulls are a mixture of softness and strength, an uncanny canine combination of fun, foolishness, and serious business, all wrapped up in love. If you ignore any of these ingredients you're cheating yourself, and your dog, of the best relationship possible. My aim with this book has been to include the same mixture. Parts of it will be fun, a few parts perhaps even foolish, and much of it serious — always with the aim of strengthening and lengthening the bond between you and dog, and ensuring the Pit Bull earns back its good name.

This is not a book meant to sit on your shelf as a collector's item. This book should have ragged pages and chewed covers, with dog hairs as bookmarks. It should have imprints of tiny puppy teeth and full grown paw prints marking the pages with your dog's progress through life, and when one day it comes time to place it back on the shelf with the last chapter christened with tears, you will have no regrets. You will have known that you and your dog shared a life of fun, foolishness, and love, all made possible because of some serious stuff. But for now, just make sure you don't get so immersed in reading that you forget to play with your dog!

The truth about Pit Bulls: If you've never been around one you might think they are bloodthirsty man-eaters on the prowl for their next meal. If you've lived with one you know they are, indeed, on the prowl for their next meal, but they plan to get it by conning you out of your dinner by doing something irresistibly cute!

Why You Need This Book

Whether this is the only dog book you'll have on your shelf, or whether your shelves are jammed with dog books, I wrote this book to be the one book you can count on when it comes to caring for and enjoying your Pit Bull. Too many dog care books are filled with unrealistic scare tactics that would cause anyone to just give up, and others are filled with hand-me-down dog lore that has no basis in reality. I did my best to make sure you won't find either of those in this book. If you want a Pit Bull book that will tell you how to fight your dog, look elsewhere. But if you want a Pit Bull book that will tell you how to love your dog, look here.

Who should read this book? The people who think Pit Bulls should be purged from the face of the earth, and especially the people who have allowed Pit Bulls to gain such a bad reputation by virtue of irresponsible breeding and irresponsible ownership. They need this book.

Who will read this book? The smart people who realize that all breeds have good and bad points, and that with sensible breeding, selection, and training you can get a Pit Bull that will be a joy to share your life with and a credit to its breed. Smart people who care enough to find out the best way to care for their dog, and who want to squeeze every ounce of fun and love into their relationship. These are the people who deserve a Pit Bull — and whom the Pit Bull deserves.

How to Use This Book

This book is a reference. The chapters are self-enclosed chunks of information that you can pretty much read in any order you wish. If you want to read the book from cover to cover, feel free, but if you just want to skip around and read the topics that interest you, be my guest. The detailed Table of Contents and the Index can help you find what you're looking for.

How This Book Is Organized

This book has 17 chapters divided into 5 parts. Here's what each part covers:

Part 1: Tough Love

Trace the origins and come to understand the forces that shaped the Pit Bull of today and why they threaten the Pit Bull of tomorrow. Familiarize yourself with the essentials of the Pit Bull physique and mystique, and finally, do some soul searching to decide if you are the right person for this breed. Once you've decided this is the breed for you, make sure you get the best dog for you. Be on the lookout for red flags and rip-offs, and be on the lookout for your new partner in adventure.

Part II: Your Pet Bull

You only get one chance to make a first impression. Here you'll find tips to get you through those difficult first days, hopefully saving your sanity, your carpets, and maybe even your pup's life. If you still have money burning a hole in your pocket, you won't when you get through buying all the stuff listed here, but you'll also get advice on what stuff you really need and what you can do without. This is the part of the book that deals with everyday life with a Pit Bull, and life with a Pit Bull every day.

Part III: Good Bull!

Dog training methods have undergone a revolution in the last few years and you can be the first on your block to train your dog the right way. Nonetheless, no matter how good a job you do, your dog is bound to develop a few bothersome behaviors — look here for the latest scientific ways of dealing with them. Pit Bulls are smart; make sure you channel their intelligence into productive activities. Your Adonis can strut in the show ring, your Einstein can shine in the obedience ring, or your Hercules can astound in the weight pulling arena — there's something for just about every Pit Bull!

Part IV: The Fit Pit

It's a little scary at first trying to decide what's normal, what's abnormal, and what's an emergency in an animal with a body so different from our own — especially when that animal can't even tell us where it hurts. Few dogs make it through life without ever getting sick or injured. You're the front line of defense when it comes to your dog's health, and this section will supply you with some formidable ammunition.

Part V: The Part of Tens

Every *For Dummies* book ends with top ten lists. I give you more than ten additional Pit Bull resources, and I offer ten ways to help improve the Pit Bull's reputation.

This book also has an appendix that explains Pit Bull terminology.

Icons Used in This Book

Throughout, the text, I use little pictures, called *icons,* to flag special bits of information. Here are what the icons represent:

Check this out for the most insidiously incorrect dogma dogging the dog world.

Just for fun: Some canine conundrums and quirky quotes.

For good, old-fashioned, helpful advice, look to this icon.

When there's a general concept that I don't want you to forget, I use this icon.

When presenting information that may protect you or your dog from harm, I give you this icon.

Where to Go from Here

If you're interested in the history of the Pit Bull breed, check out the first few chapters. Jump to part II if you need advice on choosing a Pit Bull. The rest of the book gives you the scoop on caring for and training your Pit Bull friend.

Part I
Tough Love

The 5th Wave   By Rich Tennant

PIT-BULLOON

"They're an easy breed to take care
of. Just keep them away from sharp
objects and make sure there's a sturdy
knot in their air hole."

In this part . . .

How do you design the most powerful body and spirit in the canine world? You don't. It has to evolve, forged by immense pressures. The Pit Bull evolved through generations of selection from a time when unspeakable cruelties against animals were considered entertainment, when dogs that did not deliver were scorned, and when those that turned against humans ended up dead. Yet those strong souls that emerged from this baptism of fire did so with love in their hearts and a twinkle in their eyes.

How do you know if the Pit Bull is your soul mate? You have to understand what its past means for its present — and future. No other breed has been asked to give so much, and no other breed has so ably answered the call. Now, no other breed is in such peril for its existence, discriminated against and even hated by those who don't take the time to really know it.

Chapter 1

Pitting and Petting: The Pit Bull's Past

In This Chapter

▶ Explaining the Pit Bull's origins

▶ Creating a distinct breed

▶ Going to the show ring

▶ Overcoming anti-Pit hostility

*P*erhaps no other dog breed has endured as many public misconceptions as has the Pit Bull. These misconceptions truly run the gamut: Although some people consider Pit Bulls to be the safest and gentlest companions, others regard them as evil enough to be Satan's understudies. Neither viewpoint is correct, but both have some basis in fact — and in the breed's controversial roots.

Creating Canine Gladiators

Dogs and humans around the world have long shared a special relationship — a relationship originally based on function. Early dogs who proved least useful — or who were too wild, skittish, or dumb — probably ended up in the cave man's pot, but the most helpful dogs (who were good at sounding alarms at intruders or at chasing down game) lived to produce others like them. Eventually, breed forerunners were created by breeding the best guards to the best guards and the best hunters to the best hunters. Of these, some strains proved to be especially brave and tough — valuable traits in a rough world.

Of course, these strains weren't really breeds. Few cave men had American Kennel Club or United Kennel Club papers for their dogs, so pure breeding wasn't terribly important to them. Still, with time the strains of dogs became more and more specialized. By classical Greek times, large fierce dogs called *Molossians* were so valued that Phoenician traders used them as bartering items. Because of this practice, the Molossian type was distributed along Phoenician shipping routes, some of which included stops in ancient Britain. The Molossians who ended up in Britain became further specialized and gave rise to the Mastiff family of dogs.

In Britain, Mastiffs were perfected as war dogs. When the Romans invaded Britain, they were so impressed by the Mastiff's warring ability that they brought some back to Rome. Romans valued entertainment, and the courageous dogs became infamous as gladiators who fought humans, bears, lions, bulls, and even each other in Rome's great Coliseum.

Rome was not, however, the only civilization to revel in blood sports. The British, too, placed high value on contests that featured animals fighting to the death. The spectacle of a dog killing a bull was the highest entertainment that most small villages could offer its poor inhabitants. But this kind of entertainment spanned all classes: By the 16th century, bull-, bear-, and even horse-baiting provided the finale for a royal evening of entertainment (for an explanation of bull-baiting, see the sidebar "Bull-baiting"). In the 17th century, the King even appointed a Master of the King's Games of Bears, Bulls, and Dogs.

The dogs' owners won prizes for their animals' spectacular performances, and the progeny of famous or particularly *game* dogs (meaning those dogs who refuse to quit the task at hand despite overwhelming adversity) were sought after and capable of bringing high prices. As distasteful as it sounds, these dogs produced the never-say-die stock from which today's Pit Bull claims her heritage.

An end to legal blood sports in England finally came about in 1835, but that only pushed the fans and gamblers to conduct covert matches. Staging a clandestine bull-baiting would have been difficult, but scheduling a dogfight in a barn, cellar, or back room without being discovered was quite simple.

Dog fighting favored a slightly smaller, more agile gladiator than the dogs who were adept at baiting larger animals. Most historians believe that the stocky bull-baiting dogs were crossed with the swift and agile terriers of the time to produce the aptly named Bull and Terrier, a relatively small, smart, agile, tough, and strong game dog the likes of which had never been seen before. Other breed historians contend that no such cross was made and point out that the Bulldog of the time, the Bullenbeisser, was, in fact, so similar to the modern Pit Bull that it was simply a matter of selecting the most successful fighters. Whatever the recipe, it worked.

As the Bulldogs or Bull and Terriers became known less for their bull-baiting skills and more for their fighting skills in the pits, they came to be known as Pit Bulldogs, or more simply, Pit Bulls.

Bull-baiting

Although the role of canine gladiator was the most visible job for the tough dogs of ancient Europe, it was far from their most important one. A subtype of Molossian dogs known as *Bullenbeissers* were valued for their ability to control unruly cattle, earning their keep as butcher's dogs. These dogs had to catch and grip escaping or uncooperative bulls on their way to market. The dog would hang on the bull's nose, gripping the nose without letting go until the butcher could regain control. A good butcher's dog could make the butcher's job easy; a bad dog could be killed by the bull. As with all people who depend on their dogs, butchers were proud of their best "bulldogs" and anxious to prove them better than the neighboring town butcher's dogs. So began the cruel practice of bull-baiting, in which a bull was tormented (sometimes for hours) not only for entertainment, but also in the mistaken belief that torturing the animal before killing it made its meat more tender. In fact, in some places selling meat from a bull that had not been baited was illegal.

Almost every town in England had a bull-baiting ring. One or two dogs were released, and they would attempt to grab the bull (which was usually chained to a stake) by the nose, often tormenting it for hours. The cruelties inflicted upon the poor animals (bulls and dogs alike) by people in the process were atrocious. In one well-known case, the owner of a dog demonstrated how courageous his dog was by cutting off each of her legs, one leg at a time, while she continued to drag herself to attack the bull. The dog was lost, but her offspring were in high demand.

The breed known today as the Bulldog or English Bulldog is not the same as the Bulldog of the eighteenth and nineteenth centuries. The earlier Bulldog strain is the ancestor of both the modern Pit Bull breeds and the modern Bulldog, but was more similar to today's Pit Bull than to today's Bulldog.

When English immigrants came to America, they brought with them their sport and their dogs. By the mid-1800s, dog fighting had a solid following in America. With the migration west, Bulldogs once again found themselves called upon to do the toughest jobs. They served as all-purpose farm and guard dogs, protecting families and stock from fierce wildlife, rampaging cattle, and marauding vermin. Many also served as hunting dogs, holding their own against bears, wolves, and on occasion, buffalo. Once again, the Bulldog underwent a metamorphosis — this time into a larger dog that could best serve these vital functions.

This variety of purpose is directly responsible for the great range in size of today's Pit Bulls. An example of one possible size is shown in Figure 1-1.

Figure 1-1:
Pit Bulls,
because
of their
toughness,
have been
asked
throughout
history to do
the tough
jobs.

Showing Off

In the late 1800s and early 1900s, purebred dog mania was sweeping Europe and America. Anything that looked like a pure breed — and could be paraded around a show ring — was fair game. The fighting dogs (now dubbed Pit Bulls) seemed unlikely show dogs, however, for they lacked the desired association with the upper echelons of society (any association the upper class would admit to, that is).

The American Kennel Club (AKC) was formed in 1884 to promote the interests of purebred dogs. It did so by maintaining a pedigree registry and by sponsoring performance and conformation competitions. *Performance competitions* were designed to test dogs at the function for which they were bred; for example, pointing breeds competed at pointing field trials. *Conformation competitions* were designed to compare dogs to the breed's standard of excellence, which in turn was written to describe a dog who was built to perform the job for which he was bred.

That the AKC was interested in promoting both the performance and the conformation of breeds was a problem because the job that the Pit Bull had been bred to perform was illegal. The AKC refused to endorse any aspect of dog fighting. And the old time Pit Bull fighting men weren't too interested in exchanging the excitement of the dog pit for a trot around the show ring.

Fighting words

Although dog fighting is illegal in the United States, it does occur — and it even has rules! Understanding how a traditional match was (and still is) conducted is — no matter how unsavory — essential to understanding the way Pit Bull breeding stock were selected for generations.

In the heat of battle, the dogs must discriminate between biting another dog and biting a human. Before a fight begins, each dog is washed by the opponent's handler to make sure that no drugs or toxic or foul-tasting substances are on the dog's coat. Otherwise the other dog would get the substances in his mouth. The dog is then dried and carried to his corner. During the fight, a referee and the two handlers remain in the ring with the dogs. The handlers sometimes kneel right beside the dogs; they are allowed to urge their dogs on but not to touch them. If a dog becomes "fanged" (that is, if its canine tooth pierces its lip), the handlers hold both dogs while the referee tries to push the tooth back through the lip with a stick or other utensil. The dogs are then released a few feet from each other.

True fighting dogs are eerily silent. Barking, growling, snarling, and showing teeth are threat displays that most dogs use in an attempt to discourage an opponent before a fight begins. Most dogs are more show than go, and fighting consists largely of bluffing the other dog into submission. Not so with a fighting Pit Bull. He is more likely to whine with excitement.

If one of the fighting dogs turns away from the other, the referee calls a "turn" and both handlers retrieve their dogs and take them back to their corners. The dog who turned is then released and expected to "scratch," meaning to cross the pit and attack the other dog within ten seconds. The dogs continue to take turns being released first every time one dog turns. The dog may crawl, stagger, or drag himself toward the other dog as long as he doesn't stop or hesitate. A dog who fails to scratch loses the match, and perhaps his life, as he is considered to lack gameness. A dog who is losing, but nonetheless attempts to scratch, might lose the match but may return to fight another day if his handler concedes the match.

Thus, an alternative registration body, called the United Kennel Club (UKC), was formed in 1898 to register Pit Bulls (and later, other breeds). The UKC, founded by Pit Bull owner Chauncy Bennett, emphasized function and included dog fighting as a legitimate function of Pit Bulls. To this day, the UKC remains a strong registry for many breeds — especially its banner breed, the American Pit Bull Terrier — but it no longer endorses dog fighting in any manner.

The UKC fancied up the breed's name by calling it the American (Pit) Bull Terrier, later changing the name to the now accepted American Pit Bull Terrier. As the breed's roots are mostly European, and the Pit Bull may or may not have terrier influences, the name is somewhat of a misnomer.

The first American (Pit) Bull Terrier to be registered with the UKC was Bennett's Ring, owned by UKC founder Chauncy Bennett.

Name that dog

A breed of many names, Pit Bulls have been called

- American Pit Bull Terriers
- American Bull Terriers
- American Staffordshire Terriers
- Brindle Bulldogs
- Bull and Terriers
- Bulldogs
- Half and Halfs

- Old Family Dogs (Ireland)
- Pit Bull Terriers
- Pit Dogs
- Pit Terriers
- Rebel Terriers
- Staffordshire Fighting Dogs
- Staffordshire Terriers
- Yankee Terriers

In 1909, Pit Bull proponents organized yet another registry, the American Dog Breeder's Association (ADBA). The ADBA registers only one breed: the American Pit Bull Terrier (APBT). The ADBA was traditionally the registry of fighting Pit Bulls. Although it no longer endorses dog fighting, it maintains that reputation. The ADBA instead now sponsors conformation shows and popular weight pulling contests.

Until the 1970s, neither the UKC nor the ADBA sponsored conformation shows. Yet, some Pit Bull fans wanted to try their dogs in the show ring. In 1936, Pit Bull fans who wanted to try their dogs in the show ring sacrificed the breed's name (which was unacceptable to the AKC because of its fighting connotation) and replaced it with another name: the Staffordshire Terrier. The AKC welcomed Staffordshire Terriers into its registry and show rings. This turn of events set up an unusual situation in the world of dogs. The same dog can be registered as an American Pit Bull Terrier with the UKC and the ADBA, and as an American Staffordshire Terrier (the *American* was added in 1972 to distinguish the breed from the Staffordshire Bull Terrier) with the AKC. Over the years, Pit Bull fanciers have tended to stick with one registry (and breed name) over the other.

Today, the APBT and the American Staffordshire Terrier (or *AmStaff*) have diverged somewhat. AmStaffs tend to be larger and more muscular than APBTs. ABPTs have a greater range in looks because APBT breeders traditionally breed for function in the fighting pit rather than for looks in the show ring. Although there is considerable overlap, in general, AmStaffs *look* tougher, but APBTs *are* tougher.

Becoming America's Sweetheart

In the early 20th century, Pit Bulls moved graciously from fame as pit fighters to fame as national symbols. The Pit Bull's reputation for courage and tenacity, combined with his good nature, made him a natural as the dog synonymous with the United States during World War I. A popular war poster of the period aptly captures the true Pit Bull outlook by showing a picture of a Pit Bull wearing an American flag bandana above the phrase "I'm neutral, but not afraid of any of them."

In fact, a Pit Bull (or Pit Bull mix — nobody knows for sure) named Stubby emerged from World War I as a national hero. Stubby was the unofficial mascot of the 102nd infantry, and when it came time to go overseas, the men smuggled him on board. Despite no training or experience in battle conditions, Stubby braved intense shelling to comfort wounded soldiers lying in the crossfire. He eventually participated in 18 major battles. Stubby repeatedly warned his regiment of incoming mortar shells and mustard gas attacks, and once he even prevented a spy from escaping. When Stubby was wounded, he played the role of therapy dog, cheering hospitalized soldiers. Even while recuperating in Paris, he was credited with saving a child from being run over.

Stubby was decorated by General Pershing, awarded the rank of honorary sergeant, and received by three presidents. He led more parades than any dog in history. Upon Stubby's death in 1926, his hide was mounted over a plaster form of his body, with an urn containing his ashes inside. He was displayed wearing a medal-covered coat, first at the Red Cross Museum and then at the Smithsonian Institute. Today, Stubby is largely forgotten, packed away in a crate in a back room of the Smithsonian.

The next Pit Bull to capture America's heart was Petey (officially registered as Lucenay's Pete) of *The Little Rascals* and *Our Gang* movie fame. Actually, Petey had already starred in several Buster Brown movies (as Tige) before becoming one of the most popular Rascals of all time. Whatever his role, Pete the Pup exemplified the Pit Bull in his role as the perfect buddy for any child, furthering the breed's appeal.

The Petey Papers

Like other Our Gang members, Petey's life and death is surrounded by rumors. Some reliable sources say that the original Petey was poisoned after about two years as a Little Rascal and replaced by another Pit Bull — explaining why Petey's painted-on circle around one eye switches sides partway through the series. Another piece of Petey trivia: He was the first Pit Bull to be both UKC and AKC registered.

Popular with families and welcomed throughout neighborhoods, the Pit Bull basked in his well-earned reputation as a fun-loving and patient member of the family (see Figure 1-2).

Figure 1-2:
These Pit pups would make great additions to any family.

Overcoming Pride and Prejudice

Dog breeds often wax and wane in popularity, and so it has been with the Pit Bull. After World War II, the Pit Bull gradually faded from the public eye and the family home. True devotees, however, remained as loyal to their dogs as their dogs were to them. Some of the breed remained as steadfast pets, others continued as game pit dogs — and many performed both roles admirably.

Dog fighting, although illegal, continued to be carried out with minimal interference from law enforcement until the 1970s, when the American Dog Owner's Association (ADOA) formed to lobby against dogfights. The ADOA was successful in bringing public attention to the pit — helping to push dog fighting into the shadows and propelling pit dogs into an unflattering limelight.

As with many well-intentioned laws, some unforeseen problems accompanied the crackdown on dog fighting. Dog fighting continued; it just went underground. Its illegal nature attracted patrons whose major area of knowledge was in pay-offs and threats, not Pit Bulls. Knowledgeable *dogmen* (the term for serious breeders of fighting Pit Bulls) could no longer distribute information about training methods, leaving newcomers to dog fighting — who often believed scare tactic propaganda — to experiment using cruel practices. They trained the dogs with stolen puppies and dogs in an attempt to encourage them to kill, fed them gunpowder in an attempt to make them mean, and hired strangers to beat the dogs with clubs in an attempt to make them aggressive to strangers. Not surprisingly, their dogs seldom succeeded at matches, and they were often discarded. The harm done to these dogs made them difficult to place as pets, and the harm done to the breed's reputation was immeasurable.

A certain segment of the population has always wanted to have the toughest dog on the block. Various breeds have filled these shoes throughout the years, and in the early 1980s the Pit Bull was the "tough guy" poster dog.

People who think the Pit Bull makes the ultimate macho dog don't understand the innate nature of the breed or the training the breed requires. In the quest for a bigger, badder dog, these people encourage indiscriminate aggression and even cross their dogs with larger, more aggressive breeds. The combination of bad breeding and bad training has led to instances of dog aggression that have resulted in human deaths and a media mob scene.

Because Pit Bull attacks make great stories (and because most reporters are not dog authorities), virtually every dog attack is labeled a Pit Bull attack — even if the only resemblance the perpetrator has to a Pit Bull is four legs and big teeth. The publicity has caused a public outcry from citizens who are convinced that these "killer" dogs need to be purged from society.

Legislators have been quick to jump on the bandwagon, and breed-specific ordinances banning Pit Bulls have been passed in certain communities. As these bans have begun to include other dog breeds, many dog lovers have joined Pit Bull fanciers in urging that breed-specific legislation is not only unfair, but it is less effective than laws that target irresponsible dog owners or vicious dogs in general, regardless of breed. Most breed-specific legislation has been repealed, but the struggle continues today.

The struggle is brought home whenever a Pit Bull trots politely alongside his owner, only to be met by parents who grab their children and scurry away. Pit Bull owners face a daily challenge from people who label the dogs as vicious on sight, insurance companies that refuse to cover owners of Pit Bulls, and even other Pit Bull owners who seem intent on undoing all the goodwill the responsible owners have created.

Good sports

Although illegal pit fighting still exists, Pit Bulls can legitimately compete in conformation, obedience, agility, and weight pulling competitions, and they are proving themselves helpful as boar hunters, search and rescue dogs, therapy dogs, and most of all, companions.

Owning a Pit Bull isn't easy, but that's not because of the dogs. A special commitment to the breed and a special dog owner are needed. Pit Bulls are pretty special dogs, and they have to prove it every day (see Figure 1-3).

Figure 1-3:
This sort of companion-ship is worth the effort.

Chapter 2

Sizing Up the Pit Bull

• •

In This Chapter

▶ Visualizing the ideal Pit Bull

▶ Sizing up your dog — ADBA-, UKC-, and AKC-style

• •

You wouldn't hire a Sumo wrestler to moonlight as a trapeze artist, and you wouldn't ask a ballet dancer to do double duty as a weightlifter. Different body types excel at different athletic endeavors. It's no accident that Pit Bulls look like Pit Bulls. They look like they do because they are built a certain way to do a certain job.

But looks aren't everything. The best-looking Pit Bull would, historically at least, be a dead Pit Bull if he lacked the intelligence, agility, and gameness required to make it through a match. Although most Pit Bulls today will never see a fighting pit (and will probably never so much as have a cross word with another dog), they carry with them a heritage of physical and mental characteristics that were once essential for their ancestors' survival.

Now that most Pit Bulls are no longer subject to such an unforgiving means of selecting breeding stock as pit fighting or bull-baiting, how do we ensure that the very essence of this noble breed is not lost for posterity? We do the best we can by breeding them according to a standard of perfection that — as nearly as possible — aspires to the ideal vision of a successful fighting Pit Bull.

Toughing It Out

Because dog fighting is no longer condoned in our society, the Pit Bull is among those breeds that can no longer prove its merit by performance. This doesn't mean that the Pit Bull will die out, nor does it mean that we should let it. The Pit Bull is a noble breed, a breed that provides a unique link to our own heritage (see Figure 2-1). As such, it is a sort of living antique — one that must be recreated with every generation. We can look to the fighters of the past as models by which to judge the Pit Bulls of today and by which to create the Pit Bulls of tomorrow.

Figure 2-1:
You can't
deny the
noble look
of this dog.

What did it take to win a dogfight? For the most part, it took intangible character qualities like gameness and attitude. In addition, it took wrestling ability, biting ability, and stamina — qualities based (at least in part) on the way the dog is built. Because a fighting dog is more likely to overcome shortcomings in build rather than shortcomings in character, the physique of winning fighters varied greatly from one dog to another. Nonetheless, the best of the fighters combined strong characters with strong bodies, and it is from these dogs that the ideals are drawn.

Building a Better Bulldog

The standards of the ADBA and the UKC for the American Pit Bull Terrier differ in many respects. In turn, the standard of the AKC for the American Staffordshire Terrier differs from those of the ADBA and the UKC. Yet each organization describes a dog who is built to win — and a good dog should be a good dog, no matter by which standard he is judged.

The American Dog Breeder's Association standard

The ADBA standard was written by experienced dogmen who realized that it was impossible to define the physical traits that make a dog a good fighter. Rather than try to describe every part of the dog, as do most breed standards, they focused their descriptions on those physical characteristics that they felt related the most to fighting ability, while ignoring those they felt to have little or no relationship. Thus it is less a standard of perfection than it is a checklist for evaluating a potential fighting dog.

The American Pit Bull Terrier is judged on a basis of 100 points (100 points equaling the ideal dog) that are broken down as follows:

Category	Point Value	Criteria
Overall appearance	20 points	Health, height-to-weight ratio, overall body shape
Attitude	10 points	Alertness, carriage
Head and neck	15 points	Eyes, size and shape of head and neck, teeth
Front end	20 points	Chest, front legs, ribs, shoulders
Back end	30 points	Back legs and feet, loin, hip, hock, set of tail, stifle
Tail and coat	5 points	Gloss and length of coat, length and shape of tail

The ADBA standard uses some terms that may be confusing. For example, *Bulldog* refers to the Pit Bull. *Dibo bred* refers to a particular well-known strain of Pit Bulls. A *nose-fighter* is a dog who tends to grip his opponent's nose; an *ear-fighter* is one who tends to grab the other dog's ear. *Fanging* refers to the case in which a dog bites through his own lip, getting his fang stuck in it, in the course of a fight.

The ADBA standard (with a few more of my definitions interspersed):

1. **Look at the overall profile of your dog.**

   Ideally, he should be square — that is, he should be about as long from the point of the shoulder to the point of the hip as he is from the top of the shoulder to the ground. A square dog will stand high and have maximum leverage for his weight. This means that — when standing normally with the hock slightly back of the hip — the dog's base (where his feet are) will be slightly longer than his height. Use the dog's hip and shoulder as guides to keep from being fooled by the way he is standing.

Your dog's height to weight ratio is critical. Because dogs were fought at nearly identical weights, the bigger your dog was at his weight, the better were your chances of winning. Stocky dogs with long bodies, heavy shoulders, and thick legs usually lost to taller, rangier opponents.

A tall, rangy dog is usually blessed with a fairly long neck. This is a tremendous advantage in a fight because it enables him to reach his opponent's stifle when the other dog has his front leg, to take his shorter-necked opponent's ear and hold him off, or to reach his opponent's chest when the other dog is trying to hold him off. Ideally, your dog's neck should be heavily muscled right up to the base of the skull.

The *point of shoulder* is the front of the joint between the shoulder blade (scapula) and upper arm (humerus), situated at the foremost part of the dog's body. The *point of hip* is at the rearmost part of the dog's butt.

2. **Look at your dog's back end — that's the drivetrain of any four-legged animal.**

A dog does 80 percent of his work off his hips and back legs. A long, sloping hip is most important. By its very length, it gives leverage to the thighbone (or femur). A long hip will give the dog a slightly roach-backed appearance (hence the low set tail so often spoken of). The hip should also be broad. A broad hip carries with it a broad loin and permits a large surface for the attachments of the gluteal muscles and the biceps femoris muscles, the biggest drivers in the powertrain.

The upper thighbone should be shorter than the lower leg bone (or tibia), with the stifle joint located in the upper third of the hind leg. Dogs with a low stifle are not uncommon. Although these dogs are usually impressively muscled because of their bigger biceps femoris, they are surprisingly weak and slow on their back legs because leverage is lost by a long thigh. A short upper thighbone and a long lower leg bone usually mean a well-bent stifle, which in turn leads to a well-bent hock.

A well-bent hock is critical to good wrestling ability. When a dog finds himself being driven backward, he must rely on the natural springiness of his well-bent hock and stifle to control his movement. Dogs with a straight hock (or the frequently seen double-jointed hock of many of the Dibo bred dogs) will wrestle well as long as muscle power can sustain them, but, if pushed, they will tire more quickly in the back end and will soon lose their wrestling ability.

The *stifle* is the knee of the hind legs, located at the junction of the upper thigh (femur) and second thigh (tibia and fibula). A *roach back* refers to a back that is arched dramatically upward. The *hock* is anatomically comparable to the human ankle, although dogs walk on their tiptoes all the time. The *gluteal*

muscle is the muscle just behind and below the front crest of the pelvis; the *biceps femoris* is the huge muscle making up the bulk of the upper thigh.

3. **Look at your dog's front end.**

   He should have a deep rib cage, well-sprung at the top but tapering to the bottom. An elliptical — almost narrow — chest is preferable to a round, or barrel, chest. The rib cage houses the lungs, which are not storage tanks but pumps. The ribs are like a bellows, and their efficiency relates to the difference in volume between contractions and expansions. A barrel-chested dog, in addition to carrying more weight for his height, has an air pump with a short stroke. He must take more breaths to get the same volume of air as a dog with a deeper rib cage (which has more room for large lungs).

   At the eighth rib, the shoulders should be a little wider than the rib cage. Too narrow a shoulder does not support adequate musculature, but too wide a shoulder makes a dog slow and adds unnecessary weight. The shoulder blade should be at a 45 degree (or less) angle to the ground, and it should be broad and flat. The upper arm should be at an equal angle in the opposite direction, and it should be long enough that the elbow comes below the bottom of the rib cage. The elbows should lie flat, and the upper arm should run almost parallel to the spine (not jut out at the elbows, which can give the appearance of a wide English Bulldog stance and makes a dog more prone to fractures and dislocations).

   The forearm should be only slightly longer than the upper arm, and it should be heavy and solid — nearly twice the thickness of the metatarsal bones at the hock. The front legs and shoulders must be capable of sustaining tremendous punishment, so heaviness can be an asset here. The relationship between front and back legs should be, at first appearance, of a heavy front and a delicate back. In an athletic dog, the metatarsal bones, the hock, and the lower part of the lower leg bone will be light, fine, and springy. The front legs will be heavy and solid-looking. The experienced Bulldog man, however, will note the wide hip, loin, and powerful thigh, which make the back end the most muscular.

The *metatarsal bones* are the bones leading from the toes to the second thigh, comparable to those of the human foot. The *loin* is the area just in front of the hips, over the abdominal area.

4. **Look at your dog's head.**

   The head varies more than any other part of the body in the present day Pit Bull — probably because his head's conformation has the least to do with whether he wins or loses. Certain attributes, however, do appear to be of advantage. First of all, consider the overall size of your dog's head. A head that is too large simply carries more weight and increases the dog's chances of having to fight a bigger dog. A head that is too small is easily punished by a nose fighter and is especially easy for an ear fighter to shake. In an otherwise well-proportioned dog, the head will appear to be about two-thirds the width of the shoulders, and about 25 percent wider at the cheeks than the neck at the base of the skull. The distance from the back of the head to the stop should be about the same as that from the stop to the tip of the nose. The bridge of the nose should be well developed, making the area directly under the eyes considerably wider than the area at the base of the ears.

The depth from the top of the head to the bottom of the jaw is also important. The jaw is closed by the temporal fossa muscle exerting pressure on the coronoid process. The deeper the head is at this point (that is, between the zygomatic arch and the angular process of the bottom of the jaw), the more likely the dog is to have leverage advantage both in closing the jaw and in keeping it closed. A straight, boxlike muzzle and a well-developed mandible will not have much to do with biting power but will endure more punishment. "Lippy" dogs are continually fanging themselves in a fight, much to their disadvantage. The dog's teeth should meet in the front, but more importantly the canines (or fangs) should slip tightly together, the upper behind the lower when the mouth is closed. Fangs should be wide at the gumline, taper to the end, and be sound and healthy (with none of them missing). The dog's eyes should be small and deep-set — elliptical when viewed from the front and triangular when viewed from the side. In general, the ideal head is wedge-shaped when viewed from the top or from the side, and round when viewed from the front.

The *stop* is the transition point (when viewed in profile) between the muzzle and the back of the skull. The *zygomatic arch* is the flare of bone that runs just below the lower margin of the eyes, essentially the widest bony part of the face. The *coronoid process* is the rear part of the lower jaw (the mandible) that extends upward under the zygomatic arch and has a broad area for muscle attachment. The *angular process* is the very rearmost part of the lower jaw that you can feel. *Lippy* means that the dog has loose or pendulous lips.

5. Look at your dog's appearance.

The coat can be any color or any combination of colors. It should be short and bristled. The gloss of the coat usually reflects the health of the dog and is important to an athletic American Pit Bull Terrier.

The skin should be thick and loose, but it should not fall in folds. It should appear to fit the dog tightly everywhere except around the neck and chest. Here, the skin should be loose enough to show vertical folds — even in a well-conditioned dog.

The set of the tail is also very important. It should be low, and the length should come just above the point of the hock. The tail should be thick at its base and taper to a point at the end, hanging down like a pump handle when relaxed.

The feet should be small and set high on the pasterns. The dog's gait should be light and springy.

Jaws

A popular myth is that Pit Bulls have locking jaws with 1,600 pounds per square inch biting pressure. The anatomy of the Pit Bull's jaw and skull is no different than that of any other breed. Yes, the skull is wide and the muscles well developed, but no mechanism exists that would allow the jaws to lock in place. Besides, how would the dogs eat? As for their strength, Pit Bulls do have strong jaws, but accurately measuring biting pressure in dogs is impossible — and no scientific comparisons of jaw strength have been published. With any strong dog, it's not so much the strength of the bite as it is the intentions and the determination of the dog that decide how serious a bite is.

6. Finally, look at your dog's musculature.

When you look at muscles from a breeder's standpoint, it is much more important to look at the genetic features of musculature than at those features that result from conditioning. A genetically powerful dog can be a winner in the hands of even an inept owner, but a genetically weak dog needs a good matchmaker to win — conditioning alone won't do much for him.

Imagine the bones as levers with the joints as the fulcrum and the muscles as the power source. The power being applied to the lever is more effective the farther away it is from the fulcrum. In the same way, muscles should be long, with attachments deep down on the bone and well past the joint. Short-muscled dogs are impressive looking, but they are not athletic. A muscle's power value lies in its ability to contract. The greater the difference between a muscle's relaxed state and its contracted state, the greater its power.

Above all, the American Pit Bull Terrier is an all-around athlete. His body is called on for speed, power, agility, and stamina. He must be balanced in all directions: Too much of one thing robs him of another. He is not an entity formed according to human specialists. In his winning form, he is a fighting machine — a thing of beauty.

The United Kennel Club standard

General appearance, personality, and obedience, 20 points

Head, muzzle, eyes, and ears, 25 points

✔ **Head.** Should be of medium length and bricklike in shape. The skull should be flat and widest at the ears, with prominent cheeks free from wrinkles.

- ✔ **Muzzle.** Should be square, wide, and deep. Jaws should be pronounced, displaying strength. Upper teeth should meet tightly over lower teeth, outside in front.

- ✔ **Eyes.** Should be round and set far apart, low down on the skull. Any color is acceptable.

- ✔ **Ears.** May be cropped or uncropped. Should set high on the head and be free from wrinkles.

- ✔ **Nose.** Nostrils should be wide and open. Any color is acceptable.

Body, 15 points

- ✔ **Back.** Should be short and strong. Should slope slightly from the withers to the rump. Should also be slightly arched at the loins, which should be slightly tucked.

- ✔ **Weight.** Not important. Females are preferred to weigh from 30 to 50 pounds. The preferred weight for males is from 35 to 60 pounds.

Legs and feet, 15 points

- ✔ **Legs.** Should be large and round-boned, with straight and upright pasterns. Should be reasonably strong. Feet should be of medium size. Gait should be light and springy. Dogs should not roll or pace.

- ✔ **Thigh.** Should be long with developed muscles. Hocks should be down and straight.

Neck, shoulder, and chest, 15 points

- ✔ **Neck.** Should be muscular and slightly arched. Should taper from the shoulder to the head. Skin should not be loose.

- ✔ **Shoulders.** Should be strong and muscular, with wide and sloping shoulder blades.

- ✔ **Chest.** Should be deep (but not too broad) with wide-sprung ribs.

- ✔ **Ribs.** Should be close and well-sprung, with deep back ribs.

Tail, coat, and color, 10 points

- ✔ **Tail.** Should be short in comparison to the dog's size. Should be set low and taper to a fine point. The tail should not be carried over the back. A bobbed tail is not acceptable.

- ✔ **Coat.** Should be glossy, short, and feel stiff to the touch.

- ✔ **Color.** Any color or marking is acceptable.

A nose of a different color . . .

Some people put great stock in what nose color their Pit Bull has. The color of the nose (red versus black) is determined by a gene that has nothing to do with the quality of the dog. A red nose occurs when a dog has two copies of the recessive b gene; such dogs are unable to produce black pigmentation in their skin or hair.

Breeders can fairly easily introduce the gene into or purge the gene from a bloodline without affecting other characteristics. Some very good bloodlines are known for their red-nosed dogs, but some just-as-good bloodlines have black-nosed dogs. It's all a matter of personal preference.

The American Kennel Club standard for the American Staffordshire Terrier

General Impression.

Should give the impression of great strength for his size. The dog should be well put-together — muscular, but agile and graceful — and keenly alive to his surroundings. He should be stocky — not long-legged or racy in outline. His courage is proverbial.

Head.

Should be of medium length, deep through. The dog should have a broad skull, with very pronounced cheek muscles and a distinct stop.

- ✔ **Ears.** Should be set high on the head. May be cropped or uncropped; the latter is preferred. Uncropped ears should be short and held rose or half prick. A full drop is penalized.

- ✔ **Eyes.** Should be dark and round, low down in the skull, and set far apart. They should not have pink eyelids.

- ✔ **Muzzle.** Should be of medium length and rounded on the upper side to fall away abruptly below the eyes. The jaws should be well-defined. The underjaw should be strong and have biting power. The lips should be close and even, showing no looseness. The upper teeth should meet tightly outside the lower teeth in front. The nose should be black.

Rose ears are folded back, similar to a Greyhound's ears. *Half prick ears* are erect at their base and then tip forward, similar to a Fox Terrier's. *Full drop ears* hang down, similar to a Beagle's.

Neck.

Should be heavy and slightly arched, tapering from the shoulders to the back of the skull. The skin should not be loose, and the neck should be of medium length.

Shoulders.

Should be strong and muscular, with wide and sloping blades.

Back.

Should be fairly short. Should slope lightly from the withers to the rump, with a gentle, short slope at the rump to the base of the tail. The loins should be slightly tucked.

Body.

The ribs should be well-sprung, deep in the rear, and close together. The forelegs should be set rather wide apart to permit chest development. The chest should be deep and broad.

Tail.

Should be short in comparison to the dog's size. Should be low set and taper to a fine point. Should not be curled or held over the dog's back. Not docked.

Legs.

The front legs should be straight, with large or round bones, and the pasterns should be upright. There should be no evidence of bend in front. The hindquarters should be well-muscled, let down at hocks, and turn neither in nor out. The feet should be of moderate size, well-arched, and compact. The dog's gait must be springy, but the dog should not roll or pace.

Coat.

Should be short, close, glossy, and stiff to the touch.

Color.

May be of any color. A solid, parti-colored, or patchwork coat is permissible, but an all-white (more than 80 percent white), black and tan, or liver-colored coat is not encouraged.

Size.

The dog's height and weight should be in proportion with each other. A height of about 18 to 19 inches at the shoulders for males and 17 to 18 inches for females is preferable.

Faults.

In a competition, faults are characteristics that are penalized. They include the following:

- ✔ A Dudley nose
- ✔ Light or pink eyes
- ✔ A tail that is too long or badly carried
- ✔ An undershot or overshot mouth

A *Dudley nose* means a flesh-colored nose.

Strutting His Stuff

Although many of the traits that make a good fighting dog are intangible, some physical traits are associated with fighting skill. Conformation shows provide a venue in which the physical characteristics that have been correlated with fighting ability can be evaluated. The idea is that the dog who is built the best — that is, most conforms to the standard of perfection — should be able to function the best.

Conformation shows provide one means of preserving the breed when the original job of the breed is no longer available. They do have a drawback, however. The truth is, that no matter how good the standard, you can't absolutely predict function from form. You can't evaluate the gameness, strength, endurance, or intelligence of a dog from his appearance. Some breeders fear that if Pit Bulls are bred to be show dogs, they will become caricatures of the breed. Responsible breeders use conformation shows as only one of several means of evaluating their dogs, also testing their dogs in obedience, weight pulling, and other functional competitions.

Both the UKC and the ADBA offer conformation competition for APBTs; the AKC offers classes for American Staffordshire Terriers. Because AmStaffs have had a big headstart in breeding for conformation, AmStaffs tend to win over APBTs when entered against each other in conformation shows. Remember, your dog needs to be registered with the particular organization that sponsors the shows you wish to enter. See Chapter 4 to check if your dog is eligible for AKC, UKC, or ADBA registration.

The Pit Bull's build reflects his athletic heritage (see Figure 2-2). At conformation shows, judges evaluate how well each dog conforms to the physical standard of perfection, both while standing and moving. They provide a means for preserving the breed without resorting to fighting. But you can't just show up and expect to start lugging home silver trophies, no matter how sterling your Pit Bull is.

Figure 2-2:
A natural
athlete.

Most local kennel clubs offer handling classes, in which you can learn the fundamentals of showing. Many also have occasional *match shows* — basically practice shows (even the judges are just practicing). Although match shows are usually AKC oriented, you can usually enter your American Pit Bull Terrier (APBT) as an American Staffordshire Terrier (AmStaff). Registration papers are seldom required. Don't take a match win or loss too seriously, and at any competition, no matter how obviously feebleminded the judge is, keep your opinion to yourself.

UKC conformation shows

Shows sponsored by the UKC offer the following classes:

- **Puppy:** For dogs 6 months to under 1 year of age.

- **Junior:** For dogs 1 year to under 2 years of age.

- **Senior:** For dogs 2 years to under 3 years of age.

- **Veteran:** For dogs 3 years of age and over.

- **Breeder-Handler:** For dogs over 6 months handled in the ring by that dog's breeder or a member of the breeder's immediate family

All the males are shown first. Class winners are awarded 10 points toward their Championship and then compete within their sex for Best Male of Show (worth another 15 points). Then all the females are shown, and a Best Female of Show is awarded. Best Male and Female of Show then compete for Best of Winners (worth another 10 points). This is followed by the Champion of Champions class, in which male and female Pit Bulls who have already earned a UKC Champion title compete, and then by the Grand Champion class, in which only male and female Pit Bulls who have already earned a UKC Grand Champion title compete. Finally, the Best of Winners, the Champion of Champions winner, and the Grand Champion winner compete for the Best of Breed.

It's all about the points. To become a UKC Show Champion, your Pit Bull must win 100 UKC championship points, awarded by three different judges, and win either a Best Male or Best Female of Show. Because it's possible to win points even if a dog is the only one in his class, a further requirement is that at least two of the wins must be over competition. A Grand Championship is earned by beating other Pit Bull champions (in the Champion of Champions class) in at least five shows under at least three different judges. Grand Champions compete against each other in the Grand Champion class.

The official UKC breed club, the National American Pit Bull Terrier Association, can hold a special National Grand Champion class at their fall National show, in which Grand Champions compete. The winner of this competition is declared the National Grand Champion and awarded the NTL GR CH title as part of his name.

What if you want to enter a UKC show but you haven't had a chance to register your dog? You can get a Temporary Listing from the UKC if your dog is not registered by calling the UKC at 616-343-9020 (and paying by credit card).

If you've spent any time around other dog breeds, you probably know that the AKC is the breed registry that governs most conformation dog shows in the United States. American Staffordshire Terriers are one of almost 150 breeds seen at a typical AKC show. Only a few UKC shows are for all UKC breeds, however; most UKC shows are for one or perhaps a handful of the most popular UKC breeds. Pit Bulls are one of the UKC's most popular breeds, and a large percentage of UKC shows have classes for American Pit Bull Terriers. Due to the unique history of the Pit Bull, the UKC governs most shows in which Pit Bulls compete.

Some ways in which UKC shows differ from AKC shows include

✔ **No grooming in the ring.** Grooming is not allowed in the ring. This means no brushes, cloths, or spray bottles.

✔ **No using gizmos to get your dog's attention.** You can't use squeakers, food, keys, or other artificial means of getting your dog's attention. You're allowed just your voice and your fingers.

✔ **No professional handlers are allowed in the ring.** In AKC shows, many top dogs are handled by slick pros instead of their owners.

These rules help focus the judge's attention on the dog's structure rather than on the handler's ability. Dogs in a UKC show are shown in a more natural manner than are those in an AKC show. That doesn't mean that you can just show up with an untrained dog and expect to start lugging home ribbons. Your dog will need to know how to stand still in a show pose. For the Pit Bull, this means that the front legs are perpendicular to the ground and parallel to one another, with the feet facing forward. The hocks of the rear legs are perpendicular to the ground and parallel to one another, and the feet face forward. The dog should stand straight up on his toes, and may lean slightly forward. His head should be held high. The judge will need to examine his body, so he will need to hold his pose while allowing a stranger to touch him all over. He can act neither shy nor aggressive toward the judge. He will also need to trot in a straight line at your side, neither balking, lunging, nor galloping.

AKC conformation shows

Only AKC registered American Staffordshire Terriers can participate in AKC conformation shows. AKC shows are typically larger and more hectic than UKC or ADBA shows, in part because of all the different breeds also competing.

AKC offers the following classes:

- **Puppy.** For dogs 6 months to under 12 months of age. This is often divided into a 6 to 9 month class and a 9 to 12 month class.

- **12 to 18 months.** For dogs 12 months to under 18 months of age.

- **Novice.** For dogs who have not won more than a limited number of first place awards in certain classes (the exact number depends on which class the dog's in).

- **Bred by Exhibitor.** For dogs bred, owned, and handled by the same person or an immediate family.

- **American Bred.** For dogs bred in the United States.

- **Open.** For all dogs over 6 months of age.

- **Best of Breed.** For AKC Champions (males and females compete against each other).

Except for Best of Breed, male dogs compete in all their classes first. Each class winner then competes for Winners Dog. Then the female classes are held and the winners compete for Winners Bitch. Both Winners Dog and Winners Bitch then compete against each other for Best of Winners and against the champions for Best of Breed. The best AmStaff of the opposite sex to the male or female AmStaff selected Best of Breed is awarded the Best of Opposite Sex award.

Since most AKC shows are open to all AKC breeds, they usually have further competition. Every Best of Breed winner in the Terrier group competes against each other, and the winners of all seven AKC groups (Sporting, Hound, Working, Terrier, Toy, Non-sporting, and Herding) ultimately compete for Best in Show.

An AKC Championship is earned by winning 15 points. Points are awarded to the Winners Dog and Bitch. The number of points can range from 0 to 5, and depends upon the number of dogs defeated. Many intricacies are involved in calculated points, however, so the safest bet is to check with the steward before leaving the show if you're not sure what your dog has won.

The saying "every dog has his day" no doubt came from dog shows. Sometimes, the worst mutts in the world seem to win. On other days, the judge has the wisdom of Solomon and points to your dog as the winner for first. Be prepared for anything and cultivate a sense of humor.

No matter what, don't ever allow your dog's ability to win in competition cloud your perception of your dog's true worth in his primary role — that of friend and companion. A dog who is last in his class but first in his owner's heart is far better off than an unloved dog who is first in any competition.

Chapter 3

Deciding If It's Bully for You

In This Chapter

▶ Making a commitment to a Pit Bull

▶ Knowing what bills to expect

▶ Finding out whether you're a good match

▶ Satisfying your dog's needs

▶ Being a responsible owner

*W*e research and worry and look around and test drive — all before we choose a car. Along the way, we sometimes discover that the red convertible two-seater that we've fallen in love with just doesn't fit our lifestyle, so we sigh and get a minivan instead. A Pit Bull can be that red convertible: Eye-catching and flashy, with lots of horsepower under the hood, he simply may not be the dog to fit into your lifestyle.

If you buy that red convertible, you can always resell it, but the market for used Pit Bulls is not so good. Too many Pit Bulls find themselves owned by the wrong people, then shuffled from home to home, and finally on a one-way trip to the dog pound. And some of them aren't even that lucky.

Before getting a Pit Bull, or any dog at all, ask yourself if you have the time, money, facilities, and energy to deal with a dog for the next 12 years or so. A dog is a lifetime commitment. Most adult dogs never find a second home; the situation is even more dire for adult Pit Bulls. Don't get a Pit Bull just for today; get one for all your tomorrows together. And before you search for your soulmate, do some serious soul searching.

Making a Commitment

Ask yourself if you can handle a strong dog who enjoys and needs lots of exercise. Pit Bulls love to play (see Figure 3-1). They love to exercise their bodies, their minds, and their senses of humor. Good Pit Bull owners share this sense of fun and are eager to join their dogs on a daily adventure — whether it's a run in the park, a game in the yard, or a jog around the neighborhood. If you think it's fun — and it involves activity — chances are your Pit Bull will think it's fun, too. If the idea of physical exertion horrifies you, think twice before inviting a personal fitness trainer into your home.

You need to exercise your dog's mind as well as his body. Training your Pit Bull not only tires out his brain, but it also results in a dog who is a credit to his breed. For some breeds, training is a nice option; for Pit Bulls, it is a necessity. They are too smart, too powerful, and too active to be without a leader. A poorly trained Pit Bull is an opportunity for the public to condemn "those incorrigible beasts and their irresponsible owners." A well-trained Pit Bull shows these people just how wrong they are.

Pit Bulls are geniuses and — like many gifted children — are prone to get into trouble with their great ideas. Add the Pit Bull's sense of humor, and you have a combination of a stand-up comedian and crazed inventor running through your house. Most of the Pit Bull's pranks are harmless and provide a great floor show, but a few are bound to go astray. Pit Bull owners need to have a very good sense of humor.

All dogs are expensive to keep. The American Humane Society estimates it costs an average of about $1,500 to take care of a puppy during her first year. Pit Bulls are among the healthiest and hardiest of breeds, but even so, expect to spend a lot of money at the veterinarian's office. Your dog will need vaccinations, deworming, probably heartworm prevention, and neutering or spaying. He will occasionally get sick or be injured. Pit Bulls get sick less often than most breeds, but they may get injured more often. Their disregard for danger and total immersion in every activity means they've been known to jump off rooftops after balls, fall out of trees they've climbed, race trains, tackle wild animals too tough even for a Pit Bull, and jump so wildly they damage their legs. Accident prevention will save you money in the long run, besides saving your dog.

As muscular, active dogs, Pit Bulls need quality fuel to keep them going. The average Pit Bull eats about 20 pounds of food each month. Active dogs (or dogs who spend a lot of time outside in cold weather) need more than that — and growing dogs need even more.

Like all dogs, your Pit Bull will need a place in the house he can call his own and a secure yard. Some people — who want their dog to function as a guard dog — reason that letting him sleep inside will spoil him for his duties, but your dog is far more likely to guard his family if he actually knows who his family is. The truth of the matter, however, is that if you want a guard dog, you would be better off with another breed! Most Pit Bulls are more likely to maul a burglar by licking him to death than by attacking him.

Figure 3-1:
The pups
will grow up
to be strong
dogs who
will need
lots of
exercise.

If your dog will spend a good deal of time outside, you must provide him with a warm shelter in the winter, shade in the summer, and a fenced-in yard year-round. Pit Bulls (especially bored Pit Bulls) are escape artists. And their escapes can lead them to their deaths. Loose dogs can be hit by cars, stolen, or taken to the pound — some are even killed by alarmists who think that a "savage" Pit Bull is on the loose. Letting your Pit Bull run free is one of the dumbest things you can do.

Making the Match

Sometimes, people expect the impossible when choosing a breed. They want a dog who sleeps when they do, plays when they want to play, protects them against bad guys, introduces them to handsome strangers, barks to warn of drowning children, stays quiet when the news is on, never gets sick, doesn't eat much, looks impressive, takes up no room, never messes things up, and never sheds. No such dog exists. The Pit Bull is moderately active and very playful. He's protective — sort of. He barks, but not excessively. He is impressive looking and comes in a wide size range. Most Pits are around 17 to 19 inches tall and weigh about 55 to 70 pounds, but some dogs can weigh as little as 30 pounds or as much as 100 pounds. As rambunctious, happy dogs, they sometimes create a trail of destruction when kept in small quarters.

Most often, the destruction is caused by their wildly wagging tail that clears coffee tables in a single sweep. And although their coat is very short, Pit Bulls, like almost all dogs, shed.

Pit Bulls are a delightful mixture of exuberance and serenity, obedience and mischief, challenges and rewards — topped off with a sense of humor, loyalty, and gameness. They know when to play, when to protect, and when to snuggle. Their athletic bodies can't help but elicit admiration. They are the perfect pet for many families — but not for every family.

Don't apply for Pit Bull ownership if your family:

- Already has an aggressive dog. Some Pit Bulls can't be trusted around other dogs and must never be allowed loose around them.
- Can't withstand a misinformed public's misdirected hatred of Pit Bulls.
- Doesn't have a fenced-in yard, a sense of humor, or plenty of time, energy, and patience.
- Doesn't have the ability (or desire) to make sure that your dog is well-behaved in public.

Almost all Pit Bulls share common characteristics. Whether these features are positive aspects of the dog's personality or major hindrances to the owner getting along with the pet depends on whom the Pit Bull lives with. Pit Bulls are special — and they need special people.

Read the following table to see if a Pit Bull is for you.

A Pit Bull . . .	That's great if . . .	That's terrible if . . .
Is energetic.	You are a get-up-and-go kind of person who is up for adventure with a canine accomplice.	You are already overwhelmed with work and you value what little relaxation time you have left. Or you can't stand the idea of a one-dog home demolition team.
Is strong and athletic.	You want a dog who doesn't break easily.	You break easily. Or you expect your 8-year-old to walk your dog all by herself.
Bonds deeply with his family.	You want to take your dog along on family outings.	Your plans can't include your dog.
Is very intelligent and self-assured.	You figure out how to use the Pit Bull's great play drive to channel that intellect.	You think you can manhandle your dog into compliance. Or you expect a dog to hang on to your every word.

A Pit Bull . . .	That's great if . . .	That's terrible if . . .
Loves people.	You want a dog that will threaten to drown your friends with licks and slobber.	You want a dog that won't greet a burglar that enthusiastically.
Is loyal.	You're loyal too.	You think you can invite a Pit Bull into your family on a whim — and abandon him just as easily.
Is perceived as a tough guy.	You want a dog that makes you feel safe.	You want a dog that makes you feel welcome (by others) everywhere.

Getting to the Heart of the Matter (or Your Pit Bull)

Pit Bulls are undeniably good-looking animals. But their most distinguishing feature is their personality. A Pit Bull's character is as much a signature of his heritage as is his conformation.

✔ **Pit Bulls are game.** Gameness, though hard to define, is in essence the quality of pressing on cheerfully and with gusto in the face of adversity. In everyday life, this spirit expresses itself in self-confidence, determination, and a certain _joie de vivre_. Of course, these very traits can also express themselves as stubbornness when owners attempt to work against, rather than with, their dogs.

Pit Bulls need not be aggressive. Gameness is not aggressiveness. A non-aggressive dog can be game (for example, he avoids a fight but does not back down if pressed), and an aggressive dog can be ungame (for example, he starts a fight but turns tail if the victim fights back). Some Pit Bulls are aggressive with other dogs. Others are not. But as a rule, Pit Bulls were not bred to be aggressive — they were bred to win. If challenged, they will attempt to conquer.

Pit Bulls love to play. They seem to interpret gameness as a love of games, and here the Pit Bull is master of the game (see Figure 3-2). Pit Bulls are great comedians, and they enjoy playing the clown. Their mixture of playfulness, curiosity, and intelligence sometimes gets them into some wildly humorous situations. Pit Bulls thrive on rough-and-tumble play that challenges both their physique and their psyche.

✔ **Pit Bulls are stoic.** They were bred to ignore pain and to keep their wits about them when they were hurt. They tolerate rough children like few other breeds do — and they do it with a smile that says they are not just tolerating the children, they are relishing them.

✔ **Pit Bulls are people lovers.** Pit Bulls with proper temperaments would never bite a human. In the past, Pit Bulls had to be handled during the heat of battle, and they had to refrain from biting their handlers. Those that made the mistake of biting a human were seldom forgiven, and they did not live to fight — or breed — again. Today, Pit Bulls are more likely to attack with licks and wiggles, immobilizing their victims with the 100 percent essence of dog love.

✔ **Pit Bulls are surprisingly sensitive.** Under the Pit Bull's rowdy exterior beats one of the biggest hearts in the dog world — and one of the most apt to be broken.

✔ **Pit Bulls are people pleasers.** What other breed of dog would risk its life time after time at the behest of its master? This very desire to please has — unfortunately — been at the bottom of some Pit Bull attacks on people. For some Pit Bulls, the only desire that can overpower their urge to befriend strangers is their need to please their masters. If a Pit Bull's master communicates to him that attacking a dog or person is what she desires, an attack can result — and the Pit Bull is the one who ultimately pays the price.

Figure 3-2:
Softball,
anyone?

At her best, today's Pit Bull wears her fighting heritage not as a liability, but as a badge of courage and trustworthiness. Not all Pit Bulls, however, are at their best — and when a Pit Bull is bad, she can be very, very bad. Be sure that your Pit Bull represents the very best that this noble breed has to offer by choosing the very best Pit Bull.

Brushing Up on the Law

Pit Bull owners probably know more about dog law than do any other kind of dog owners. They have to. Too often, Pit Bull owners have been the victims of breed-specific legislation that targets their dogs, attempting either to place restrictions on them or to ban them altogether.

However, a five-year study (published in the *Cincinnati Law Review*) concludes that statistics do not support the assertion that any one breed is dangerous. And the study finds that when legislation is focused on one breed, the legislation fails because it is not enforceable, it is confusing, and it is costly. Furthermore, focusing legislation on breeds that are labeled as vicious only distracts attention from the real problem — irresponsible dog owners. Banning a breed does not stop people from getting that kind of dog, but it does force them to buy their dogs from irresponsible sources — and it prevents them from obtaining the proper socialization, training, and medical care for their dog.

Fighting breed-specific legislation, however, doesn't mean burying your head in the sand and denying that Pit Bulls (and other dogs) can seriously injure — and even kill — people. In a six-year study of fatal dog bites that occurred between 1989 and 1994, more than half of the victims were children under ten — and more than half of the attacks occurred on the dog owner's property. The breed most commonly indicted in the study was the Pit Bull, which was responsible for 24 deaths. The problem with this study is that people tend to mislabel any mixed-breed dog a Pit Bull. But whether or not all these dogs really were Pit Bulls, Pit Bulls are the ones getting blamed — and you and your Pit Bull are paying the price.

Finding out about your community's laws before getting a Pit Bull is a good idea. If anti-Pit Bull legislation is in place (and you aren't the kind of person who likes a hassle), you might do better with another breed. If, however, you are half as game as your Pit Bull is, you will join others to oppose the unfair legislation. Dog groups around the country have successfully replaced breed-specific laws with laws that target dangerous dogs and their irresponsible owners, no matter what the breed.

Chapter 4

Shopping the Bull Market

. . . .

In This Chapter

▶ Separating good breeders from bad breeders

▶ Looking for a good Pit Bull

▶ Considering the used or abused

▶ Registering your new Pit Bull

▶ Picking the dog who's best for you

. . . .

*Y*ou probably want a Pit Bull because you like the way they look and the way they act. So make sure that the dog you get looks like a Pit Bull and acts like a Pit Bull. Equally important, you want to make sure that the dog you get will live a long and healthy life. You've chosen a great breed that has the misfortune to have some not so great breeders. Take your time and get the Pit Bull you deserve.

Avoiding Bad Blood

The best way to get a good Pit Bull is to find a good breeder. The problem is that virtually all the people who ever let two dogs of the same breed mate consider themselves to be expert dog breeders. In reality, Pit Bulls are too often bred by the wrong people for the wrong reasons. Beware of breeders who:

✔ Raise Pit Bulls for fighting or think Pit Bulls should be aggressive. Pit Bulls can be game without being specially bred for aggressiveness.

✔ Treat their dogs without respect, love, or kindness.

✔ Sell cheap puppies. Expect to pay from $200 to $300 for a registered pet-quality pup, and an average of $300 to $500 or more for show quality. Male and female pets should cost the same. Raising healthy puppies takes a lot of resources, and cheap pups probably are cheap because the breeder has cut corners.

✔ Are ready to send pups home with you before the pups reach eight weeks of age.

- Can't compare their dogs to the UKC, ADBA, AKC standard, don't know the standard, or scoff at the standard.

- Think bigger is better, or worse, meaner is keener.

- Are unfamiliar with any Pit Bull health concerns, or insist that they don't have to screen because their dogs are free of problems. All Pit Bull breeders should have their dogs screened for hip dysplasia. The best breeders will have their dog's hips evaluated and the results on file with hip registries such as Orthopedic Foundation for Animals (OFA) or PennHip.

- Insist that you view the puppies at a place other than their home or don't allow you to see the dam of the litter. Such breeders are often hiding a small-scale puppy mill or large-scale dog fighting operation.

- Have no pedigree, photos, or videotapes of both parents and of other relatives. Good breeders know every dog in their pedigrees and will have you running for the door when they go to retrieve yet another album or videotape.

- Ask you no questions. Good breeders consider placing a puppy as no less a responsibility than arranging adoption for a baby (well, maybe that's an exaggeration). They ask about your facilities, dog and Pit Bull experience, and your plans for your Pit Bull.

- Think Pit Bulls are ideal for everyone. They're not! But breeders in search of a buck would have you think so.

- Tell you that you can make your money back by breeding your Pit Bull. Does the breeder look rich?

"Whoever said you can't buy happiness forgot little puppies." — Gene Hill

Searching High and Low

The most common sources of cuddly Pit Bull puppies are newspaper ads, friends, pet stores, hobby breeders, and rescue groups. Of these, I recommend hobby breeders or rescue organizations. But since newspaper ads are still the most popular source, I look at them first.

Classified information

"Enjoys quiet evenings by the fire, strolls on the beach at dawn, and fine dining. Looking for a lifetime partner."

Despite the convenience, finding your new family member in the classifieds is seldom a good idea. Some things in life shouldn't be easy, and buying a dog is one of them. Although reputable breeders sometimes advertise in the newspaper, most ads are placed by *backyard breeders* — novice breeders who naively breed the family pet or think that they can make a quick buck by throwing a few dogs together. They seldom have the knowledge or resources to produce healthy, well-adjusted puppies or to adequately evaluate your chances for a happy life with the dog; even worse, in some cases, they don't care.

Other newspaper ads are placed by large-scale breeding operations that churn out litter after litter with profit the sole motivation. Some ads may also be placed by breeders who cater to the fighting Pit Bull market, who produce Pit Bulls that don't have the desirable temperament for a trusted companion. Individual dogs or puppies advertised in the paper may have originally come from these poor sources; now, their new families find they cannot deal with them. Their problem may become yours. Use extreme caution when considering a Pit Bull advertised in the newspaper.

Kennel review

Hobby breeders who place advertisements in all-breed dog magazines, or especially in Pit Bull–only magazines, tend to be serious about their dogs. The same is true for those who have kennel pages on the Web. You can generally find a wide assortment of quality dogs from breeders who either have a Web page devoted to their dogs or who know enough to advertise in all-breed or breed-specific magazines — although there's no guarantee that these people are good breeders. Some may still be motivated by profit, and these breeders may put up a good front.

Try to visit the facilities personally and see for yourself if the dogs are being treated like livestock, producing machines, or fighting animals. If you are not allowed to visit, look elsewhere.

Keep an eye out for clues that the breeder is breeding fighting dogs. Fighting operations often have all their dogs tethered on heavy chains. They often have treadmills, springpoles (see Chapter 5), and other muscle-building equipment. However, these "clues" are also found in the operations of breeders who are *not* raising fighting dogs. Many show breeders condition their dogs with treadmill running, and many pet owners have springpoles for their dog's enjoyment and exercise.

Old scars on a dog may indicate that they have been fought, but they could also indicate some chance encounters with housemates. If every dog has such scars, especially located around the face, they more strongly suggests a fighting history — or a very careless owner. Photos, videos, and magazines about fighting are a strong clue that the breeder may have fighting interests, but don't expect such clues to be left in the open. In some cases, even having the intention to fight dogs can be prosecuted, and every clue mentioned here can be used as legal evidence of intention. A good rule may be: If the breeder seems suspicious of you, be suspicious of him.

Know what you're looking for and don't hesitate to make your wishes known to the breeder. A breeder of fighting dogs should have the good sense to discourage you from coming to visit if you want a cute dog for the kids, and a breeder of pet dogs certainly doesn't want to send a pup home with you if you have any notion of fighting her. Being honest with the breeder gets you the best dog for your needs and, in the long run, is the best route for you, the breeder, and the dog.

But what are you looking for? If you want a conformation show dog, you need to find a breeder who competes successfully in conformation. The dogs in the pedigree should be either AKC Champion AmStaffs or UKC Champion or Grand Champion APBTs. If you want an obedience or agility competitor, find a breeder who competes in these sports and has breeding stock with obedience or agility titles. If weight pulling has caught your fancy, find a breeder with successful weight pulling dogs. Although it's possible for a dog without a background in any of these areas to excel in them, your odds of competing successfully are far greater if your dog's ancestors have also been successful.

Even if your only goal is to find the best companion on earth, a hobby breeder has invested the same time and energy into your pup that he has in every other potential winner. Take advantage of it.

Check out advertisements in all-breed magazines, such as *Dogs USA, Dog World,* and *Dog Fancy.* Beware of dog magazines catering to dog fighting enthusiasts; you don't want to get a Pit Bull from fighting lines and you don't want to encourage their breeders.

Expect a lot from hobby or professional breeders; they should have dogs boasting titles in conformation, obedience, or pulling, and certifications for clear hips (see the description of hip dysplasia in Chapter 13).

Also, expect to pay more for these puppies. Here is where it gets a little tricky. How much is too much? Some breeders charge outlandish prices for pups because they claim their dogs are the salvation of the breed. In general, be cautious of a breeder whose dogs are priced well over or under the average price. There's no such thing as the "chance of a lifetime" litter, puppy, or dog — although chances are that whatever dog you choose will be a once-in-a-lifetime friend.

Join an Internet Pit Bull discussion list for more information and leads. Several Pit Bull lists can be found by searching for "Pit Bull" at www.egroups.com and at www.k9web.com/dog-faqs/lists/email-list.html.

To the rescue

What about rescue Pit Bulls? Many Pit Bulls are in need of permanent homes. Most of them will make loving, trustworthy companions, but a few may need special care to help them recover from their past experiences.

National Pit Bull rescue groups usually have Pit Bulls available who have been screened for health and temperament problems, but the best organizations are as picky about prospective homes as the best breeders are. Experienced foster groups can evaluate the needs of each dog in their care and help you choose a dog who fits well with your circumstances. Choose a rescue dog just as carefully as you would any other. This dog has already been shuffled around from home to home; make sure that your home will be his last.

Some Pit Bulls are in rescue for a reason; perhaps they didn't get along with other dogs, cats, or children. They may need special circumstances or a more experienced owner. Some Pit Bulls have been rescued from fighting operations and need some extra care and rehabilitation. Most Pit Bulls, however, are in rescue simply because their first owners didn't think it through when they decided to get a Pit Bull.

Use the Web to search for a rescue group in your area. Simply type "Pit Bull Rescue" into a search engine, and you should get many matches.

You can contact your local animal shelter and ask to be alerted if a Pit Bull should become available, but many animal shelters have become wary of Pit Bull inquiries that, too often, come from people who aren't suited for Pit Bull ownership. You may need to convince shelter workers of your sincerity by visiting repeatedly and discussing your intentions for your prospective dog. Some shelters never or seldom adopt out Pit Bulls because of bad experiences with people using them for fighting. Another concern shelters have is liability, should a dog that was previously used for fighting bite someone.

Checking the Bona Fidos

You may not particularly care whether your Pit Bull is a blue blood or purple ribbon bred. Her value as a beloved companion isn't altered by the presence or absence of papers. Registration papers are one sign of responsible breeding, however, and responsible breeding is of such critical importance in this breed. Papers are also crucial if you intend to breed or compete with your Pit Bull.

Your dog generally needs to be registered with each organization in which you wish to compete with her. This means that if you dream of running around the show ring at Westminster (an AKC show), you need to get an AKC registered AmStaff; if you wish to earn a Grand Championship, you need to register your dog with the UKC. Some organizations recognize dogs registered with other organizations, but some do not.

The largest registries of Pit Bulls in the United States are the United Kennel Club (UKC) and the American Dog Breeders Association (ADBA), both of whom refer to the dog as an American Pit Bull Terrier. The American Kennel Club (AKC) version of the Pit Bull is called an American Staffordshire Bull Terrier. Note that I use the abbreviations *APBT* for the American Pit Bull Terrier and *AmStaff* for the American Staffordshire Terrier.

ADBA registration

Unlike the AKC and UKC, The ADBA registers only one breed: the American Pit Bull Terrier. The ADBA has been historically associated with dog fighting, and although it no longer officially endorses the practice, it still has not shaken the reputation as a fighting dog registry.

If your new Pit Bull's parents are both registered with the ADBA, then the breeder should have registered the entire litter with the ADBA by the time you take your pup home. You should receive a tan registration certificate (not a photocopy) from the breeder to return to the ADBA with your chosen name for the dog. If the parents of your dog are registered with the ADBA, but your pup hasn't already been registered, you need the signatures of the dogs' owners on your registration application to verify that the breeding between those two dogs did take place.

Even if your dog does not come from ADBA registered parents, you can *single register* her with ADBA if the dog's ancestors have been registered with another organization. To single register, you need to supply a three-generation pedigree with the complete registered names of all the dogs in the pedigree, and also submit a copy of your dog's registration papers if she is registered with another organization, such as the AKC or UKC.

The ADBA's recognition of dogs from UKC or AKC stock sometimes makes things a little tricky. Remember that the AKC recognizes American Staffordshire Terriers, not American Pit Bull Terriers. However, the UKC recognizes AKC-registered AmStaffs as UKC registered APBTs. If dogs originally registered as AKC AmStaffs are registered with the ADBA, they are indicated by an asterisk (*) on the pedigree, denoting that they are technically AmStaffs.

UKC registration

If the sire and dam of your puppy are registered with the UKC, the breeder should give you a green puppy-registration certificate when you buy your dog, which you fill out with the name you choose for the dog and return to the UKC. If your Pit Bull is a purebred but isn't registered with the UKC, you can single register your dog by submitting the proper documentation, as long as she is registered with another organization. APBTs registered with the ADBA and AmStaffs registered with the AKC can be registered after they've been inspected by a member of the National American Pit Bull Association to confirm that they meet the standard and exhibit proper temperament.

If your dog is a purebred but isn't registered with any registry, or even if your dog isn't a purebred, you can apply for a UKC *Limited Privilege Listing* or AKC *Indefinite Listing Privilege.* These listings require proof of spaying or neutering (rendering your dog ineligible for conformation showing), but allow you to compete in obedience and agility trials.

You may see the following terms on a UKC registration: The designation of *Purple Ribbon (PR)* is given to UKC registered dogs who have 6 generations of known ancestors and whose 14 ancestors within the last 3 generations are all registered with the UKC (all the parents, grandparents, and great-grandparents). The UKC also offers the *Performance Pedigree* (PAD), which lists the number of offspring produced and the number of degrees earned for all 14 ancestors in the 3 generation pedigree. The UKC marks all registration papers as *inbred* when the breeding is the result of a mother-son, father-daughter, or brother-sister mating. *DNA-P* indicates a DNA profiled dog and *DNA-VIP* indicates that the dog and both of her parents are DNA profiled, so that the dog has *verified, identified parentage* (VIP). (DNA samples are obtained by swabbing the inner surfaces of the lips.)

AKC registration

The AKC registers American Staffordshire Terriers, and does not recognize either UKC or ADBA registered Pit Bulls as AmStaffs. AKC registration papers consist of a registration certificate or application form, which you complete and send to the AKC to register the dog in your name. If these papers are not available when you buy the puppy, the breeder is required by AKC rules to give you a signed statement or bill of sale that includes the breed, sex, and color of the dog, her date of birth, the breeder's name, and the registered names of the dog's sire and dam (with numbers if possible). A breeder who is concerned that a non-breeding quality AmStaff might be bred rather than neutered or spayed may sell a dog with a *Limited Registration,* which means that if the dog is bred, her offspring will not be registered by the AKC. Dogs with limited registration can still compete in AKC competitions (except for conformation). Limited Registration *can* be changed to regular registration, but only by the breeder, not by the owner.

Note that a dog born of an AKC-registered dam to a UKC-registered sire (or vice versa) will not be recognized as pure by the AKC. An AKC registered AmStaff must have both parents AKC registered as AmStaffs.

Your dog's AKC registered name cannot be changed, so choose carefully. A UKC registered name can be changed up until the time the dog becomes a UKC champion.

All this is pretty complicated, so I'll summarize some of the important points:

- The AKC does not recognize UKC or ADBA registrations.
- The UKC recognizes AKC and ADBA registrations.
- The ADBA recognizes UKC and AKC registrations.

Picking Your Pit

Both Pit Bull males and females make equally good companions. Pit Bull males are slightly larger than females. Some males mark their territory inside your house by urinating on walls and furniture, a behavior that can be difficult to thwart. Males may fight with other males, especially other male Pit Bulls. Females, too, can fight with each other, but are somewhat less likely to do so. Their main drawback is that they come in *estrus* (also known as *season* or *heat)* twice a year. Estrus lasts for three weeks. Neutering usually solves these problems.

Try to choose the best Pit pup, with the best parents and grandparents, you can find. If looks are important to you, be sure they have the look you like. Consider the essentials of the Pit Bull standard. The Pit Bull is a grand athlete, a combination of lithe movement and rippling musculature. The Pit Bull should give the impression of strength, agility, speed, and stamina, without sacrificing one for another. If you plan to show your dog, have somebody familiar with the Pit Bull standard come with you and evaluate the ancestors and puppies. If you don't plan to show, simply go with what pleases your eye (see Figure 4-1).

If temperament is important to you — and it should be — be sure you like how the adults act. The adult Pit Bull should display a great joy of life, enthusiasm for adventure, desire to please, and courage in the face of adversity. These same traits should be evident in the puppy you choose. The dog who comes to greet you, tends to follow you around, and doesn't object to being held occasionally is your best choice for a stable companion. Be sure that the breeder interacts with the pups with kindness; early experiences can have lifelong consequences.

Your pup has a better chance of living a long, healthy life if her relatives have also had long and healthy lives. Ask how old the parents are and how long the grandparents or great-grandparents lived. It's a plus if the parents and grandparents have normal hip ratings from the Orthopedic Foundation for

Animals (OFA), but it's no guarantee your pup won't develop hip dysplasia as an adult. Have your puppy checked by your veterinarian within a day of bringing her home.

Even the most carefully bred and chosen pup may not develop as hoped concerning conformation, temperament, or health. Discuss with the breeder what, if any guarantees are provided, and consider whether you can handle returning a pup to whom you've become attached if that is part of the bargain. If having a successful competition dog is of vital importance to you, consider buying an adult who has already shown potential.

Pit Bull pups require constant attention, careful supervision, and endless work. Consider whether you will have the time and energy to devote to a puppy. If not, consider getting an older dog from a breeder or rescue group. One of the many Pit Bull perks is that adults maintain their puppy playfulness for many years. If you have children, an older Pit Bull may be less likely to bowl them over with her exuberance. She will either be housebroken or be very easy to housebreak. She will have less tendency to chew. And don't worry: She'll bond to you as though she had always owned you. Oops, as if you had always owned her. You may find that the best way to ensure many years of pleasure is to start with an adult Pit Bull. Of course, you still have to do your part by providing the best care possible.

Figure 4-1:
All puppies
are cute.
Take care to
choose the
one that's
best for you.

Photo courtesy of Cindy Noland.

Part II
Your Pet Bull

In this part . . .

Puppy proofing your home will be a lot easier if you do it before your new Pit pup is underfoot undoing everything as fast as you can do it. Roll up your sleeves, get out the credit card, and practice your meditation, because the more you do now, the better your chances of saving your home, your dog, and your sanity.

After the home front is conquered, you're ready to share the wonders of the world with your new buddy. Say good-bye to your old life — things will never be the same! But, hey, isn't that why you got a Pit Bull in the first place? Read on to find out the best way to prepare for a walk on the wild side.

Chapter 5

Pit Projects

● ●

In This Chapter

▶ Puppy-proofing your house

▶ Going on a Pit Bull buying bonanza

▶ Making and buying Pit Bull toys

● ●

So, you're about to add a baby Pit Bull to your life.

Exited? Scared? You'd better be both. Take a last look around your home so you can remember how it looked BP (Before Pup). Heck, take a picture for posterity. You won't see it looking like this for about another year — maybe ten. After you take your pictures, roll up your sleeves and get to work. Channel your excitement into preparation, and get ready for your new pet before he arrives. When your new dog enters your home, you'll be too busy having fun to get any work done — and what little you do accomplish, your little troublemaker will undo faster than a speeding Pit Bullet.

Once home, your new Pit Bull faces the transition from canine litter member to human family member, a pretty remarkable change. Every new day is full of novel experiences and strange rules. Your Pit pup is naturally inquisitive and needs for you to safeguard him from danger and guide him toward becoming a well-mannered member of the household.

Avoiding Dangerous Pitfalls

A Pit Bull puppy is like a super baby. Imagine a baby who can run faster than an adult, jump his own height, and chew through wires: That's a Pit Bull baby. Because Pit Bull puppies are even more active than human babies, you have to be even more diligent in puppy-proofing than in baby-proofing. If you've never had a dog before, you may have some home improvement projects on your hands before your home is safe enough for a mischievous Pit Bull. Using your own imagination and diligence is the best way to insure your pup's safety.

Anyplace your Pit Bull may wander must be puppy-proofed, just as you would baby-proof your home and yard for a new child. Crawl around on the ground at puppy level to see what dangers beckon. You may as well get used to it down there — you'll be sprawling there with your pupster soon enough. In addition to baby-proofing your home, you need to be alert to these factors:

- Doors are a danger area:
  - Puppies can be injured running into clear glass doors. Attach stickers at puppy eye level to avoid such accidents.
  - Everyone in your family must be made to understand the danger of slamming a door — the pup may be in the way.
  - Never close a garage door with a puppy darting about.
  - Doors leading to unfenced outdoor areas should be kept securely shut. A screen door is a vital safety feature.

- Puppies love to chomp on electrical cords and lick electrical outlets. Such oral exploration can result in death from shock, severe burns, and loss of jaw and tongue tissue. Pups can also pull electrical appliances down on themselves by pulling on cords.

- Pups can pull over unstable objects, causing the object to come crashing down on the pup.

- High decks, balconies, and staircases are bad news. Use baby gates, temporary plastic fencing, or chicken wire (if needed) to prevent the puppy from accessing these dangerous areas.

- Careless people can undo all your safety efforts. Impress upon family members the dire consequences that can occur if they allow the dog to dance around the lawn mower, conduct target practice with the dog in the area, leave a puddle of antifreeze on the garage floor, and on and on. Everyone in the family needs to consider what consequence their actions may have on the pup. Keep chemicals, drugs, cleaners, sponges, small objects, strings, and coins out of reach of a puppy's adventurous mouth.

- Check the yard for poisonous plants, bushes with sharp, broken branches at a Pit Bull's eye level, and trees with dead branches or heavy fruits in danger of falling. If you have a pool, school your dog on how to find the steps so that he can get out.

Fencing In Your Pit Bull

Good fences really do make good neighbors — and live dogs (see Figure 5-1). The number-one Pit Bull lifesaver is a securely fenced yard. In today's world of suburbs and automobiles, a loose dog is, at best, an unwelcome visitor, and more often road kill. Even a friendly Pit Bull intent on playing with passersby can be interpreted as a dog looking for trouble and reported to animal control or law enforcement. Roaming Pit Bulls can find themselves accused of various misdeeds, damaging the breed's reputation and possibly resulting in legal action against you. Pit Bulls can be gifted jumpers, climbers, diggers, and wrigglers, and are often tempted by the greener grass on the other side of the fence. Running dogs, playing children, racing bicycles, or just the call of the wild may prove irresistible to your dog. Privacy fences (such as stockade fences without cracks for a dog to peek through) are the best choice because they prevent your dog from being swayed by such temptations, and prevent potential dognappers from seeing your Pit Bull.

Figure 5-1:
A fenced yard is a safe playground for your Pit Bull.

"He lived and died without knowing that twelve- and sixteen-foot walls were too much for him. Frequently, after letting him try to go over one for a while, we would have to carry him home. He would never have given up trying. There was, in his world, no such thing as the impossible." —James Thurber on his childhood Pit Bull, Rex.

What about those invisible containment systems, in which dogs wear a device that gives them an electronic shock when they cross a certain boundary? They aren't as good as an old-fashioned fence. Because they work only with a dog who is wearing a special collar that's activated by the buried boundary wire, they can't keep out stray dogs that aren't wearing such a collar, nor can they keep out unscrupulous dognappers. In addition, an excited or determined Pit Bull can be over the boundary before he has a chance to stop. An excited Pit Bull won't let a little shock stand in the way of a good adventure!

Keeping your dog in a tiny pen on the far side of the yard is scarcely better. Pens do have their place for containing dogs securely, however. Such a pen should be at least 6 feet high or, preferably, have a solid top to keep out rain and sun and keep in climbing Pit Bulls. The pen must have both shade and shelter. Dogs can get more exercise in a long, narrow pen than in a square pen of equal area. If you place a doghouse within the pen, be sure that the dog cannot jump on the top of the house and then out of the pen. The most convenient pens have a doggy door leading inside the house or garage so that the dog has shelter. The pen can provide a secure area for your Pit Bull when you are away from home, but is not a substitute for taking your dog into your home and giving him regular exercise.

If you don't want to welcome your Pit Bull as a real member of your household, you'll be missing out on the best this breed has to offer. Pit Bulls raised as part of the family are more obedient, trustworthy, and protective. Reconsider getting a Pit Bull if you plan to exile him to a life of solitary confinement.

Pit Bulls may be tough, but they're not built to withstand either excessive cold or heat. Their hair is too fine and short to afford protection from the elements, and they don't take hot weather particularly well, either. If you wouldn't be comfortable sleeping outside in either hot or cold weather, neither will your Pit Bull. A Pit Bull is not a dog who should be expected to live outside!

Providing a Cozy Doghouse

If your dog will be spending a lot of time outside, he may need a doghouse. The best doghouses have a doorway system that prevents wind and rain from whipping into the sleeping quarters. This means a design with two offset doors and an "entrance hall." One of the doors should have a hanging rubber or fabric flap like doggy doors have. The floor should be slightly raised and soft bedding should be in the sleeping quarters. For warm weather, shade must be available.

A great summertime cooler is a kiddie wading pool. Introduce your Pit Bull as a pup and he'll learn to lounge in the water to keep cool on hot days. Be sure to change the water regularly as it stagnates quickly.

Lying Down with Dogs

Do you have a bed? Well, what about your dog? You'd be surprised how many people go off to bed at night and leave their dog wandering aimlessly around the house, without a bed to call his own. When these people discover the dog sleeping on the sofa, they label the dog as "sneaky," but your Pit Bull needs a comfortable bed just as much as you do. You can choose from several sleeping options for your Pit Bull.

Bull dozers

Decide now if you want to share your bed with your dog. Remember that your pup won't understand why he was welcome in your bed last night (after you gave him a nice bath) but not tonight (after he gave himself a nice mud bath.) Whether you're willing to share your bed or not, your dog should also have his own bed. A bed can be a folded blanket, a crib mattress, a big cushion, a fancy bed made just for dogs, or anything moderately soft — and preferably washable. It can be placed in a corner, a box, a dog crate, or anywhere out of the way of drafts and excitement. Whatever you use and wherever you put it, the most important thing is that the bed is a place your dog can call his own. The next most important thing is that you don't use the traditional wicker basket bed, unless you have an insatiable desire to play a mind-boggling game of pick-up sticks.

Even if you don't share your bed, one of the best parts of having a Pit Bull is the chance to snuggle. Cuddling with your dog in front of the fire or the television is fun, so throw a blanket on the floor and share it with your dog.

Crates can be great

The crate is a popular and useful dog bed and training tool. Many new dog owners are initially appalled at the idea of putting their pet in a crate as though he were some wild beast. At times, though, your Pit Bull *is* a wild beast, and a crate (or crate) is one way to tame the beast.

Your pup needs a place that he can call his own, a place he can seek out whenever the need for rest and solitude arises. The crate can be that place (see Figure 5-2).

Think of the crate as the canine equivalent of a toddler's crib. It's a place for naptime and a place where you can leave your pup without worrying about him hurting himself or your home. It is not a place for punishment, nor is it a storage box for your dog when you're through playing with him.

Rethink getting any dog if you plan for him to live in a crate. Don't expect your dog to stay in a crate all day, every day, while you're at work. To lock an intelligent, active being in a crate without stimulation is not only cruel, but can also lead to behavior problems.

You can't just stuff your Pit Bull in a crate when you feel like it and expect him to take it lying down. In fact, if you do that he will do everything but lie down. Start by placing the crate where the pup won't feel secluded from the rest of the family. Place him in the crate on a soft blanket when he begins to fall asleep, and he will become accustomed to using it as his bed. Add a chewbone or favorite toy to keep him company. If you time it right, you should not have to worry about a crying puppy begging to be let out; if you time it wrong, you may have to steel yourself to his pleas until he finally falls asleep.

Most crates are either of the wire variety or the plastic variety. Wire crates provide better ventilation and view for your dog, and most (especially the suitcase models) are easily collapsible for storage or transport. However, they can be drafty and don't provide the coziness of plastic crates. Dogs can strain an amazing assortment of items through the gratings, so take care about what items you set on or near a wire crate. Most wire crates are not approved for airline shipping.

Plastic crates are relatively inexpensive. They don't provide ventilation as well as wire crates do, but they can be cozy, especially in winter. They take up more room when storing as they only break down into halves; however, each half can be used as a bed.

Whatever type of crate you choose, pay special attention to the latching mechanism. Make sure a determined dog can't spring the door. The ideal crate is large enough for a puppy to stand up in, but not large enough for the puppy to walk around in. Crates that a dog can walk around in tend to be used as bathrooms. If you plan to travel with your crate, make sure it can fit into your car and that it is easy to transport.

If money were no object, then you could keep buying ever-expanding crates as your pup got bigger. A more realistic option is to buy a large crate and then place a divider in it that you gradually move to accommodate the growing pup. The adult crate can be larger once your dog is housebroken.

Figure 5-2:
A crate can be your Pit Bull's sanctuary.

The bull pen

Exercise pens (or *X-pens*) are transportable, wire, folding playpens for dogs, typically about 4 x 4 feet. X-pens are like having a little yard and are perfect for puppies. They provide a safe time-out area when you just need some quiet time for yourself but don't wish to confine your dog in a small crate.

Don't forget baby gates! They are better than shut doors for placing parts of your home off-limits. Do not use the accordion style gates, in which a dog can get his head stuck and asphyxiate.

Making Bull Buys

Besides the big ticket items, don't forget all the little things that make life sweet for your sweetie. Start with toys, chewies, toys, food, toys, and a few more toys. The best places to find a selection are discount dog catalogs, vendors at dog shows, and large pet supply stores.

Pit Bulls, balls, and other toys

Toys play an important role in mental and physical stimulation and help keep your home in one piece. Dogs that have toys are less likely to destroy inappropriate items. A stroll down the toy aisle of any pet shop will have your pup choosing every one in reach.

Pit Bulls love balls, especially big, bouncing balls. Hard rubber balls are ideal for tough-playing puppies. A large, partially deflated soccer ball also makes an ideal plaything.

Small balls (such as golf balls and jack balls) can be swallowed or inhaled, and soft rubber balls can be chewed to bits.

Rubber tug toys are great favorites with Pit Bulls, but use them sparingly with youngsters. Constant pulling on immature canine teeth and jaws may cause occlusion problems. This kind of play may also foster a sense of physical competitiveness that may not be appropriate in a full-grown Pit Bull. That doesn't mean you can never play tug games with your dog; just do so sparingly and intersperse other, more cooperative, activities.

Most squeaky toys are poor choices for Pit Bulls. Many are made of plastic that can be easily chewed and swallowed. In most of them, the squeaker is easily dislodged and also swallowed. Don't leave your dog unsupervised with a squeaky toy. These are toys, not chewies, and should only be used when you are playing with the dog.

Fleece toys are relished by most Pit Bulls, but some dogs are too rough with them and rip them apart. Again, these are not chew toys, and your dog should not be allowed to play unsupervised with them if he may chew them up. Children's stuffed toys are a good alternative for some dogs, but most Pit Bulls will have the room festooned with toy stuffing in short order.

Pit Bulls can destroy most normal dog toys, so you may have to invest in a heavy-duty toy (see Figure 5-3). The best choices are those made of durable rubber in which food (such as peanut butter or dog kibble) can be placed — such as the Kong or the Buster Cube. The dog then can spend a long time extracting the food from the toy. These toys are great for times when you must leave your dog alone.

Figure 5-3:
Make sure
to select
durable,
heavy-duty
chew toys.

Homemade toys are a great option. Stuff a sock with a couple of other socks or a tennis ball, knot it near the end, leave a long "leg" for throwing, and you have one of the best toys money can't buy. Stuff a long sock with a several balls all in a line and let your dog work to get each ball out, one by one. Take an old plastic milk jug or soda bottle, and you have a wacky, noisy throw toy that bounces erratically. Throw in a few dog biscuits or kibble and you have a challenging food puzzle. Small rubber tires are sturdy, roll erratically, and can be carried by a strong dog. Thick sections of rope can also be fun.

Don't forget the traditional stick. Make sure the ends are blunt and that it is not long enough that the dog can jab one end into the ground if it is holding the other end in its mouth — many dogs have jabbed a hole in the roof of their mouth that way. Of course, make sure your dog doesn't eat the stick!

Toys designed to withstand the average dog's destructive ability are child's play to a determined Pit Bull. If your dog likes to destroy and eat toys, you can't leave them with him. Homemade toys are especially ill-advised for these dogs. Dogs that swallow material can swallow long socks, causing a severe intestinal blockage in which the intestines bunch up around a long object. Dogs that munch plastic or wood can swallow shards of plastic containers or sticks. Super toy destroyers need super sturdy toys from pet catalogs or pet stores.

Pit Bulls especially enjoy games of strength, and toys involving jumping and tugging are great favorites. A homemade springpole is a great way for your Pit Bull to entertain himself. Springpoles can be simple or fancy; the basic design is a rope attached to an overhanging limb or arch with a heavy cloth attached to the rope by a big spring. The dog is encouraged to bite and pull on the cloth, and when he lets go, the cloth springs away and the dog tries to catch it. Start with the cloth at about the same level as the dog's head. Adult dogs can graduate to a higher placed cloth so they have to leap for it, but puppies should not be encouraged to jump high or hang from the cloth as doing so could injure their immature joints or teeth. Make sure your dog can't catch his teeth in the spring, and start slowly with the game. You don't want your Pit pup to become bored or exhausted.

Another fun toy is a pole lure, which is essentially a stick about 6 feet long or so with a string of equal length tied to the end and a toy or ragged cloth tied to the end of the string. The object is for you to run around and drag the toy, changing direction and generally trying to keep your dog from catching it. Don't let your dog get hurt by jumping too erratically after the toy, however. The toy will bounce around and the dog will have a great time trying to catch it as it bounces, changes direction, and goes up in the air. Your neighbors, of course, will think you're insane.

"Old shoes make great dog toys." Pit Bulls are smart, but they can't tell the difference between last year's styles and this year's styles — and when they come across your open closet, they may think they've truly hit the jackpot if you've conditioned them to chewing on shoes.

Chewies for choosy Pit Bulls

Like all dogs, Pit Bulls love to chew. They love to chew hands, feet, shoes, furniture, walls, sticks, logs, trees, cars, and heavy equipment with a natural born talent that would put a beaver to shame. Chewing is natural for all dogs. Pit Bulls just happen to be very good at it. You will be far more successful redirecting your dog's chewing than trying to abolish it. The most popular chew items are those made of rawhide, which you should avoid. Some rawhide is processed with poisonous substances. Dogs who swallow hunks of rawhide can choke or develop serious intestinal obstructions. A variety of vegetable-based chews are available. For gator-jawed dogs, hard rubber or nylon bones can last a long time and provide good dental cleaning.

Pig ears are a great treat but have high fat content and can cause diarrhea. Hooves tend to splinter and have been implicated in some problems. Hooves and bones have both caused cracked teeth and many veterinary dentists advise against their use.

Bull bowls

Your dog needs food and water bowls, and although you could just let him use yours, most people prefer for the dog to have his own. Your choice of materials is plastic, ceramic, or stainless steel. Forget plastic. Pit Bulls can chew it up and many dogs are allergic to it. It's also hard to keep clean. Ceramic is also not a great choice, simply because it can be awkward to clean and, if it cracks, harbors germs. Stainless steel bowls are best because they resist breaking and are easily washed.

A flat, wide bowl works best with Pit Bulls. To thwart ants if you ever feed your dog outside, place the bowl in a shallow pan of water so that the ants have to cross a moat to get to the food. If you plan to keep your bowl outside in freezing weather, be sure not to use metal (which the dog can get his tongue stuck to) and consider getting a bowl heater that keeps the water from turning to ice.

Collars for your Pit Bull

One size does not fit all, and your Pit Bull will be served best by a collar that fits his neck and your abilities. The three major collar styles are buckle, choke, or martingale.

Buckle collars

Every dog should have a traditional buckle collar (a flat collar that buckles) to wear around the house. Your dog's license tags (preferably the flat, plate type) should be on it. You will have to buy several buckle collars as your pup grows, but the little nylon puppy collars don't cost much. When your dog reaches maturity, you can splurge on a handsome leather or nylon collar.

Even though they look tough, you should probably resist the temptation to get a collar with spikes on it. They're not very comfortable for your dog and give a poor impression of the breed in public.

Buckle collars can have some shortcomings. For one, buckle collars with plastic clasps are notoriously unreliable; the clasps often break when the dog lunges against them, setting the dog free at the worst possible time. For another, the large neck of many Pit Bulls means that the collar has to be so big it is apt to slip off, over the dog's head, if he pulls back against it. Finally, buckle collars give the handler little control if the dog is strong and stubborn. This is especially true for a bull-necked Pit Bull.

Choke collars

For this reason a choke (or *slip*) collar may be a better choice while walking the dog. Choke collars come in nylon or chain, with chain giving a little bit more control. The main problem with choke collars of any type is their tendency to literally choke dogs to death. That's a mighty big problem. Countless dogs have gotten their choke collars caught on sticks, fences, car interior parts, or even a playmate's tooth and died — sometimes in front of their desperate owners, who couldn't rescue the dog because of the dog's frantic actions.

Never leave a choke collar on a dog. It's like sending your child out to play with a hangman's noose around his neck.

Martingale collar

A compromise between a buckle and choke collar is the martingale collar. It tightens when pulled, but can only tighten so much when properly fitted. Most martingale collars are nylon. A special type of martingale is the metal prong collar. These collars have links with prongs that bite into the dog when the collar tightens. Needless to say, their use is controversial. In some cases (in which the handler is physically unable to control the dog), they may be the only safe choice. Any person using a prong collar needs to get professional advice on the collar's proper use in training the dog.

Other choices

A problem with any kind of collar is that controlling a dog by his neck is somewhat difficult. When the collar slips down low on the neck, the dog can throw his weight into it and pull with reckless abandon, oblivious to all your pulling. The Pit Bull's muscular neck renders him especially impervious to tugging. Head collars (also called *head halters*) can control your dog better, by controlling his head. They work on the same principle as a horse halter; where the nose goes, the body follows. Head collars are a humane and effective alternative for headstrong Pit Bulls. The only problem with them is that to the uninitiated onlooker, it appears that you have a muzzle on your dog, thus reinforcing the vicious Pit Bull stereotype.

Harnesses that fit around the chest can be a good alternative. In most dogs, they are less effective than collars. But most dogs don't have the strong necks that Pit Bulls have. If you plan to compete in weight pulling, your Pit Bull will need to get used to wearing a harness. Besides, a Pit Bull looks quite handsome in a harness! A special type of harness (sometimes called a *Lupine harness*) is available that tightens when the dog pulls. It's sort of like a choke harness, except it tightens around the chest and shoulders. It can be a good choice for walking a strong Pit Bull.

A leash on life

Many Pit Bull owners reason that they have a strong dog, so they'd better get a strong leash. True. Then, they reason that the strongest leash of all is one made of chain. Not so true. Sure, the chain part is strong. But the part where the chain is attached to the handle is usually just a weak rivet, making the weakest link in this chain very weak indeed. Add to this the fact that you can't grab the chain part of the leash or wrap it around your hand because it would really, really hurt, and you should realize that a chain leash is a bad choice for a strong dog. Get a sturdy braided, nylon, or leather leash — anything but chain! All dogs should have a four- or six-foot leash. Shorter leashes are better when walking in crowed places.

Keep in mind that your dog is a Pit Bull. No matter how sweet and well-trained he is, some people are going to be terrified if they see him unleashed and trotting down the street with a silly grin on his face. You have even more reason than other dog owners do to keep yours on a leash.

Retractable leashes are very popular and useful, but are often carelessly used. They're not for use around other dogs or people. Using them in a congested space can create a terrible tangle. Nor are they for use next to a road; dogs are too apt to run onto the road before you can put the brakes on, and dogs can be just as dead if they're hit by a car when on-leash as when off-leash. Finally, they pose a hazard to the dog's owner too! Several people have lost finger parts when the line whipped across their hands.

Remember, too, that a Pit Bull can build up a tremendous amount of momentum if he runs at full speed to the end of the leash. Whereas, in most dogs, such a charge would probably lead to the dog being snapped suddenly back, with a Pit Bull it can knock the leash from your hand or even snap the line. In addition, if you drop one of these leashes they retract toward the dog, which can cause the dog to think a monster is chasing him, creating a horrifying chase in which the panicked dog runs faster and faster in a futile attempt to get away. You can buy an additional part that prevents the leash from retracting uncontrollably, but that sort of defeats the purpose of the leash!

Retractable leashes are great, but they should be used with care.

Brush up on grooming supplies

Your new Pit Bull will need a few health and beauty aids to keep him looking and feeling his best. Being a Pit Bull, he doesn't need all the frou-frou type beauty aids of some other dogs, but he still needs a few essentials. For coat care, a natural bristle brush is ideal. Although Pit Bulls don't get tangled hair, a brush helps remove dead hair, stimulates the skin, and distributes oils. Brushing your Pit Bull also helps you bond. Don't forget the dog shampoo; although you can use people baby shampoo, dog shampoo is your best bet. Be sure to get some rinse-free shampoo for quick fixes. A good-smelling dog deodorant is also useful.

Get your dog used to having his teeth brushed while he's still a puppy. Get a soft doggy toothbrush or a child's toothbrush. In fact, many dogs seem to enjoy the sound and sensation of electric toothbrushes with rotating bristle heads. Add some meat flavored doggy toothpaste and you'll have a Pit who can show off his gleaming choppers for his entire life.

Nail clippers are absolute essentials. Two types are available: guillotine and scissors. Both are good. Be sure to get heavy-duty nail clippers for an adult Pit Bull.

The scoop on poop

A poop scoop may not be an exciting thing to buy, but it is an item you will appreciate for years to come. If you have a yard, don't try to clean it with makeshift shovels and buckets. Use something designed to make the job easy and less yucky. Get a poop scoop! The two-part ones are easier to use than the hinged ones. The ones with a rake are better for grass, and the flat ones are better for cement.

Then what to do with the scooped poop? You can flush it down your own toilet as long as you haven't stockpiled it, you can bag it and put it with the garbage (illegal in some places), or you can dig a hole and bury it (also illegal in some places). If none of these sound appealing, you can throw it into your neighbor's yard (illegal in all places). Another option is to buy a doo-doo disposal unit, which is a basically a buried bucket with bacteria that digests the waste into a sludge.

If you're walking your dog in public areas, a number of poop baggy systems are available. Use them.

Chapter 6

Living with Your Pit Bull

In This Chapter

▶ Learning the house rules

▶ Interpreting what your dog is trying to tell you

▶ Making introductions with babies and children

▶ Walking (and running and swimming) your dog

▶ Traveling with your canine copilot

From the moment you bring your Pit Bull home, you and your family have to adjust your lifestyle to accommodate the new dog. From house training to walks in the park, this chapter shows you what you need to do.

Acting Like a Pit Bull in a China Shop: House Rules

Your home may be your castle, but it's your Pit pup's playground. As cute as he may be the first time your Pit pup storms your castle, it will quickly dawn on you that this can't continue. Pit Bull pups don't wipe their feet, they chew like beavers, and they are not overly particular about where they deposit bodily wastes. A Pit Bull who's running amuck in your home is a mobile set of barracuda teeth set on auto-chew, powered by four mud-tracking pistons, and armed with a variety of orifices prone to randomly squirt out assorted yuck when you least expect it.

Unless you're trying to make sure your in-laws and neighbors quit coming over, you have to set up some house rules for your new family member or your new family member will rule the house. Your puppy is a natural-born explorer, and his exploratory tools are his teeth. But any chewed items left in his wake are your fault, not your pup's — you are the one who should have known better. Harsh corrections are no more effective than a tap on the nose along with a firm "No," and replacement of the item with a legitimate chewable. If you come across one of your cherished items chewed to bits and feel compelled to lash out, go ahead — hit yourself in the head a few times for slipping up. It may teach you a lesson!

Sprays and liquids are available that have a bitter taste that dissuades (sort of) dogs from chewing surfaces upon which they've been applied.

"Discipline a puppy by grabbing him by the nape of his neck and shaking him, just like his dam would do." Nonsense. Mother dogs may grasp a pup by his neck, but they don't shake his neck as a means of correction. Shaking a puppy (or adult Pit Bull) is no safer than shaking a human baby. It's a good way to cause neck injuries or brain damage. It's also a good way to get bitten.

Taking the Pit Stop Outside

Don't think that you can raise a puppy without learning the secrets of cleaning a carpet. Still, you can spend less time scrubbing if you devote a little more time to housetraining. Start by restricting your pup's freedom in the house. Your pup is less inclined to relieve himself near his bedding area, and if you can restrict him to that area when he's not supervised he'll be more likely to hold himself. But don't make him wait too long. Even strong Pit Bull puppies have very weak control over their bladder and bowel, so if you don't take them to their doggy outhouse often and whenever they need to go, they may not be able to avoid soiling. At the slightest hint of pending elimination, go outside with your dog and stay with him until he has done his deed. When the puppy does relieve himself in his outside toilet, remember to heap on the praise and let your pup know how pleased you are. Adding a food treat really gets the point across. Keep some tidbits in a jar near the door and always accompany your pup outside so that you can reward him for being such a smart Pit Bull.

Don't ask more from your pup than he's physically able to give. A good rule is that a puppy can, at most, hold his bowels for as many hours as the pup is months old. This means that a three-month-old puppy can hold it for three hours (but note that there are limits — your 12-month-old Pit Bull can't hold it for 12 hours). If the pup is forced to stay in the house or in a cage longer than you can reasonably expect him to hold it, you're causing an accident and teaching your pup to go in the wrong place. A doggy door is an invaluable aid in housetraining. Once your pup gets the general idea, he will usually elect to let himself out to do his duty while you are gone.

When a pup soils in the house, he labels that area as his bathroom and is likely to go there again. If your pup does have an accident indoors, clean and deodorize the spot thoroughly and block the pup's access to that area. If you catch your dog in the act, say "No" and scurry him outside. Harsh corrections won't help, and may even hinder your training as he may confuse the act of relieving himself at all in your presence with punishment. Punishment after the fact is totally in vain, and serves to only convince your pup that you are unstable.

"Every dog may have his day, but it's the puppies who have weak ends." — Unknown

"Rubbing a dog's nose in its mess is the best way to teach him a lesson." That's a lot of bull! It doesn't work, and besides, it makes kissing your dog no fun at all!

No matter how biddable your Pit Bull is, don't expect miracles. Housetraining takes time and patience. Like all youngsters, your Pit Bull will have accidents, but he will learn, and he will learn more quickly if you do your part.

When the Plumbing's Broken

What happens when your housetrained dog appears to have forgotten his training? If your adult Pit Bull soils the house, the inappropriate elimination could be due to a physical or emotional problem. A physical examination is warranted any time that a formerly housebroken dog begins to soil the house. You and your veterinarian need to consider the following possibilities:

- Older dogs may simply not have the bladder control that they had as youngsters; a doggy door is the best solution.
- Older spayed females may dribble; ask your veterinarian about drug therapies.
- Several small urine spots (especially if bloody or dark) may indicate a bladder infection, which can cause a dog to urinate frequently.
- Sometimes, a housetrained dog is forced to soil the house because of a bout of diarrhea, and afterwards he'll continue to soil in the same area. If this happens, restrict the dog's access to that area, deodorize the area with an enzymatic cleaner, and revert to basic housetraining lessons.
- Male dogs may lift their leg inside of the house as a means of marking it as theirs. Castration often solves this problem, as long as it's performed before the habit has become established; otherwise, diligent deodorizing and the use of some dog-deterring odorants (available at pet stores) may help.
- Submissive dogs, especially young females, may urinate upon greeting you; punishment only makes this submissive urination worse. For these dogs, be careful not to bend over the dog or otherwise dominate the dog. Keep greetings calm. Submissive urination is usually outgrown as the dog gains more confidence.

✔ Some dogs defecate or urinate due to the stress of separation anxiety; you must treat the anxiety to cure the symptom. Dogs that mess their cage when left in it are usually suffering from separation anxiety or anxiety about being closed in a cage (claustrophobia). Other telling signs of anxiety-produced elimination are drooling, scratching, and escape-oriented behavior. You need to treat separation anxiety and start cage training over, placing the dog in the cage for a short period of time and working up gradually to longer times. Dogs who suffer from cage anxiety but not separation anxiety do better if left loose in a dog-proofed room or yard.

Trying Your Patience

These next few months are going to be a time of incredible fun and hair-pulling frustration. Your Pit pup will have flashes of intelligence and obedience, matched by periods of apparent dim-wittedness and disobedience. No matter how wonderful your dog is and how careful you are, you will lose a few cherished possessions and more than a few good nights' sleep. This is part of raising any puppy. You can go berserk and undo every bit of good training you've managed, or you can count to three, and then thirty-three, and end up with a far better trained dog in the long run. Dogs can't understand English, and they can't understand you losing your temper. They really do want to please you, but it's a strange world with strange rules that don't always make a lot of sense to a fun-loving pup. It will get better, so make sure you can look back at these precious months and remember the fun parts without regretting your own lack of control. Your Pit Bull puppy will never be a puppy again. They really do grow up too fast.

Understanding Pit Talk

Say something to your Pit Bull and she will prick her ears, perhaps cock her head, and try her hardest to decipher what all that "blah, blah, blah wanna go out blah blah " means. Not only does your Pit Bull try her hardest to understand you, but she also tries to talk to you. You need to try to understand her as well. As much as they've shaken off their wild vestiges, Pit Bulls still speak the ancestral language of wolves:

✔ A wagging tail and lowered head upon greeting is a sign of submission (see Figure 6-1.)

✔ A lowered body, tucked rear, urination, and perhaps even rolling over is a sign of extreme submission.

✔ A yawn is often a sign of nervousness.

- Drooling and panting can indicate extreme nervousness

- Exposed teeth, raised hackles, very upright posture, stiff-legged gait, and direct stare indicate very dominant or aggressive behavior (see Figure 6-2).

- Exposed teeth along with the submissive signs create the submissive smile, often used in greeting.

- Elbows on the ground and rear in the air, is the classic *play-bow* position, and is an invitation for a game (see Figure 6-3).

Figure 6-1:
A
submissive
Pit Bull.

What Pit Bulls see

Dogs see well at night because they have highly light-sensitive rod retinal as well as a shiny layer (the tapetum) in the back of the eye that reflects light back onto the retina (causing the eyeshine that dogs sometimes have at night). But dogs have poor vision for fine details or color. Their color vision is like that of a red-green colorblind person: They confuse shades of yellow-green, yellow, orange, and red, but can readily see and discriminate blue, indigo, and violet from all other colors and from each other.

Figure 6-2:
An
aggressive
Pit Bull.

Figure 6-3:
A playful
Pit Bull.

"A dog can express more with his tail in minutes than his owner can express with his tongue in hours." —Unknown

Becoming a Social Animal

As puppies open their eyes and begin to explore the world, they can't afford to be afraid of every new thing they see because everything that they see is new. So when they're very young, up to the age of about 12 weeks, puppies take new experiences right in stride. Totally fearless puppies don't usually survive to become adults, however, so starting at around 12 weeks puppies begin to get a little more suspicious. The suspicious part of their nature continues to become more pronounced as they get older. Pups should be exposed to as many novel experiences as early in puppyhood as possible, while they're still fearless explorers.

Bear in mind that a bad experience is even worse than no experience at all. Puppies are just as likely to learn that new situations are dangerous as they are that new situations are safe. Be very careful that your pup doesn't get hurt or frightened. Don't think that if a little is good, a lot is better. If you want your pup to enjoy a stroll downtown so that she can meet new people, great. But avoid the Macy's Thanksgiving parade.

You won't be doing your puppy Pit Bull any favors if you scare her silly. You'll be overwhelming your pup and achieving the opposite of the result you'd planned on. Remember that the idea is not to overwhelm but to expose, and not to merely expose, but to make the exposure a good experience. Stuff a pocket with treats and hand them out liberally. Fortunately, it's a rare Pit Bull who's lacking in the confidence department, at least once you give your pup a fair chance to be out and about. Nonetheless, every Pit Bull is different and you need to go at different paces with different dogs.

You must balance the benefits of early socialization with the threat of communicable disease. Fortunately, it takes only a few exposures to most situations to achieve good socialization. Take your pup a few times to an area in which unvaccinated dogs or puppies are unlikely to have been. If you expose her to other puppies, make sure they have been vaccinated.

Many dedicated Pit Bull owners expose their new pup to _everything_ they can think of. The pup may go with them to work, then to class, and so on, with a novel experience every day — but these dedicated owners forget one thing. They forget to expose the pup to being by herself. Part of the fun of having a new pup is spending every moment with her. But because separation anxiety is one of the largest sources of dog behavioral problems, neglecting to teach your Pit Bull to be by herself is a serious omission. Most dogs don't like to be alone, but most dogs have to be alone at one time or another.

If your puppy is crate trained, you can start by placing her in her cage when she is tired and leaving for a few minutes. Even if you don't have a cage, you can leave her alone in a secure room or yard. Giver her a special toy or chew-bone so she doesn't feel abandoned and bored. Leave her only for a little while. Don't sneak out, but don't make a big deal of leaving either. Just non-chalantly leave and return. Work up to longer times. If she goes crazy howling and trying to escape, try to wait for a moment when she is quiet and quickly return. You don't want her to think she summoned you back, even though she did. Again, just ignore her when you return. Then take a step backward in your training and leave for a shorter time period.

Has your Pit Bull pup been exposed to all of these?

- Bathing and grooming procedures
- Being alone
- Being in a cage
- Car rides
- Cats and other pets (see Figure 6-4)
- Children
- Games
- Loud noises
- Other dogs
- Strangers, both men and women
- Swimming
- Traffic
- Training commands
- A variety of surfaces to walk on

Figure 6-4:
Dogs and cats can get along.

Photo courtesy of Ann Childs.

Going to Kindergarten

Puppy kindergarten classes provide a great opportunity to expose your pup to nice people and to other pups her own age. Especially if yours is the only dog in your household, she may not have many opportunities to interact with other dogs. But running amuck with her new buddies isn't necessarily a good thing. If your dog gets beat up or is the bully, you're not teaching her good social behavior. Just as human kindergarten students need to learn how to interact nicely, canine students also need guidance to learn proper canine social skills. At the same time, your pup can start practicing her first simple obedience exercises and learn to control herself in public. You can also get advice about some common puppyhood problems. Good classes and bad classes are out there, so check it out first and don't be shy about complaining or quitting if things don't seem right to you once you're enrolled. Contact your local kennel club, veterinarian, or obedience school to find a kindergarten class in your area.

Meeting the Children

Many a devoted Pit Bull owner has been known to get rid of the dog when a new baby comes home, often because of the stories the new parent has heard about what dogs can do to babies. Just as many Pit Bull owners glibly bring the new baby home and hand the babe over to the dog to guard.

Neither is the correct response. Dogs can hurt babies. They can also protect babies. The way you introduce the dog to the baby may make the difference.

Pit Bulls have always had a special affinity for children, seeming to relish their comical antics and to feel protective of them (see Figure 6-5). The Pit Bull's close relative, the Staffordshire Bull Terrier, is nicknamed "the nanny dog" in England because of its reputation as a babysitter for the family children. Many a Pit Bull has been credited with saving a child's life. Unfortunately, many Pit Bulls have also been charged with ending a child's life. Give your Pit Bull a chance to be a good guy, but don't give her a chance to be the bad guy.

A few Pit Bulls may be wary of children, either because they don't understand what they are or because they've had bad experiences with them. Introduce dogs and children carefully, encouraging the child to be gentle and to offer the dog a treat. Do not allow young children to sit on a dog, fall on her, or pull her hair, ears, or tail. Instruct children that they are never to run from a dog, scream shrilly around her, stare at her, or hurt her. It's not fair even to the most saintly of dogs to allow her to be picked on. Never take chances with a child's safety, but do give your dog a chance — safely.

Things to keep in mind as you prepare to bring a baby and a Pit together:

- The dog should know how to "Come," "Sit," "Stay," and "Lie Down" on command.

- Keep the dog on-leash when first introducing her to the baby. If you're uneasy, you can muzzle the dog, but you don't want the dog to associate muzzling with the baby. She should already be familiar with the muzzle before the baby comes home, and she should sometimes wear it when she's not around the baby.

- When first bringing the baby home from the hospital, keep the dog away. Let her get used to the sound and odor of the new family member. Some dogs may not understand this is a small human and not a prey animal, so be very careful at this time.

- Have the dog "Sit" and "Stay," bring the baby in the room, and reward the dog for staying. Gradually move the baby closer, all the while rewarding the dog for her good behavior.

- Only when you feel confident about the dog's comfort level with the baby should you allow her to sniff the baby.

- Do not leave the dog and baby alone together.

- Always praise and pet the dog when the baby is present. Never shuttle the dog out of the room because the baby is coming in. You want the dog to associate the baby with good things and not be jealous or resentful of the baby. Remember that your dog probably used to be the "baby" of the family.

Figure 6-5:
These two
look like
they'll be
friends
for life.

Photo courtesy of Ann Childs.

Teach children not to stare at a strange dog. Staring directly at a dog is interpreted by the dog as a threat. It can cause a fearful or dominant dog to bite.

Going for a Bull Run

One of the great joys of living with a Pit Bull is the chance to watch your dog run and jump with the enthusiasm and gusto that only a Pit Bull can muster. But you can't just open the door and let your Pit Bull run amuck. You need to take precautions to make sure your dog's exercise is both safe and fun. Many Pit Bull owners think that because their dog is so smart and trustworthy, she's reliable off-leash. That may be true 95 percent of the time. But it's what happens in the other 5 percent of the time — when another dog attacks, a cat runs underfoot, or a hot dog vendor's cart careens out of control — that can be deadly. Whatever the reason, the trustworthy dog forgets herself for just a moment — and that's all it takes to run in front of a car, scare a child, or run away.

Never unhook the leash until you know everything about the area. Look out for cliffs, roadways, and drainage culverts. Avoid parks and public areas where your Pit Bull, no matter how friendly, could be a nuisance or perceived as a threat. Avoid wilderness areas during hunting season. Could your dog be tempted into chasing wildlife? Watch for animals and dogs that could attack your dog. Watch for animals and dogs that your dog could chase or attack.

Going hog wild

Catching and holding strong wild game is one of the oldest uses of bulldogs, and Pit Bulls are still used for this sport in some parts of the world. The southern part of the United States is home to huge wild boars that are among the most formidable of opponents. Hunters employ hounds to track the boar by scent and chase him until they can bring him to bay. The hounds are no match for a wild boar, however, so the hunter either needs to bring in reinforcements to bring down the hog — enter the Pit Bull. Usually, the hunter keeps the Pit Bull on-leash and unleashes him only when the hog has turned to face the hounds.

Hog catching Pit Bulls have to be tough and courageous; they also must discriminate between the hog and the other dogs. Some inexperienced Pit Bulls may attack a baying hound instead of the hog, harming the dog and allowing the hog to escape. Hog catching can be dangerous; many dogs are injured or killed.

I know how you feel: "Because my dog so loves to run free, she should have that right!" No matter how trustworthy your dog is, you're breaking the law in many places when you allow her to be off-leash. If your Pit Bull is off of her leash and somebody trips over her, or she causes a bicyclist to fall or a car to swerve and crash, or if she harms a child or another animal, you are legally — and morally — responsible. You will almost certainly be sued, and you will almost certainly lose. You'll also have put dogs one step closer to being banned altogether from public places. You will have endangered your dog's life and possibly endangered human lives. And you will have given Pit Bulls an even worse name.

In some areas, no safe or legal place exists to let your dog run loose. You can still do a good job of exercising her on-leash, however. Taking the dog for a walk is an excellent low-impact exercise for both of you, and is especially good for dogs who aren't quite in prime physical condition. Retractable leashes are great for walks, but you must be especially vigilant when using them. Dogs can still dart out into the path of traffic. Keep an eye out for loose dogs and cats, and hold your dog close around stray animals and passing pedestrians.

 Never hold a leash with just your hand or fingers around the loop because your dog can pull the leash right out of your hands. The best way to hold a leash securely is to insert your entire hand through the loop and grasp the leash just above the loop handle.

Start with a short walk and gradually work up to longer distances. An adult Pit Bull should walk at the very (very) least a half mile daily, and would be better off walking several miles. Puppies should never be walked long distances, as they can damage their developing bones if they're overtaxed. Older or obese dogs must not be asked to walk farther than they can comfortably manage.

Cleaning up your act

It never fails. Your dog has been denying that she has any bodily functions for the past day. Now she decides that the ideal time to defecate is when you're in the middle of a crowd of people. Should you smile nonchalantly and drag your dog along as though you don't notice, leaving behind an implicating trail? Do you kick the evidence off into the gutter? Do you let go of the leash and pretend she's somebody else's dog? While each of these ideas is tempting, you will no doubt get caught and look even worse than you already do; besides, it's people who don't clean up after their dogs who have caused dogs to be banned from so many public places. The biggest dog lover in the world doesn't love stepping in dog excrement. In fact, it's illegal in many places to not clean up dog feces.

But what to do with doo-doo? If you regularly walk your dog in a city, you may have one of those fancy poop picker-uppers. Just as easy to use, though, is a sandwich bag or plastic bag. Put your hand in it and use it as a glove to pick up the pieces, and then turn it inside out and dispose of it.

Jogging can also be fun for your dog, but you must work up to longer distances gradually and avoid jogging with your dog in hot weather. A quick look at one should confirm that Pit Bulls weren't built to be marathon runners. They can't cool themselves as well as humans can, and heatstroke has taken the lives of far too many jogging dogs. Avoid jogging your dog on hard surfaces, which are jarring to the joints. Check the footpads regularly for abrasions, gravel, tearing, or blistering from hot pavement. In the winter, check between the pads for balls of ice and rinse the feet when returning from walking on rock salt.

Beware of walkin' in a winter wonderland. Don't let your dog walk on thin ice and check between her pads for ice balls when your dog walks on any ice or snow. Also, remember to never jog with or otherwise overexert a Pit puppy.

Making a Splash

A body of water is great for keeping your dog's body exercised, yet cool. Swimming is ideal exercise for dogs with joint disorders, dogs who are recovering from injuries, or any dog in hot weather.

If your Pit Bull is hesitant about swimming, you need to entice her into the water a little at a time. Get right in the water yourself. The first time your dog goes in over her head, she may splash and become frightened. Her front feet will usually be too high to swim effectively, reaching above the water surface with each stroke. You can help by elevating her rear so that her front feet stay under the water's surface. Most Pit Bulls take only a few practice sessions before they get the drift. Many Pits become especially excited at the opportunity to retrieve a favorite toy from the water. But be careful that you don't send an exhausted dog out into deep water or into water with an undertow. Dogs do drown.

Hitting the Road

Pit Bulls make excellent road buddies. They agree with everything you say, they're always up for a side trip, they give you a good excuse to stop and enjoy the scenery, and they scare away all the bad guys. Traveling with your Pit pal can be fun. But if you don't plan ahead, traveling with your Pit Bull can be mistake.

If you're traveling by car, consider whether you have enough room for your dog, or better, your dog in her cage. Does she behave when she's left in a cage? What will you do with your dog when you need to stop to eat, use the restroom, shop, visit friends, or sightsee? If the weather is hot, you can't leave her in the car. You can't leave her tied next to the car. And in many cases, you can't take her with you.

Why can't you leave her in the car with the windows down? If your dog is sufficiently suspicious and tough looking, this may work — but even the toughest dog can be a target for dognappers or weirdos. If you have a cage, you can place your dog in it, then padlock the cage door and padlock the cage to the car for security. Never leave your dog tied to your car. Many a dead dog has been found hanging out the car window after being tied inside. One other warning: In this litigation-crazed society, it's not unheard of for somebody whose *own dog* has bitten him to seek out an unsupervised dog and claim "dog bite!" Because you own a Pit Bull, your dog is an especially tempting target for someone who's seeking compensation for a dog attack that never happened. The moral: You never know what may happen if your dog sticks her head out of the window of your car while you're shopping.

Every year, dogs die from being left in cars while their owners run inside the store for "just a minute." If it's at all warm outside, the car acts like a hothouse and the temperature rises quickly. Meanwhile, the dog's owner is inside an air-conditioned store and forgets how hot it is outside. The owner decides to shop for just a few more minutes. Then the checkout line is long. The temperature in the car rises to well over 100 degrees F, to 120 degrees F or more. The dog pants, then drools, and then finally goes into convulsions. The owner returns to the car and rushes the dog to the emergency clinic, where she requires days of intensive care for liver, heart, and brain damage — or dies. The shopping excursion ends up costing thousands of dollars, if it doesn't cost the life of a beloved pet.

This Pit Bull's owner knows that not all Pit Bulls need to be macho.

Athletic dogs like Pit Bulls enjoy the outdoors. A fenced-in yard makes a great playground.

Even tireless Pit Bull puppies need a break sometimes.

Giving your Pit Bull puppy appropriate toys — such as a sturdy ball that's too large for her to swallow — helps to create a well-adjusted, healthy, obedient adult.

How could anyone think that Pit Bulls are vicious after seeing this youngster's face?

Like most terriers, Pit Bulls are curious and self-assured.

This Pit Bull is six months old. Dogs this age should be learning all the basic obedience commands.

Is it any wonder that many people confuse Boxers and Pit Bulls? The cropped ears that are common in both breeds create an alert expression.

Pit Bulls come in almost every color and combination of colors imaginable. This Pit Bull has a bit of the Dalmatian's flair.

This Pit Bull sports a permanent black eye. Many Pit Bulls have distinct facial markings.

A well-groomed, well-trained Pit Bull is a splendidly dapper dog.

Many Pit Bulls are devoted family dogs. This breed was developed to be extremely loyal.

Pit Bulls are very responsive to obedience training; this dog is heeling beautifully.

Pit Bulls are one of the most energetic and athletic breeds — another reason they can make such a great pet for a family.

You may want to keep this photo handy — just in case you're ever asked whether Pit Bulls can get along with other pets.

Photo courtesy of Cindy Noland.

Your Pit Bull will want to share in all your holidays.

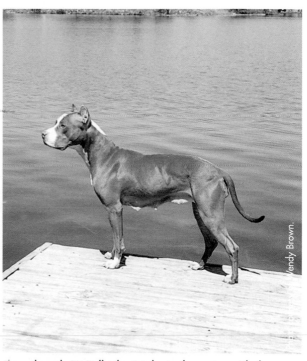

Wendy Brown.

Even though Pit Bulls don't take to the water with the enthusiasm of some other breeds, many Pit Bulls do enjoy water activities.

A Pit Bull can be a star in your life.

Keep your head and paws in the car at all times . . .

For a dog, bliss is a ride in the car, with the wind in her fur and bugs in her teeth, as she hangs her head out of the window and enjoys!

It's fun while it lasts. But it may not be long before your dog is thrown from the car, gets her nose stung by a bee, or gets her eye put out by a rock. Human children would also love to run around the car and hang their heads out of the windows, but you wouldn't dream of letting a child do that. People who let their Pit Bulls ride in the back of a pickup truck may think they look cool, but they may as well have a Pit Bull–sized bumper sticker that reads "Moron at the Wheel." No matter how well balanced your Pit Bull may seem to be, she can't stay in the pickup bed if you slam on your brakes, swerve suddenly, or get in an accident. She'll be thrown from the truck and is likely to be killed.

Doggy seatbelts are available at pet stores and through pet catalogs. Many Pit Bulls have learned to wear them. Don't think tying your dog in place by her collar will do just as well — that's a good way for your Pit Bull to get a broken neck. You can improvise by fitting your dog with a harness and attaching the harness to the seatbelt. The back seat is safer than the front, and the front seat is absolutely off-limits if your car has passenger-side airbags.

You can also keep a sturdy cage in your car. Cages have saved many a dog's life. Cages can go flying, too, so remember that the cage should be securely fastened to the car for human as well as canine safety. A sticker or tag should be on the cage that reads "In case of an accident: Take this dog to a veterinarian, then contact the following persons (list names and phone numbers), who guarantee payment of all expenses incurred." Remember that you may not be able to speak for your dog in the event of a serious accident, so have a document attached to the cage that speaks for you.

Consider where you'll be staying when you think about going on a road trip with your Pit pal. Your friends may not appreciate having a strange dog in their home, and your dog may not get along with their pets or children. Many motels do not accept dogs. Several books are available listing establishments that accept pets, so if you're traveling with a pet, buy a book that helps you plan. If you do find a dog-friendly motel, keep your dog in her cage or on your own clean sheets from home. Don't be tempted to leave your dog alone in your motel room. The dog's perception is that you've left her in a strange place and forgotten her; she either barks or tries to dig her way out through the doors and windows in an effort to find you. The odds are pretty good, too, that she becomes upset and relieves herself on the carpet. Not only will you be left holding a sizable bill, but you'll also have helped to ban dogs from yet another establishment.

If you're staying at a campground, keep your dog on leash or in an X-pen at all times. Other campers may have tiny dogs that your dog may chase, and many campgrounds have wild animals wandering through that could prove too tempting for your Pit Bull. Walk your dog away from campsites and always clean up after her.

Always keep a couple of plastic bags in your pocket. Dogs can decide to relieve themselves when and where you least expect it! Changes in water or food, or simply stress, can cause diarrhea, so be particularly attentive to taking your dog out often.

Always walk your Pit Bull on-leash when away from home. If she's frightened or distracted, your dog could become disoriented and lost. Retractable leads are perfect for traveling.

Your Pit Bull will need her own suitcase full of supplies. Pack with your dog's health and safety in mind, and consider packing:

- Bedding
- Bottled water or water from home — many dogs are very sensitive to changes in water and can develop diarrhea
- Bowls for her food and water — paper food bowls may be an easy solution to washing
- Bug spray or flea spray
- A cage
- Chewies and toys
- Collar with license tags listing the phone number of somebody who can be reached while you're on your trip
- Dog biscuits and other treats (in addition to plenty of her regular food)
- A flashlight for night walks
- Flea comb and brush
- Health and rabies certificates
- Medications, especially anti-diarrhea
- Moist towelettes, paper towels, and self-rinse shampoo
- Plastic bags or other poop disposal means
- A recent color photo in case your Pit Bull somehow gets lost
- Short and long leashes

Finding a Pit-Sitter

You may have gathered by now that sometimes you and your dog are both better off if you take your trip alone. Should you leave your dog with just a giant pile of food, hire a dog sitter, or use a boarding kennel?

If you are only going to be gone overnight, have a doggy door and an Alcatraz-like yard or kennel, and a dog that doesn't engorge herself and is healthy, then — and only then — can you leave a good supply of food and water, wave on your way out the door, and come back the next morning. But too many dogs will eat the entire supply of food as soon as you step out of the door, which could even bring on a severe case of gastric distress. You can get a feeder that's on a timer, but a determined Pit Bull may be able to break into it.

If you're going away for a day or more and not taking your dog with you, consider a pet-sitter service. Your dog will be more comfortable in her own home. You need a pet-sitter who isn't afraid of Pit Bulls and a dog who accepts strangers in the home. Good pet-sitters will want to make friends with the dog *before* you leave home. Hire a bonded, professional pet sitter. The kid next door is seldom a good choice for this important responsibility. Unless the kid next door is an experienced dog person, it's too easy for the dog to slip out of the door or for signs of illness to go unnoticed. The pet sitter should come twice a day to feed and water your dog and briefly visit with her. This works best if you have a doggy door and secure fence.

Your Pit Bull may be safer if you board her at a kennel. The ideal kennel is approved by the American Boarding Kennel Association, has climate-controlled accommodations, and keeps your Pit Bull either indoors or in a combination indoor/outdoor run. The run should be covered so that a climbing or jumping dog cannot escape, and an extra security fence should surround the entire kennel area. Someone should be on the grounds 24 hours a day.

Whatever you decide to do with your Pit Bull, always leave emergency numbers and your veterinarian's name. Make arrangements with your veterinarian to treat your dog for any problems that may arise. This means leaving a written agreement stating that you give permission for treatment and accept responsibility for charges.

Finding a Lost Love

Pit Bulls usually stick pretty close to their owners. But sometimes the unforeseeable happens, and you and your dog are suddenly separated. The best time to find a dog is right after she's lost. Too many people take too long to realize their dog is really not coming back on her own, time in which they probably could have found their dog.

"Pit Bulls can navigate home using mysterious powers." Only in the movies! Most incredible journeys are undocumented and impossible to prove. Even if they were true, 99 percent of the dogs in the world have no such powers and get lost a block away from home.

If your Pit Bull gets lost:

- ✔ Start your search at the very worst place you can imagine your dog being, usually the nearest road.

- ✔ Post large posters with a picture of your dog or a similar looking Pit Bull.

- ✔ Distribute fliers with her picture at the local animal control and police department, parking lots, veterinary clinics, and in your neighborhood.

- ✔ Take out an ad in the local paper.

- ✔ If your dog is gone overnight, consider camping out where she was last seen. If you must leave the area in which your dog was lost, try to leave her cage, blanket, some of your personal belongings, or even your open car in case the dog returns while you're gone.

Personally go to every animal shelter within at least 50 miles; talk to as many employees as you can, leave photos with them, and impress upon them that this is your *beloved* pet. Some animal shelters have rules discriminating against Pit Bulls. You must make sure that yours receives fair treatment if she's picked up.

Call every Pit Bull breeder you know, even unsavory sorts who are involved in dog fighting. Get the word out to them that you are offering a large reward, just in case somebody has taken your dog with the idea of using her for breeding, fighting, or training another dog to fight.

Proper I.D.

Your dog should always wear identification tags. In addition, she should be tattooed on her inner thigh with her registration number or microchipped or both. A microchip contains information about the dog and is placed under the dog's skin with a simple injection. Some early microchips could migrate several inches from their original site, but changes in their design have made them relatively immobile. Their shortcoming is that they require a special scanner to be read. The number is registered with one of the microchip dog-recovery agencies, which contact you if your dog is reported.

Part III
Good Bull!

The 5th Wave   By Rich Tennant

PAVLOV'S DOG

"Watch—I can make him ring that bell just by drooling a little bit."

In this part . . .

For years and years, dog training was a battle between man and beast. When that beast was a Pit Bull, guess who won? It's a wonder any dog ever learned anything, and training time was a dreaded part of the day. New training methods are easy, fun, and most of all — they work. Do both yourself and your dog a favor and work with your Pit Bull, not against it. You'll learn how here.

Learning a few tricks is worthless if your dog acts like a psychopath otherwise. Behavioral problems are one of the major causes of dog death in this country, and the results can be disastrous when that dog is a Pit Bull. Too many dogs are given up because their owners didn't know how to cope with a behavior problem, yet many times these problems could have been solved had only the right advice been available.

Once your Pit Bull prodigy has shown its potential, you can show it off in all sorts of competitions and do-gooder activities. So read on to educate your Pit Bull.

Chapter 7

Coping with a Pit Bull Terrorist

. . . .

In This Chapter

▶ Loving your dog but hating what he does

▶ Explaining why what you're doing isn't working

▶ Biting, barking, digging, peeing, pooping, jumping, and escaping — all in a day's work!

. . . .

Misbehavior is the most serious disease among dogs in this country. It accounts for more dog deaths than any sickness. This disease thrives on misinformation — and it is indeed thriving. The last decade has seen significant advances in applied animal behavior. Veterinarians or behaviorists specializing in animal behavior problems can offer the latest advice when dealing with many serious behavioral problems.

Fighting Like Cats and Dogs

Can you have more than one Pit Bull? It depends. Can you have a Pit Bull and a dog of another breed? It depends. Can you have a Pit Bull and a cat? It depends. It depends on the individual dog involved, her early exposure, and your commitment to keeping peace in the family.

Cats

Pit Bulls are generally no more aggressive toward cats and other pets than any other breed of dog would be. Aggression toward other pets is usually associated with a high *prey drive*. All dogs have a certain amount of prey drive, with hunting breeds generally having the highest. Pit Bulls have been used as hunting dogs in their past history; some are still used as hog-catching dogs. But they were never used to catch small mammals and cats hold no special allure for them. Nonetheless, any dog that hasn't been raised around members of other species may fail to identify them as fellow pets and give chase. If you want your Pit Bull to live peacefully with your other pets, your best bet is to make the introductions when your dog is still young. Introduce your Pit Bull and your cat inside or in some place where a high-speed chase could not occur. The cat should have an escape route, however, or start out on a high perch or in a cage. Feed them in the presence of one another so they associate each other with special treats. If you're still uneasy about how your Pit Bull will act, consider using a muzzle for the first face to face meeting. Be just as careful that your cat doesn't scratch your Pit Bull! Don't leave the animals together and unsupervised until you're absolutely sure that they're getting along; even then, it's seldom a good idea.

And dogs

Aggression toward strange dogs is a normal trait of canines. It's in their blood. This trait was accentuated in the early breeding of fighting Pit Bulls. Unfortunately, it can sometimes be a difficult trait to have in today's world. Pit Bulls were bred for generations to be fighting dogs. This doesn't mean that they're vicious. It does mean that many are naturally inclined to behave confidently and sometimes aggressively toward other dogs, and most are naturally inclined to try to win a fight should another dog start it. Pit Bulls from lines that recently were producing fighters may have this tendency more than Pit Bulls from lines that have not been selected for fighting in recent generations. No matter how long it's been since your dog's ancestors were used for fighting, the ability to fight another dog is one of the Pit Bull's original reasons for existence. Remember, also, that Pit Bulls were bred for *gameness*. The mellowest Pit Bull, who would never even dream of starting a fight, may also never dream of backing down from one that another dog's started.

Denying that the Pit Bull's heritage creates game and tough dogs is like denying that a retriever has a tendency to retrieve. Retrievers aren't the only breed with an inclination for retrieving, nor are Pit Bulls the only breed with an inclination for fighting. But taken as a whole, each breed has a tendency to do what its genes tell it to do. If you're vehemently opposed to owning a dog who carries sticks around, you would be ill advised to get a retriever; if you are vehemently opposed to the possibility of dog fights in your home, you would be ill advised to get more than one Pit Bull. As in any breed, there's a good deal of variation; some Pit Bulls make wonderful friends with other dogs and some make mortal enemies with them. Although dogs raised in fighting environments and from fighting lines are most likely to be dog-aggressive, even dogs raised in the best of homes and from the gentlest of lines may not tolerate other dogs. Having said this, many breeds exist that are far less tolerant of living with other dogs than Pit Bulls are. A dog with the desirable Pit Bull temperament is possessed of such self-confidence that she doesn't need to prove herself or pick fights. Even if challenged by another small dog, she will ignore him or retaliate only enough to send him on his way; he is not worth her fighting effort. But if she is challenged by a worthy opponent, she will not back down and will do what it takes to win.

The chances of dogs getting along are better if they're of opposite sexes. Two males are most likely to fight, but two females can also be antagonistic. Neutered males are less likely to fight, but spaying females doesn't have the same effect — although many females are particularly aggressive during their estrus season. Having two dogs also works best if one dog is older than the other, so that the older dog is clearly the leader of the pack. Puppies tend to get along well with their elders. Seniority counts for a lot in the dog world, and a young pup will usually grow up respecting his elders. Sometimes, a youngster gets aspirations to be top dog, however, or two dogs of about the same age never quite decide which one is leadership material. Then the trouble starts. Remember to first decide if this is natural rough play behavior between the two. An occasional disagreement, too, is normal. A disagreement that draws blood, leaves one dog screaming, or in which the two dogs cannot be separated, is a potential problem. Such disagreements, if repeated, spell trouble. Sometimes, having two dogs works out best if only one of them is a Pit Bull.

If you have an adult dog who's never been around other dogs, you need to test your Pit Bull to see how she reacts to being around another dog. Make sure that both dogs are securely restrained, not just the Pit Bull. Test the dogs on neutral territory. You can place your Pit Bull in a kennel or on a short, secure chain and walk the strange dog into view. Some dogs are actually somewhat more aggressive when in a kennel or on a chain, so if your Pit allows the other dog to approach and still acts friendly, this is a very good sign.

The next step is to put both dogs on sturdy leashes and walk them alongside each other, letting them focus on a lot of diversions. Hand out plenty of treats, but don't make them compete for them. If you're introducing a new dog into your home, ignore the newcomer around the resident dog, and praise and show affection for the resident dog whenever the new dog comes around. You need to reinforce the resident dog's feelings of leadership by always petting her and feeding her first, and letting her know that she's still the special one.

Sometimes housemates will have dominance spats. Soothing the underdog and punishing the bully is human nature, but you wouldn't be doing the underdog any favors. In the dog world the dominant dog gets the lion's share of the most precious resources. Your attention is the most precious resource your dog can have. If you give your attention to the loser, the winner will only try harder to beat the daylights out of the loser so that your attention will go where he thinks it should go — to the dominant dog. You do your losing dog a favor if you treat the winning dog like a king and the losing dog like a prince. This means you always greet, pet, and feed the top dog first. It goes against human nature, but it goes quite well with dog nature.

Even if you have two bosom-buddy dogs, you're well advised to separate them when you're not around to supervise. Little spats can arise over possession of a toy or one dog can accidentally irritate the other, leading to an escalating fight. Unlike human friends, dogs can't be trusted to back off and be polite. Every dog has the potential to get into a fight. The difference is that Pit Bulls were bred for generations to win them. Don't give your dogs a chance to get a fight started.

Aggression toward strange dogs can be more difficult to work with. This is more often a problem with males; neutering these dogs may help. The most basic "cure" is to avoid other dogs and always walk your dog on-leash. Don't allow your male to mark on trees (or anything) along your route; in doing so, he is claiming that tree, shrub, or bench as his territory, and will be more likely to defend it. Train your dog so that he knows the basic obedience commands, including the "Come," "Sit," and "Stay" commands. Bring tidbits, and when your dog sees another dog, have him perform these exercises and reward him. Don't wait until he acts aggressively to give the commands, as this only rewards the dog for his aggressive actions.

Many people pet and speak soothingly to their dog when he begins to act aggressively, but this only gives the dog the message that he's doing the right thing and encourages him to be aggressive. Similarly, don't yell and scream. To the dog, these actions indicate that you're entering the fray and are attacking the other dog as well. Don't run toward the other dog for the same reason; your dog will interpret your behavior as an attack and will be only too happy to help.

Remember that your Pit Bull's ancestry can actually help you to control her. A confident Pit Bull has no reason to pick fights, and most Pit Bulls get along well with other dogs. Pit Bulls are extremely eager to please. Fighting Pit Bulls who couldn't work with their handlers were usually not kept on, and as a result today's Pit Bull is among the most responsive of dogs. A well-trained Pit may make moves toward another dog, but should bow to her owner's wishes and cease such behavior when her owner makes it clear that such actions are not desirable.

Finally, keep in mind that many breeds of dogs are more dog-aggressive than Pit Bulls. Pit Bulls just get blamed for it more, and are better at doing something about.

Aggression toward other animals doesn't mean a dog will be aggressive toward people. Remember that Pit Bulls were developed to be dog-aggressive but people-passive.

Saving Your Home

Perhaps the most widespread behavioral problem in all breeds of dogs is that of home destruction. Pit Bulls are no more likely to engage in destructive behavior than any other breed, but they do happen to be very good at it. Shredded papers, emptied trash cans, chewed shoes, and plowed flowerpots are signs of a dog just having dog fun (see Figure 7-1). It's expected behavior for puppies, and it's also seen in bored dogs. The best cure is to take everything you need to save out of reach of your dog, and replace it with a variety of toys. The other way to prevent such behavior is to make sure your dog is too tired to go crazy when you don't want him to. Exercise his body and mind regularly so he's content to rest when inside.

Figure 7-1: If your puppy thinks it's okay to chew on boots, she won't discriminate between old and new.

Not all home destruction stems from wanton misbehavior. The most serious cases more often stem from separation, which occurs when you leave your dog alone. Pit Bulls love to be with their people; as social animals, they can become anxious if left alone. They try to get away and find you by eating and digging their way out of the doors or windows. Unlike the dog who is having a blast ripping your garbage to shreds, the dog with separation anxiety is often panting and drooling with nervousness. They may be so nervous they urinate and defecate on the floor. These dogs only tend to get worse; you need to teach them that being left alone is no big deal. Make sure your partings and reunions are low key, and leave your dog with a special treat. Start by leaving your dog alone for only a few minutes and gradually increase the time once your dog is calm for a short duration. Your veterinarian can help with drug therapy that can help you calm your dog's fears and facilitate training.

"Dogs will redecorate the house to spite their owners for leaving them alone."
Wrong! Dogs never destroy out of spite. Owners who consider this erroneous
idea to be true never cure their dogs.

Calming the Raging Bull

Let's face it — many people are afraid of Pit Bulls. Some Pit Bull owners
derive immense (if perverse) enjoyment from this, but most protest that their
puppy dogs are just big pussycats. They're usually right. Nonetheless, some
Pit Bulls can be aggressive, and their large size and powerful jaws make this
sort of behavior too dangerous to take lightly. The first step in understanding
aggression is distinguishing between play biting and real biting.

All in good fun?

Puppies and dogs play by growling and biting. Young puppies play with their
littermates this way, but once a dog has left the litter, you're the next best
thing (see Figure 7-2). So many people have seen horror stories about Pit
Bulls that if the dog growls and bites they immediately overreact and label
him as vicious. You need to know the difference between true aggression and
playful aggression. Look for these clues that tell you it's all in good fun:

- A wagging tail
- Down on elbows in front, with the rump in the air (the *play-bow* position)
- Barks intermingled with growls
- Lying down or rolling over
- Bounding leaps or running in circles
- Mouthing or chewing on you or other objects

Look for these clues to know if you'd better watch out:

- A low growl combined with a direct stare
- Tail held stiffly
- Sudden, unpredictable bites or attacks
- Growling or biting in defense of food, toys, or his bed
- Growling or biting in response to punishment

Figure 7-2:
Playful, non-aggressive interaction like this is the behavior to encourage in your dog.

Just because your dog is gnawing at you in fun doesn't mean you should let him use you as a chewie. When your pup bites you, simply say "Ouch! No!" and remove your limb from his mouth. Replace it with a toy that's not made of flesh and bone. Hitting your dog is uncalled for — your dog was just trying to play and meant no harm. Hitting is also a form of aggression that could give your dog the idea that he had better try (bite) harder next time because you're playing the game a lot rougher. You don't want to encourage playful aggression, but you don't want to punish it, either. You want to redirect it to inanimate objects. Take your dog out to play with his toys or let him burn off some energy running.

Biting the hand that feeds

Aggression toward humans is one of the most severe behavioral problems any dog can have, and it's especially dangerous in Pit Bulls. The potential for human endangerment often leads to the dog's demise. Many times, the dog is dearly loved, but the owner can no longer cope with the threat to the safety of humans.

Dog aggression toward humans can be roughly divided into aggression toward family members and aggression toward strangers. Because of the gravity of this problem, the best advice is to seek the counsel of a certified companion animal behaviorist if your dog displays any aggression toward humans.

It bears repeating: If you think that your dog displays any signs of being people-aggressive, take action. Go and see an expert behaviorist. If no behaviorists practice in your area, seek help from a veterinarian experienced in behavior or from an experienced dog trainer. Take no chances.

A decade or so ago it became the fad to train dogs as though they were puppies and to establish dominance over them using what were claimed to be the same methods a wolf parent would use. Such methods included rolling the dog on its back and pinning it there until it gave up, grabbing it by the neck and shaking it, and even biting it. The end result was a disaster. Dogs weren't fooled; they knew the difference between a person and a fellow canine. Some dogs were transformed into cowering wimps. Many more dogs took it and took it until they could no longer stand it and then they rebelled with disastrous results. The technique has probably been responsible for more dog bites to adult family members than any other.

True, it's important to be the dominant member of your pair, but bullying your way to dominance is not the answer. You place yourself in a dominant position by treating your dog gently but letting him know he's not the king. After all, you control all the valuable assets in your home, including food and attention. What would convince a dog that he ranked over a human? Actions such as:

- Petting the dog on demand
- Feeding the dog before eating your own meal
- Allowing the dog to go first through doorways
- Allowing the dog to win at games
- Allowing the dog to have his way when he acts aggressively
- Fearing the dog
- Not punishing the dog for initial instances of aggression

Dominance aggression most often occurs as a result of competition over a resource. If you try to remove food or a toy, encroach on your Pit Bull's sleeping quarters, or even try to step past your Pit Bull in a narrow hall, the dog may interpret your actions as aggressive and respond in kind. The dog may also respond aggressively toward a display of dominance by the owner (even an activity that seems harmless like petting or grooming, but also scolding, leading, or bending over the dog). Dogs may act more aggressively toward family members than strangers, and treat the family members in a dominant way, such as walking stiffly, staring, standing over them, and ignoring commands. Punishment usually only elicits further aggression.

Treatment consists of putting the dog in his place, without direct confrontations. Your dog has the ability to win in a serious direct confrontation with you. If you try to beat him into submission, you will just as likely end up the loser. At least at first, avoiding situations that may lead to a showdown is wise. If, however, your dog only growls, and *never* bites, you may be able to nip the behavior in the bud before you get nipped yourself by scolding or physically correcting the dog. If your dog is likely to bite, but you still want to try, talk to your veterinarian about temporary drug therapy to calm it sufficiently during initial training and consider having your dog wear a muzzle. If you think that you, or anyone else, may be in any danger from your dog, get professional help to retrain your Pit Bull.

You must cease and desist any of your behaviors that tell the dog he's the boss. As much pleasure as you may get from petting your dog absentmindedly as you watch TV, you can't. No more free lunches, and no more free pets, for your dog. From now on, your dog must work for his petting, his praise, and even his food. The work will be simple — just obeying simple commands from you. He must sit when you tell him to sit and wait until you've gone through doorways first. When your dog thrusts his head into your lap to be petted, you must ignore him. When you want to pet your dog, you must first have him obey some simple commands, and then pet him sparingly as a reward. Yes, it's tough love — but it may be your dog's only chance. The stakes are too high.

"You should roll a dominant dog over on his back into a submissive position." Wrong! Attempting this with a dominant dog is a good way to get bitten!

Dominance aggression is more common in males than females; occasionally (but not always) castration can help. Your veterinarian can give your intact (unneutered) male dog a drug that temporarily causes his hormonal state to be that of a neutered dog as a test to see if castration may help. Spaying a female will not help (and may even hinder) curing dominance aggression.

Owners of such dogs inevitably feel guilty and wonder "Where did I go wrong?" The fault is not entirely the owner's. Some of the owner's actions may have helped produce the problem, but dogs that exhibit dominance aggression normally have a predisposition to the problem. The owner merely added fuel to the fire by treating the dog as if the dog were king.

Fear is another cause of aggression toward people. The owner may be bitten if the dog has come to fear overzealous physical punishment, or a stranger may be bitten if she approaches and tries to touch the dog and the dog is fearful of her. In both cases, the dog bites out of self-defense — even though no real threat existed. Obviously, punishment will only make matters worse. The cure is to refrain from placing the dog in situations that make him afraid or to try to alleviate the dog's fears.

Beware of dog

A Pit Bull's aggression toward strange humans is not only dangerous, but it's also a lawsuit waiting to happen. Some dogs may be afraid of strangers and bite when approached by them. Others actively go after strangers, treating them as they would intruding dogs. Still others bite visitors to their home. Each case must be treated differently. The fear biter must have his fear treated and should never be put in a situation in which a stranger is forced upon him. The dog who goes after strangers is very likely being territorial. He must be corrected and scolded. When a stranger appears, the dog should be required to perform a few obedience commands and be rewarded with a tidbit for good behavior. The dog who attacks visitors should also be corrected and required to do some simple obedience when visitors come. Shuttling the dog into another room only increases his aggressive tendencies. You want your dog to associate visitors with good times. Eventually, you may even have your visitors give your dog treats. Regardless, don't take chances. If you worry what your dog will do, keep him on-leash at all times around strangers.

Plucking up Courage

Strangely enough, many Pit Bulls are shy of people or afraid of other dogs. Every so often a particularly imaginative Pit Bull comes up with a bizarre fear all his own, but the phobia can usually be treated using the same general concepts that I present in this section.

"The best way to deal with a scared dog is to inundate him with the very thing he's afraid of, until he gets used to it." Wrong! This strategy, called *flooding*, doesn't work because the dog is usually so terrified that he never has the opportunity to realize that the situation is actually safe. The cardinal rule of working with a fearful dog is to never push him into situations that might overwhelm him.

Don't coddle your Pit Bull when he acts afraid, because coddling reinforces the behavior. If your Pit Bull is in a situation where he's anxious, try giving him a few commands. When he performs the exercises correctly, you have a reason to praise your dog (which comforts him) and the dog's sense of security increases after he does the exercises because he knows what's expected of him. Whether it's a fear of strangers, other dogs, car rides, thunder, or being left alone, the basic concept is the same: Never hurry and never push the dog to the point that he's afraid.

Pit Bulls are characteristically gregarious with strangers, but once in a while a shy Pit Bull comes along. Shy dogs are like shy people in some ways: They're not so much afraid of people; it's more like they're afraid of being the center of people's attention. Unfortunately, the most common advice given to cure shyness in dogs is to have a lot of strange people pay attention to the dog. This usually does little except petrify the dog and further convince him to be afraid of strangers. The shy dog is learning that, for some reason, strangers seem alarmingly interested in him!

Never force a dog who's afraid of people to be petted by somebody he doesn't know; this contact in no way helps the dog overcome his fear, and is a good way for the stranger to get bitten. Strangers should be asked to ignore shy dogs, even when approached by the dog. When the dog gets braver, have the stranger offer him a tidbit — at first, while not even looking at the dog.

In the worst-case scenario, the dog is petrified at even the lowest level of exposure to whatever he's scared of. You may have to use anti-anxiety drugs, in conjunction with training, to calm your dog enough to make progress. You need the advice of a behaviorist if you think your dog may need medication.

Fear of thunder or gunshots is a common problem in older dogs. To see a normally courageous Pit Bull quivering and panting in the closet at the slight rumblings of a distant thunderstorm is a sad sight, and the fear only gets worse with time. The time to do something about this fear is at the first sign of trouble. Try to avoid fostering these fears by acting cheerful when a thunderstorm strikes and playing with your dog or giving him a tidbit.

Once a dog develops a noise phobia, try to find a recording of that noise. Play it at a very low level and reward your dog for calm behavior. Gradually increase the intensity and duration of the recording. A program of gradual desensitization, with the dog exposed to the frightening person or thing and then rewarded for calm behavior, is time-consuming. But it's also the best way to alleviate any fear.

"The scientific name for an animal that doesn't either run from or fight its enemies is lunch." —Michael Friedman

Corralling the Escape Artist

How would you teach a dog to climb over, tunnel under, or gnaw through fences? You'd start gradually, with short fences, fences with little gaps under them, and fences with weak spots. Once your Pit Bull mastered getting through these fences, you would gradually make the fence taller, snugger, and stronger, and keep improving it step by step. You'd make sure the dog had a lot of motivation to get to the other side, maybe by leaving him there all alone with nothing to do, or by making sure that all sorts of activity was visible on the other side of the fence. Being a Pit Bull, your dog would catch on fast and would be a well-educated escape artist in no time. The funny thing is, the process I just outlined is basically what many people do who *don't* want their dog to escape from the yard. If you want your dog to stay in the yard, make your yard escape proof from the very beginning.

If your dog is a digger, try burying a wire mesh fence under the ground for a foot or two inside the fence's perimeter. As a last ditch effort for an incorrigible fence jumper or digger, you may have to string electric wire just inside your fence.

Digging Up Some Dirt

I hope you took a picture of your manicured yard before your Pit Bull came along. Most Pit Bulls consider it their mission to turn a yard into a wasteland with all the charm of a toxic dumpsite. Be grateful that your yard will have personality, unlike the neighbor's cookie-cutter, boring green lawns. In case you haven't gotten the hint yet, you may as well give up on keeping your yard pristine.

Curing digging is almost impossible, but the damage is confinable. Encourage your dog to dig in a sandbox or other area of the yard shielded from the neighbors' judgmental stares. The best cure is lots of exercise. With age, most Pit Bulls seem to realize that all that digging never gets them anywhere and they lose their ardor for tunneling.

"You can teach a dog to quit digging by filling the hole with water and half-drowning the dog in it." Wrong, wrong, wrong! It doesn't work, it's cruel, and it's dangerous.

Tales from the Bark Side

The surest way to make your neighbors hate your dog is to let him bark and bark day and night. There's a big difference between a dog who warns you of a suspicious stranger and one who warns you of the presence of clouds in the sky. You may worry that you'll ruin your dog's watchdog ability by discouraging barking. But the opposite is true: A watchdog who cries wolf is useless.

Allow your Pit Bull to bark momentarily at strangers, and then call him to you and praise him for quiet behavior, distracting him with an obedience exercise if need be. If your dog won't stop barking when you tell him to, distract him with a loud noise of your own. Begin to anticipate when your dog will start barking, distract him, and reward him for quiet behavior.

Isolated dogs often bark from frustration and loneliness. Even if the attention gained includes punishment, the dog will continue to bark in order to obtain the temporary presence of the owner. A dog stuck in a pen or tied to a chain in the backyard *will* bark. What else is there to do?

The simplest solution is to move the dog's quarters to a less-isolated location. Let the dog in your house or fence him in your entire yard. Take the dog for long walks, during which he can interact with you and other dogs. If your dog barks when you put him to bed, move his bed into your bedroom. If this isn't possible, the dog's quiet behavior must be rewarded by your presence, working up to gradually longer and longer periods of quiet separation. The distraction of a special chew toy, given only at bedtime, may help alleviate barking. Remember too, a sleeping dog can't bark, so exercise can be a big help.

Chapter 8

Training the Teacher's Pit

In This Chapter

▶ Learning why fun training works

▶ Exploring why timing is everything

▶ Teaching your new dog old tricks

Dog training is an area filled with misinformation, myth, and mystery. The very thought of it so intimidates some people that they give up before they start. Don't despair! Dog training now is easier, more effective, and more fun than ever.

You're one of the lucky ones. Pit Bulls love to please people and they're eager pupils. Most cases of Pit Bull misbehavior stem not from dumb dogs but from dumb — no, make that misinformed — trainers.

Some Pit Bull owners get a perverse pleasure in how poorly trained their dog is, as though the dog's wildness were a sign of machismo. Others think training involves dominating the dog into submitting to their will. Both methods are great recipes for creating Pit Bulls who are nuisances — and even potential dangers — to others. I feel like a broken record, but: Training your Pit Bull is even more important than training most dogs, because you have to make sure that your dog never gives people the idea that Pit Bulls are bad dogs.

Besides, training's fun!

Training Your Pit to Wag Her Tail

Look at the best obedience dogs, the best drug-detection dogs, the best weight-pulling dogs — even the best fighting dogs. They all have one thing in common when they're at work: Their tails are wagging. Were they dragged, slapped, and choked until their tails just couldn't stop wagging? Of course not!

These animals enjoy every minute, not only because the work itself has been made pleasurable, but because the reward following it is also fun. Their trainers knew how to make training into a *game*. Sometimes the game may be challenging, but it's always winnable. After all, they don't describe Pit Bulls as game for nothing! Pit Bulls love a game and they love to win. Just like people, they may go through the motions of a job they're forced to do, but they'll never do it well unless it's fun.

In the old days, dog training consisted of pulling, jerking, and praising. But these old-fashioned dog-training methods based on force were difficult, ineffective, and no fun for either the dog or the trainer. Punishment may tell a dog what not to do, but it can't tell a dog what it should do. Punishment definitely can't make a dog *want* to do anything. Besides, since when has a Pit Bull been bothered by a little distraction like punishment? Pit Bulls were bred to continue on in the face of adversity; punishment is just as likely to result in them setting about doing whatever it was they were doing wrong with even more dogged determination.

Simply because you don't use punishment, that doesn't mean that your dog will be trained only with praise. Praise is essential, but not always sufficient, for training.

Pit Bulls like praise, but not as much as food and games. Praise can become a stronger motivator if you always praise immediately before you give an even stronger motivator. This way, praise signals a reward and gains strength as a secondary motivator. It may (eventually) be substituted as the only reward.

But first, you have to decide what to use as your dog's primary reward. It may be a yummy treat, a thrown ball, a quick game of tug, or a good neck scratch. Whatever it is, it will be your secret training weapon. Save this special reward for training.

Think of your Pit Bull's tail as a monitor of brain activity. When it's wagging, her brain is turned on. When it's still, her brain is in neutral. Your job is to keep it wagging while she's learning.

Working for food

Animal training has been done with force for centuries. The idea that dogs should never be trained with food has been popular for most of that time. Now, professional animal trainers and animal-learning scientists have shown that food training produces superior results. Only recently has food-motivated training become accepted in training the family dog, and owners are finding that dogs learn faster, mind more reliably, work more eagerly, and have a more trusting dog-owner relationship.

At first, use food to guide your dog into position, and then as a reward when she's in place. After your dog knows what's expected, hold the food out of sight and only give it as a reward. Gradually give the food as a reward fewer and fewer times, so that the dog is always wondering if this will be the lucky time. This is the same psychology used (very effectively) to induce people to put money into slot machines.

Making ideas click quick

Professional dog trainers go one step further. They use a signal (such as a click sound) to instantly tell the dog when she's performed correctly. The signal is then followed by a food reward. A clicker signal is used because it's fast, noticeable, and something the dog otherwise does not encounter in everyday life. In order to apply this technique to the following training guidelines, whenever giving a treat or praise is mentioned, you should precede the treat or praise with a clicker signal.

Here's an example of how to use a clicker. First, teach your dog that the clicker signals a reward. Do this by clicking and then rewarding her several times, until when she hears the click she looks expectantly at you for her treat or toy. Now that she knows about the good things that come from the clicker, say "Sit." Instead of forcing her rear down, lure her front up by holding a treat above and behind her muzzle. If she jumps up for it, don't give it to her. Only when she bends her rear legs do you click and reward. Then do it again, clicking and rewarding for successively closer approximations to the sit position. Finally your dog sits, you click, and then reward. Your dog thinks she's trained you, so she's happy, and you think you've trained her, so you're happy.

The clicker is such an effective training tool because it conveys to the dog, almost instantly, when she's on the right track. It's not so much the clicker itself that's effective, but the timing involved. Great dog trainers have great timing.

Clickers are great gadgets that make training your Pit Bull much easier. They can be found in most pet supply catalogs.

Getting the Timing Right

The crux of training is anticipation: A dog comes to anticipate that after hearing a command, she will be rewarded if she performs some action. She will eventually perform this action without assistance from you. A properly issued command has four parts:

1. **Your dog's name.** You probably spend a good deal of your day talking, with very few words intended as commands for your dog. So you need to alert your dog that these words are directed toward her.

2. **The command itself.** Make sure you use consistent terms for the desired action (not alternating, for example, "Sit" and "Down" to mean the same thing). Use an authoritative but not bullying tone.

3. **The reaction by the dog.** Many trainers make the mistake of simultane-ously saying the command word and at *the same time* placing the dog into position. *This is incorrect.* The command comes immediately before the desired action or position. When the command and action come at the same time, not only does the dog tend to pay more attention to your action of placing her in position, and less attention to the command word, but the command word loses its predictive value for the dog.

4. **The reward.** This should be presented as soon as possible after the dog has performed correctly.

Remember: name, command, action, reward!

Following the Ten Commandments

You'll do well to keep the following guidelines in mind as you train your Pit Bull.

1. Thou shalt not live in the past

Dogs live in the present; if you punish or reward them, they can only assume it's for their behavior at the time of the punishment or reward. So if you dis-cover a mess, drag your dog to it from her nap in the other room, and scold her, the dog thinks that she's being scolded for napping or that her owner is mentally unstable. Good lesson!

2. Thou shalt not train your dog to be bad

Dogs repeat actions that bring them rewards, whether or not you intend for them to. Letting your Pit Bull out of her cage to make her quit whining may work momentarily, but in the long run you end up with a dog who whines incessantly every time you put her in a cage. Make sure that you reward only those behaviors you want to see more often. When your dog misbehaves, sometimes the best thing for you to do is to stop for a second and ask your-self how you would train your dog to beg at the table, run away, jump up on you, bark to get out, or whatever bad thing she's doing. Often you will see you've been inadvertently using exactly that same method. You may have been teaching your dog to be bad.

3. Thou shalt not confuse

Lapses in consistency are unfair to the dog. If you feed your dog from the table "just this one time" because she begs, you've taught her that, even though begging may not always result in a handout, it just may pay off tonight. And this intermittent payoff produces behavior that's very resistant to change — just like the occasional slot machine jackpot keeps gamblers coming back time and time again. You could hardly have done a better job of training your dog to beg if you tried.

4. Thou shalt not speak in tongues

Your Pit Bull takes commands literally. If you've taught her that "Down" means to lie down, what must the dog think when you yell "Down" to tell her to get off the sofa — where she was already lying down!

5. Thou shalt not use force

Dogs already want to please you; your job is simply to show them the way. Forcing them can distract or intimidate them, actually slowing down learning.

6. Thou shalt not hurt thy friend

Striking, shaking, choking, and hanging are extremely dangerous, counter-productive and cruel; they have no place in the training of a beloved family member. Plus, they are the hallmarks of a dumb trainer because they don't work. Owners sometimes try to make "a correction the dog will remember" by ignoring or chastising the dog for the rest of the day. The dog may indeed realize that her owner is upset, but she won't know why. Besides, chances are that you're the one who's doing things the wrong way, not your dog.

7. Thou shalt not beat a dead horse

Your Pit Bull will work better if her stomach isn't full and will be more respon-sive to food rewards. Never try to train a sleepy, tired, or hot dog. You, and your dog, have good days and bad days. On bad days, quit. It makes no sense to continue when one or the other is not in the mood. Do one simple exercise and then go do something else. Never train your dog when you're irritable or impatient.

8. Thou shalt not end on a low note

Begin and end each training session with something the dog can do well. Keep sessions short and fun — no longer than 10 to 15 minutes. Dogs have short attention spans, and you'll notice that after about 15 minutes your dog's performance begins to suffer unless a lot of play is involved. Training a dog who's tired or bored encourages bad habits and resentment in the dog and frustration for the trainer. Quit while you're ahead — especially when training a young puppy or when you only have one or two different exercises to practice. Keep your Pit Bull wanting more and you'll have a happy, willing, and obedient partner.

9. Thou shalt not go crazy

Repeating a command over and over, or shouting it louder and louder, never helped anyone, dog or human, understand what's expected of them. Your Pit Bull isn't hard of hearing. If she acts like she is, you need to guide her toward the correct behavior, and probably need to back up a step in your training.

10. Thou shalt not lose your patience

Remember that nothing will ever go as smoothly as all of the training instructions predict. Although there may be setbacks, you *can* train your dog. Just be consistent, firm, gentle, realistic, patient — and have a good sense of humor.

"Did you ever walk into a room and forget why you walked in? I think that's how dogs spend their lives." —Sue Murphy

Going to School

Most of your training will be done in your home or yard, where your dog can concentrate on the lessons instead of new surroundings. But obedience is pretty useless if it only works at home. Once your dog learns a task, you can take her to slightly more distracting places. One of the most distracting, but useful, places to go is obedience school.

Obedience classes are filled with people who share many of your same interests. They're a great place to learn about dogs, share your dog's latest cute story with people who actually think it is cute, and meet a lot of really nice people. If you take the plunge into competition, classes are a place to celebrate wins and to laugh about failures.

A class, with its many distractions, is no place to teach your dog something new. Your dog's training should always be done at home. Use the class to practice, perfect, and troubleshoot. Class is also the place where your dog gets to show all her new friends just how smart she is.

Sometimes, your Pit will be the star pupil. Other times, you'll feel like your dog is the class dunce. If you have a particularly unruly dog, your goal may be to have your dog stand calmly beside you at the end of the course. Each dog will progress at her own pace; every dog will improve. Many dogs profit from repeating the same class, using the first time through as a warm-up.

If you plan on competing in obedience, a class is a necessity. Obedience trials are held amidst great distractions. Your dog has almost no chance of passing unless she has some experience working around other dogs.

Not all obedience classes are created equal, and some should never have been created at all. To find a good one, ask someone with a well-trained dog — preferably a Pit Bull — where they attend class. Talk to the instructor and get an idea about his or her experience with Pit Bulls. Will your dog be discriminated against? Most experienced instructors are careful about safety, so some safety precautions should be applauded. Just make sure they apply to all the dogs equally. Most experienced instructors also know how good Pit Bulls can be at obedience with the right training. Ask what techniques are used in class. If possible, sit in on the class. If the class is still using outdated yank and jerk methods, look elsewhere. If you are ever in a class and you're asked to do something to your dog that you don't feel comfortable doing, just say no. Your friend's well-being is worth too much.

Getting the Right Stuff

You can go out and spend a few hundred dollars on a radio-controlled collar, but your dog won't learn any more than if you used an old rope. The secret isn't the tools; it's the trainer. Still, having the right tools can make things go a bit easier. Besides, they make you look like you know what you're doing.

Basic training equipment usually includes a short (six foot) *lead* (another term for a leash), a long (about 20 foot) lightweight lead, and a collar. Traditionally, a choke collar has been used; most trainers now prefer a buckle collar and many are finding that the halter-type collars are best for Pit Bulls.

A choke collar is not for choking! In fact, it's more correctly termed a *slip* collar. The proper way to administer a correction with a choke collar is with a *very* gentle snap, then immediate release. The choke collar is placed on the dog so that the ring that has the lead attached to it comes up around the left side of the dog's neck and through the other ring. If the collar is put on backwards, it won't release itself after being tightened (since you will be on the right side of your dog for most training).

Never leave a choke collar on a dog!

Starting Basic Training

It's never too early or too late to start the education of your Pit Bull. If you're training a very young Pit Bull, train her for even shorter time periods than you would an adult. By the time your Pit Bull reaches six months of age, she should know "Sit," "Down," "Stay," "Come," and "Heel."

I demonstrate how easy training can be by training an imaginary pup named Sweetlips.

A common problem when training any dog is that the dog's attention is elsewhere. You can teach your dog to pay attention to you by teaching her the "Watch me" command. Say "Sweetlips, watch me," and when she looks in your direction, give her a treat or other reward. Gradually require Sweetlips to look at you for longer and longer periods before rewarding her. Teach "Watch me" before going on to the other commands.

Coming to terms

If your dog knows only one command, that command should be to come to you when called (see Figure 8-1). Coming on command is more than a cute trick; it could save your dog's life. You never know when your dog could slip out of the door or escape from her collar. Being able to call her back to you is imperative.

Sweetlips probably already knows how to come; after all, she comes when she sees you with the food bowl, the leash, or a favorite toy. You may have even used the word "Come" to get her attention; if so, you have a head start. You want her to respond to "Sweetlips, come" with the same enthusiasm she has for her supper. In other words, "Come" should always be associated with good things.

Think about what excites your Pit Bull and makes her run to you. For most young Pit Bulls, chasing after you is one of the grandest games ever invented. And, of course, most young Pit Bulls jump at the chance to gobble up a special treat. Use these two urges to your advantage when you teach your Pit Bull to respond to "Come."

Figure 8-1:
These Pit
Bulls come
when
called.

The best time to start training is when your Pit Bull is a young puppy, but it's never too late. You will need a helper and an enclosed area — a hallway is perfect for a very young pup. Have your helper gently restrain the puppy, while you back away and entice her. Do whatever it takes to make Sweetlips come to you: Ask Sweetlips if she wants a cookie, wave a treat or a favorite toy, even crawl on your hands and knees. The point is to get her attention and to get her struggling to get away from your helper so that she can get to you. Only at this point should you call out "Sweetlips, come!" with great enthusiasm, at the same time turning around and running away. Your helper immediately releases Sweetlips. Allow her to catch up to you. Reward her by playing for a second, then kneel down and give her the special treat. Repeat this exercise several times a day, gradually increasing the distance that the puppy has to travel and taking care never to practice past the time when your pup begins to tire of the game. Always keep up a jolly attitude and make the pup feel lucky to be part of such wonderful fun.

Once your puppy has learned the meaning of "Come," move your training outdoors. With the pup on a six-foot leash, enthusiastically call "Sweetlips, come!" Quickly run away. When she reaches you, praise and reward. If she ignores you for more than a second, tug on the lead to get her attention. Don't drag her as that doesn't teach the Pit Bull anything positive and a simple tug should suffice.

Your dog should understand that responding to "Come" can't be put off until she feels like coming. The longer you separate the tug from the command, the harder it is for your pup to relate the two, and, in the long run, the harder the training is on the youngster. After the tug, be sure to run backwards and make the pup think that it's all part of a grand game.

Next, attach a longer line to Sweetlips. Allow her to meander about, and in the midst of her investigations, call, run backwards, and reward. After a few repetitions, drop the long line, let her mosey around a bit, and then call. If she begins to come, run away and let her chase you as part of the game. If she doesn't come, pick up the line and give a tug, and then run away as usual.

If, at any time, Sweetlips runs the *other* way, don't chase her. The only game a Pit Bull likes more than chasing you is being chased by you. She will always win. Chase the line (not the dog), grab it, give it a tug, then run the other way.

As your dog becomes more reliable, you should begin to practice (still using the long line) in the presence of distractions such as other leashed dogs, unfamiliar people, cats, and cars. In most of these cases, you should not let the dog drag the line the way you've been practicing. Hold on just in case the distractions prove too enticing.

Some dogs develop a habit of dancing around just out of reach, considering your futile grabs to be another part of this wonderful game. You can prevent this habit by requiring your dog to allow you to hold her by the collar before you reward her. Eventually, you may even want to make her sit in front of you before you reward her — just remember to keep it fun.

This may seem like a lot of work to teach a simple command that your dog can almost teach herself, but following this system, in the long run, saves you a lot of wasted time and perhaps a lot of grief. Besides, it should be fun for you too, not just your dog!

Never have your dog come to you and then scold her for something she's done. In her mind, she's being scolded for coming, not for any earlier misdeed. Talk about mixed messages! Nor should you call your dog to you at the end of an off-leash walk. You don't want her to associate coming to you with relinquishing her freedom. Call her to you several times during the walk, reward and praise her, and then send her back out to play. (Always keep in mind that your dog shouldn't be off-leash anywhere that's not completely safe.)

Sitting bull

"Sit" is the mother of all dog commands, and with good reason. It's a simple way of controlling your dog. It's easy to teach. Plus, a Pit looks so cute and innocent when she sits.

The easiest way to teach "Sit" is to stand in front of your pup and hold a tidbit just above her eye level. Say "Sit" and then move the tidbit towards her until it is slightly behind and above her eyes. You may have to keep a hand on her rump to prevent her from jumping up. If she backs up instead of sitting down, place her rear against a wall. When she begins to look up and bend her hind legs, say "Good!" then offer the tidbit. Repeat this, requiring her to bend her legs more and more until she must be sitting before receiving the "Good!" and the grub.

Teach stationary exercises, like "Sit," "Down" (see Figure 8-2), and "Stay," on a raised surface. Using a raised surface allows you to have eye contact with your dog and gives you a better view point from which to help your dog learn. It also helps keep your little one from being distracted and taking off to go play. One other tip for these stationary commands: Don't precede them with your dog's name. When your dog hears her name, she has a tendency to jump up in anticipation — defeating the whole purpose of the command!

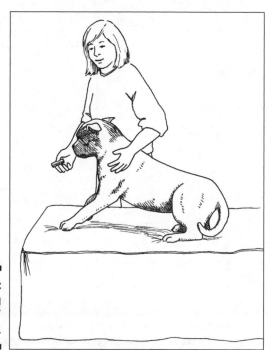

Figure 8-2:
Teaching
the "Down"
command.

Staying power

You may be able to get your dog to sit — but then she bounces back up once you've rewarded her. Require her to remain sitting for increasingly longer times before giving the reward. You can also teach "Stay," which is another very handy command for your dog to know.

A dangerous habit that many dogs have is to bolt through open doors, whether from the house into the outdoors or from a car. Teach your dog to sit and stay until you give the release signal. Only then can she walk through the door or exit the car.

Have your dog sit and then say "Stay" in a soothing voice. If your dog attempts to get up or lie down, gently but instantly place her back into position. Work up to a few seconds, give a release word ("Okay!") and praise and give a tidbit (see Figure 8-3). Next, step out from "Heel" position (starting with your right foot) and turn to stand directly in front of your dog while she stays.

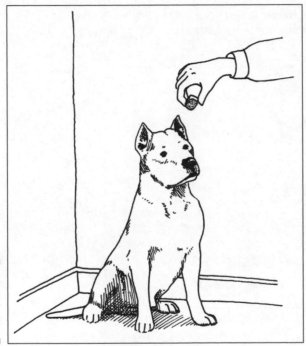

Figure 8-3:
Teaching
the "Stay"
command.

By stepping off with your right foot when you want your dog to stay and your left foot when your want your dog to heel, you give your dog an eye-level cue to compliment your verbal command.

Work up to longer times, but don't ask a young puppy to stay longer than 30 seconds. The object is not to push your dog to the limit, but to let her succeed. To do this, you must be very patient and you must increase your times and distances in very small increments. Finally, practice, with the dog on-leash, by the front door or in the car. For a reward, take your dog for a walk!

Staring into your dog's eyes as if hypnotizing her to stay is tempting, but this really will have the opposite effect! Staring is perceived by the dog as a threat and can be intimidating. The dog may squirm out of position and come to you, her leader!

Learning ups and downs

When you need your Pit Bull to stay in one place for a long time, you can't expect her to sit or stand. This situation is when "Down" command really comes in handy.

Begin teaching "Down" with the dog in the sitting position. Say "Down" and then show her a tidbit and move it below her nose toward the ground. If she reaches down to get it, give it to her. Repeat, requiring her to reach farther down (without lifting her rear from the ground) until she eventually has to lower her elbows to the ground. Never try to cram her into the down position, which can scare a submissive dog and cause a dominant dog to resist. Practice "Down-Stay" just as you did "Sit-Stay."

Walking well-heeled

Walking on a leash is the obedience exercise your Pit Bull will probably do most often, especially if you live in a place where you can walk your dog in a public area. Walking nicely beside you will take considerable practice, however (see Figure 8-4). If walking on a leash is a new experience for Sweetlips, she may freeze in her tracks once she discovers her freedom is being violated. In this case, don't simply drag her along. Instead, coax her a few steps at a time with food. When she follows you, praise and reward. Doing so helps her to realize that following you while walking on-leash pays off.

Figure 8-4:
This Pit Bull knows how to heel.

Once your pup is prancing alongside, it's time to ask a little more of her. Even if you have no intention of teaching a perfect competition "Heel," you need to teach the command as a way of letting your Pit Bull know it's your turn to be the leader.

Have your Pit Bull sit in the heel position; that is, on your left side with her neck next to and parallel with your leg. Lining up your feet and your dog's front feet is close enough. Say "Sweetlips, heel," step off with your left foot first, and continue walking. During your first few practice sessions, keep her on a short lead, hold her in heel position, and, of course, praise. The traditional method of letting the dog lunge to the end of the lead and then snapping her back is unfair if you haven't first shown the dog what is expected. A better alternative is that after a few sessions of showing the dog the proper heel position, you give her a little more loose lead and use a tidbit to guide her into correct position.

If your Pit Bull still forges ahead after you've shown her what's expected, pull her back to position with a quick, gentle tug, then release, of the lead. If, after a few days' practice, your dog still seems oblivious to your efforts, then turn unexpectedly several times. Doing so teaches your dog that it's her responsibility to keep an eye on you.

As you progress, you'll want to add some right, left, and about-faces to your walks. Also try walking at all different speeds. Then practice in different areas (still always on-leash) and around different distractions. You can teach your Pit Bull to sit every time you stop. Vary your routine to combat boredom, and keep training sessions short. Be sure to give the "Okay" before allowing your dog to sniff, forge ahead, and meander on-leash.

Keep up a pace that requires your Pit Bull to walk fairly briskly. Too slow a pace gives your dog time to sniff, look around, and in general become distracted; a brisk pace focuses the dog's attention upon you and generally aids training.

One of the many nice things about having a dog is taking her out in public. You know that you and your Pit Bull cut a sharp image as you stroll along with the dog at your side. That image is none too sharp if your dog is dragging you along behind her as she visits every fire hydrant in sight. Not only that, but your dog will be perceived as a menace and you will be exhausted by the end of what should have been a pleasurable walk if you don't teach your dog "Heel." Walking alongside of you on-leash may not come naturally to your Pit Bull, but it can come easily.

Trying Every Trick in the Book

The only problem with basic obedience skills is that they don't exactly astound your friends. For that, you need something flashy — some incredible feat of intelligence and dexterity. You need a dog trick. Try the standards: "Roll over," "Play dead," "Catch," "Shake hands," and "Speak." All these tricks are easy to teach, with the help of the same obedience concepts outlined in the basic training section.

- ✔ **"Roll over."** Teach your dog to roll over by telling Sweetlips to lie down, and then saying "Roll Over" and luring the dog over on her side with a treat. Once she's reliably rolling on her side, use the treat to guide her onto her back. Then guide her the rest of the way, eventually giving the treat only when she's rolled all the way over.

- ✔ **"Play dead."** Teach your dog to play dead by teaching your dog to lie down from a standing position. You can do this by guiding her with a treat. Require her to drop quickly in order to get the reward. Then lure her over on her side, requiring her to stay down for longer periods before getting the reward. Getting the head down is the hard part. You can try placing the reward on the floor and not giving it unless she places her head down, but you may have to use your hand for a little extra guidance.

- ✔ **"Catch."** Teach your dog to catch by tossing a tidbit or ball in a high arc over your dog's face, so that it would land just behind her nose. If your dog doesn't catch it, grab it off the ground before your dog can reach it. Eventually, your dog figures out that to beat you to the bounty she'll have to grab it before it reaches the ground.

  Do not try this teaching technique with a dog who tends to be possessive of her food!

- ✔ **"Shake hands."** Teach the shake hands trick by having your dog sit. Say "Shake" and hold a treat in your closed hand in front of your dog. Many dogs will pick up a foot to paw at your hand. These are the naturals! With other dogs, you have to give a little nudge on the leg or lure her head far to one side so that she has to lift the leg up on the opposite side. As soon as the paw leaves the ground, reward! Then require the dog to lift the leg higher and longer.

- ✔ **"Speak."** Teach this trick by saying "Speak" when it appears as if your Pit Bull is about to bark. Then reward. Don't reward barking unless you've first said "Speak."

Keep this in mind about tricks: If your dog can physically do it, you can teach your dog to do it on demand. Just use your imagination (and your patience). And have fun!

Chapter 9

Going Out to the Bull Games

In This Chapter

▶ Testing your dog's gameness the legal way

▶ Evaluating your dog's genius

▶ Competing in all the games that Pit Bulls play

Pit Bull competitions probably got their start when early butchers tried to prove to one another that their bulldog was the best. The breed was developed to its fullest when owners let their Pit Bulls fight it out in the pits. Pit Bull people, like their dogs, are a competitive bunch. Although bull-baiting and pit fighting are no longer legal, plenty of other ways of proving your Pit Bull's mettle exist today. Conformation shows are one way to compete with your dog, but your Pit Bull will probably enjoy the various competitions that encourage him to use his body and mind even more than he'll enjoy showing off in the conformation ring.

Pulling His Weight . . . and More

How can you prove your Pit Bull's mettle if you're not into dog shows and want to test working ability instead of looks? Weight pulling is the best way to ethically test your dog's athletic ability and gameness. And it's great fun!

Weight pulling is becoming accepted as the best substitute for dog fighting, as it provides a legal alternative for testing gameness. *Gameness does not mean aggressiveness*. Gameness refers to the ability to continue in the face of adversity, to continue trying no matter how difficult the task becomes. Not only is weight pulling a test of gameness, but it also tests your Pit's strength.

Weight pulling competitions stem from competitions between sled dogs, and some weight pulls are still held on snow. More often, they're held on a hard or earthen surface. The dog is attached by a harness to a cart with wheels. Weight is added to the cart and the dog is asked to pull the cart a short distance. Weight pulling competitions are sponsored by several organizations, including the ADBA.

Training to pull

Chances are, you've spent a good deal of time training your Pit Bull not to pull when he's on leash. And if he's spent any time tied out (although I don't advise the practice, I acknowledge that a lot of Pit Bull owners chain their dogs), he's taught himself that pulling is useless — so the first step in training your dog to be a champion weight puller is convincing him that sometimes it's good to pull. You'll need to buy a harness for your dog. One is shown in Figure 9-1. He will soon learn that when he's in harness, he's not only allowed, but also expected, to pull. You can get a custom fitted harness from one of the harness makers linked to the International Weight Pull Association Web site (www.iwpa.net) or one of the makers listed in ads in dog sport enthusiasts' magazines. A custom fit enables your dog to pull harder with greater comfort. You can also buy or build a cart if you want to go whole hog, but you don't have to.

As with most training and conditioning paradigms, the secret to weight training is to start slowly and avoid letting your dog fail. A dog who's used to succeeding tries to succeed. A dog who's used to failing gives up. Even if your Pit Bull is a strong dog capable of pulling you down the street, start him off with a light load. A cinderblock or tire works well. Your goal at this point is to teach him the concept of pulling when asked to do so, not to test his strength. If your dog already knows how to "Stay" and "Come" you're ahead of the game. Attach his harness to the tire, tell him to stay, walk in front of him, and say "Pull!" Encourage him to come to you. When he does, praise him lavishly. Continue to practice until you can call him from 15 feet away.

Figure 9-1:
A Pit Bull
and his
weight-
pulling
harness.

Why all this attention to training? A well-trained dog understands what's being asked of him and pulls more decisively. He is less likely to injure himself because he isn't lunging against his harness. He's learned how to use his body effectively, pulling slowly, steadily, and strongly. He's developed the confidence that he's doing what is expected and that he can succeed in what you've asked him to do.

Careful training, however, is only half the equation for producing a successful pulling dog. Your dog needs to develop his strength and stamina before tackling higher weights. Take your dog for a brisk walk while he drags a tire. Work up to a longer distance of about a mile. Once he's strutting along easily, add slightly more weight. Your dog should be conditioned using long walks with light loads before you ask him to try his first heavyweight pulls.

Add extra weight by adding additional tires or packing tires with bricks. When working with heavy weights, build up gradually. Remember: The heavier the weight, the shorter the distance you should ask your dog to walk. Make your dog quit while he still feels like a winner. Start with only a couple of pulls per day, and don't weight train every day. Muscles need a chance to recuperate after weight training; challenging them every day tends to break them down, not build them up.

Feed your dog a well-balanced diet that's slightly higher in protein than you would feed him if he were not working. Weight pulling is an athletic event; treat your competitor like the athlete he is.

One more type of training is in order. Your dog will have to wait for his turn in a holding area along with other dogs. He must wait politely, neither growling nor behaving aggressively toward the other dogs. If you cannot control him, he may be asked to leave.

ADBA weight pulling competition

To enter an ADBA weight pulling competition, dogs must be ADBA registered, at least nine months old, neither spayed nor neutered, not in heat, and not aggressive to people. Dogs compete within their weight ranges and males and females compete together. The weight ranges are as follows:

- 35 pounds and under
- 35 to 45 pounds
- 45 to 55 pounds
- 55 to 65 pounds
- 65 to 75 pounds
- 75 to 90 pounds

Although you can borrow a harness at the pull, your dog will be more comfortable in his own custom-fitted harness. The harness attaches to the cart by means of *traces,* or connecting lines, between 4 and 6 feet in length. To qualify, dogs must pull the cart and weight a total of 15 feet in 60 seconds. You can entice your dog forward with a toy or other incentive, but you can't use food, a live animal, anything that encourages aggression towards humans, or anything that could give the breed a bad image. Fouls are called if you push or drop the dog at the start, touch the dog or cart while he's pulling, allow the dog to touch the toy or incentive during the pull, act aggressively to the dog, or if the dog runs out of time. Three fouls and you're out!

Placements within each class are determined by the most weight pulled per pound of body weight. Points are given for first place (8 points), second place (5 points), and third place (3 points). An additional award is made to the dog pulling the most weight. Ten points are given for Most Weight Pulled and for Most Pulled per Pound. To win the ADBA (or, technically, the ADBSI, for American Dog Breeders Show Inc.) weight pulling title of *Ace* your dog needs a total of 100 points.

Once your dog is an Ace, he can compete in the Ace class. It, too, is divided by weight: 44 pounds and under; 44 to 64 pounds; and 64 pounds and over. Points are given out as follows: 1st: 10 points; 2nd: 7 points; 3rd: 4 points; Most Weight: 15 points; Most Weight per Pound: 15 points. Your dog is an Ace of Ace once he wins 100 points in the Ace class. After that, each additional 100 points in the Ace class advances the title. An Ace of Ace I has a total of 300 points. An Ace of Ace II has a total of 400 points, and so on.

IWPA weight pulling competition

The International Weight Pull Association (IWPA) is open to all dogs. IWPA rules make it more difficult for an untrained dog to compete, so dogs are typically more experienced and polished than at ADBA pulls.

Your dog must be between 12 months and 12 years of age to enter. Pregnant females or females in estrus cannot compete. Six weight classes are offered:

- 35 pounds and under
- 36 to 60 pounds
- 61 to 80 pounds
- 81 to 100 pounds
- 101 to 120 pounds
- 121 pounds and over

An IWPA weight pull differs from an ADBA weight pull in several respects. The handler can't entice the dog with toys or even stand right in front of the dog.

Instead, the handler must stay behind the front of the cart or behind the finish line. Whereas two handlers are allowed at an ADBA pull, only one is allowed at an IWPA pull. The dog may begin a pull with as much as one foot of slack in the line at an ADBA pull; at an IWPA pull only enough slack is allowed to prevent the dog from accidentally moving the cart before the start. The dog must pull the weight 16 feet in 60 seconds.

Placements are awarded within each class on the basis of maximum weight pulled. Points are awarded as follows: 5 points for first place, 3 points for second place, and 1 point for third place. In addition, each qualifying dog receives 1 point for every dog he defeats, with the last place dog getting ½ point. Dogs compete for season's standings on the basis of their five best pulls made during the IWPA pulling season of September 1 to March 31. For your dog to earn points, you must be a member of the IWPA.

Working dog certificates are awarded for pulling a certain percentage of the dog's own weight. To earn the Working Dog (WD) title, a dog must pull 12 times his own weight on four occasions during the pulling season. To earn the Working Dog Excellent (WDX) title, a dog must pull 18 times his own weight four times during the season. To earn the Working Dog Superior (WDS) title, a dog must pull 21 times his own weight three times during the season.

The next time that you're taking your Pit Bull for a walk and you feel like you're being dragged behind him, remember that Pit Bulls are *very* good at pulling. They hold the following International Weight Pulling Association all-breed records:

- ✔ For dogs between 20 and 29 pounds: 1580 pounds
- ✔ For dogs between 30 and 39 pounds: 2000 pounds
- ✔ For dogs between 40 and 49 pounds: 2030 pounds
- ✔ For dogs between 50 and 59 pounds: 2879 pounds

Want to try to beat 'em? Contact the ADBA or IWPA to get started. Visit the International Weight Pull Association at www.iwpa.net or e-mail it at info@iwpa.net; ADBA pulling rules can be found at members.aol.com/bstofshw.

Staying in Step with Obedience

Think your Pit Bull's gifted? What to prove it? You don't have to send your dog to graduate school to adorn his name with degrees. An obedience trial is your chance to earn titles that attest to your dog's genius. You just need to teach your dog some simple exercises (and then teach him some really hard ones).

You can teach the exercises at home, but you should also enroll in a good competition-centered obedience class. Although most classes are aimed at

AKC trials, just a few modifications are needed to train your dog for UKC trials. Classes are a valuable source of training advice and encouragement from people who are experienced obedience competitors. They provide an environment filled with distractions — similar to the environment that you'll encounter at an actual trial. And perhaps most of all, they provide a ready source of shoulders to cry on for the all those trials you should have passed but somehow didn't.

The purpose of obedience trials is not to show how you can dominate your dog and have him obey your every word. Rather, it's to demonstrate teamwork while performing certain progressively more difficult exercises. A happy Pit Bull who makes a few errors should be preferred to a cringing dog who goes through the exercises error-free.

Unless both you and your Pit Bull are prodigies, expect to fail a few trials. Failing a trial, in the grand scheme, is an insignificant event. Your dog will forgive you for the times it was your fault; be sure that you can do the same. Don't let a ribbon or a few points become more important than a trusting relationship with your companion. The UKC awards four obedience titles: Companion Dog (U-CD), Companion Dog Excellent (U-CDX), Utility Dog (U-UD), and Obedience Champion (U-OCH). Titles are awarded after a dog qualifies at three trials, which means passing each exercise while getting at least 170 total points out of 200 possible points.

"I think animal testing is a terrible idea; they get all nervous and give the wrong answers." —Unknown

Novice (U-CD) exercises

The Novice exercises are those that any well-behaved dog should know. With a little training, and a little more polishing, the U-CD title is within reach of almost every Pit Bull, no matter how inexperienced the trainer. The single caveat is that the dog must be absolutely trustworthy around other dogs, as he will be in the ring off-leash with strange dogs. Never take chances for the sake of a title. Most Pit Bulls have no trouble behaving themselves with other dogs and enjoy the chance to compete.

Open (U-CDX) exercises

The Open exercises ask more of the dog than the Novice ones. Whereas Novice exercises emphasize basic control, Open exercises ask the dog to work away from the handler and to perform exercises he might not otherwise do in everyday life. Most Pit Bulls are capable of completing the title, but it does take a lot of work.

Utility (U-UD) exercises

Utility exercises ask the dog to perform tasks that could, under certain circumstances, be valuable to the handler. Although most Pit Bulls are capable of learning them, not all Pit Bull trainers are capable of teaching the exercises. Years of hard work are often required to earn a U-UD, making it one of the most illustrious titles in the dog world.

The UKC Obedience Champion (U-OCH) title is awarded after the U-UD. A combination of a special dog, a skilled handler, and immense dedication is required to win this award.

Pit Bulls may not seem like obedience whiz dogs at first glance, but once you see a good one in action you'll stand in awe at their ability. Unfortunately, too many Pit Bulls are never given the chance to prove that their brains equal their brawn. Most dogs kept for fighting purposes were trained only for fighting, and otherwise spent their time chained away from the family. Pit Bulls are portrayed as mindless fighting machines by the media, to the extent that even Pit Bull owners didn't bother to try training them. Even some obedience classes, where they should know better, discriminate against Pit Bull students. Yet those Pit Bulls who have taken the obedience challenge have demonstrated that they can compete with the best of them. Their happy, attentive attitude makes them eager to learn the most challenging exercises. Their gameness gives them the fortitude to keep on trying, even when the lessons become frustrating. Their physique gives them the stamina to keep practicing when other dogs have fallen by the wayside. The truth is, Pit Bulls almost have an unfair advantage in obedience trials.

What are you waiting for? Even if you turn up your nose at the idea of pursuing titles with your dog, the competitions are fun and the training brings you and your Pit Bull even closer together.

The AKC also offers obedience trials for American Staffordshire Terriers. The exercises and titles are roughly similar to the UKC exercises.

Overcoming Obstacles

For all of their brawn, Pit Bulls are amazingly agile. Not surprisingly, they excel at the new sport of . . . agility! Agility (the sport, not the attribute) also puts to good use the Pit Bull's never-ending quest for a challenging game. In the sport, dogs face an obstacle course they run through as fast as possible, while jumping, balancing, climbing, weaving, running through tunnels, and having lots of fun.

In competition, various obstacles are arranged in various configurations that vary from trial to trial. Handlers can give unlimited commands, but they can't touch the obstacles or the dog. Points are lost for refusing an obstacle, knocking down a jump, missing a contact zone, taking obstacles out of sequence, and exceeding the allotted time limit.

The obstacles vary depending on the type of agility competition you and your dog enter, but could include jumping over fences and bushes, going through tunnels, walking over a teeter totter, traversing bridges, and weaving through poles. The height of the jumps and the size of the tunnels are adjusted according to the height of your dog at the withers and the depth of his chest.

Many obedience clubs are now sponsoring agility training, but you can start working on some of the fundamentals at home. Entice your dog to walk through a tunnel made of sheets draped over chairs; guide him with treats so that he weaves in and out of a series of poles made from several plumber's helpers placed in a line; get your dog comfortable with walking on a wide, raised board; teach him to jump through a tire and over a hurdle. Make sure that he knows the basic obedience commands ("Sit," "Down," "Come," and "Stay") and makes sure that he's comfortable and controllable around other dogs.

Remember that agility training is for agile dogs, and agile dogs are athletic dogs! Don't think you can have your Pit Bull waddle into an agility competition. You don't want to hold your breath as he walks on a plank, hoping that it won't break. You need to condition your Pit Bull like the athlete he is. You also need to have a vet check his health beforehand, to make sure that your dog isn't dysplastic, arthritic, or visually impaired.

High jumping and vigorous weaving can impose undue stress on immature bones. These activities should be left until adulthood.

The UKC offers progressively more difficult levels of competition.

- **Agility I** (U-AG I) consists of 13 obstacles. Six of these are non-hurdles, six are hurdles, and one is a pause table (where the dog must sit or lie down for several seconds).

- **Agility II** (U-AGII) consists of 16 obstacles, including seven non-hurdle obstacles, eight hurdles and a pause box, all arranged in a more challenging fashion than in Agility I.

The AKC and several other organizations also offer agility competitions.

Staying on Track

Neither the UKC nor the ADBA offer tracking trials. This is too bad, because Pit Bulls are excellent trackers when given the chance. Schutzhund clubs do offer the FH tracking title to all Pit Bulls, but for tracking competitions, the AKC is probably your best bet. It offers several tracking titles.

- ✔ The Tracking Dog (TD) title requires the dog to follow an approximately 500 yard track with three to five turns laid by a person from 30 minutes to 2 hours before.

- ✔ The Tracking Dog Excellent (TDX) title entails following a longer and older trail with more turns and more challenging circumstances.

- ✔ The Variable Surface Tracking (VST) title requires trailing over a variety of surfaces, such as might be encountered when tracking in the real world.

The younger your Pit is when you teach him to follow his nose, the easier your training is. One way to train your Pit Bull to track is to drop little treats along your trail as you walk, and then let the dog follow along your trail and find them. The dog will soon learn that he can find treats simply by following your trail. As training progresses, the treats get dropped farther and farther apart, until eventually only one big reward waits at the end of the trail. Another way to train is to hide from your dog and have a helper release him to go find you. Once you've taught your dog to follow his nose, you're on the right track to a tracking title.

Getting a Grip on Schutzhund

Although Pit Bulls aren't the first breed that comes to mind when the topic of Schutzhund training comes up, they are capable of doing well in Schutzhund. Schutzhund (which means *protection dog* in German) was developed primarily to test German protection breeds in tracking, obedience, and protection.

A Schutzhund dog must show courage — holding his grip on the subject even when the subject deals him a few blows with a stick. Pit Bulls define courageous, so they seldom have problem with this. A Schutzhund dog must also have gripping power, enabling him to hold on despite the subject's attempts to be freed. Pit Bulls are unsurpassed when it comes to grip. A Schutzhund dog must be obedient. Pit Bulls are intelligent and eager to please.

The importance of finding an experienced instructor — who emphasizes obedience and dog control — cannot be overemphasized. It's best if the instructor has experience training Pit Bulls, as the techniques that work with the more popular Schutzhund breeds often don't work with Pit Bulls. For example, compared to other Schutzhund breeds, many Pit Bulls are more reluctant to bite a human. (Don't worry: The people being bitten wear a special padded sleeve that teeth can't go through.)

Several levels of Schutzhund competition are offered, progressing in difficulty from Schutzhund One (SCH I) on to Schutzhund Two (SCH II) and Three (SCH III). Several organizations offer Schutzhund competition, but some only allow American Staffordshire Terriers (or require that you label your APBT as an AmStaff), and some don't allow Pit Bulls to compete.

The sport of Schutzhund is controversial in America because many people perceive it as attack dog training. Training a controversial breed, such as the Pit Bull, in this controversial sport is something to be wary of. Many Pit Bull owners worry that the image of a Pit Bull biting a person in protective garb will further the image of the Pit Bull as a vicious dog. Those who train their Pit Bulls in Schutzhund contend that the high degree of responsiveness necessary for these dogs to compete should give the opposite impression: that of a highly trained dog who can be called off an attack.

One important fact: Attack or protection training without obedience training is not Schutzhund! It's a dangerous imitation, and you're better off not to train your Pit Bull at all than to train him only partially in Schutzhund.

Rounding Up a Herding Title

The idea of a Pit Bull working as a herding dog may seem odd at first, but recall that one of the Pit Bull's first jobs was as a stock dog, assigned the task of keeping unruly bulls marching to slaughter. Still, don't expect to see a Pit Bull at one of the Scottish herding trials, where Border Collies put sheep through a complex series of maneuvers. Pit Bulls work best when confronted with unruly stock. However, some Pit Bulls have earned herding titles with a variety of animals, including cattle, sheep, and even ducks.

Training a dog to herd takes a lot of work. If you think your Pit Bull may have potential, find somebody with stock who can show you the ropes. See if your Pit Bull can earn the entry-level title of Herding Certified, which means the dog moves to gather or drive the stock without attempting to attack or scatter them. A variety of more advanced titles are available from the American Herding Breed Association.

Part IV
The Fit Pit

The 5th Wave   By Rich Tennant

AFTER CHASING THE RABBIT FOR MANY HOURS, BUSTER FOUND HIMSELF VERY FAR FROM HOME INDEED

In this part . . .

Pit Bulls are healthy critters! They can be even health-ier if you take good care of them. Here, you'll find the real skinny on dog foods, beauty secrets, and preventive health care, and how to tell when things aren't right and what to do. Your dog depends on you for this; don't let him down. There will be a test!

The worst kind of test is the pop quiz of an emergency. Make sure you've studied the first aid chapter ahead of time because you never know when it will spring, and a failing grade here has dire consequences.

I hope you will keep your dog its entire life, and I hope that will be a long time. You're just the sort of person who deserves a great dog and the sort of person a great dog deserves. Great dogs and great people experience great sorrow with the loss of the other, but that is part of having a great relationship.

Chapter 10

Feeding a Bottomless Pit Bull

In This Chapter
▶ Walking down the pet food aisle
▶ Avoiding foods that are bad for dogs
▶ Giving the scoop on natural diets
▶ Reading the label
▶ Losing weight or putting it on

The Pit Bull is a great animal. Potentially, she has a powerful physique, an energetic psyche, and surprising longevity. One of the factors that influences whether your Pit Bull can reach her full potential is the food that you place in front of her. The fact that most dogs are usually fed one type of food makes choosing that food even more important and intimidating. All it takes is one dizzying trip through the dog food section of a supermarket, pet supply store, or dog show vendor aisle to leave you utterly baffled and feeling like the worst dog owner ever created. Are the cheap ones really poisoning your dog? Are the expensive ones really providing better nutrition via bee wings, armadillo milk, or whatever other esoteric ingredients have convinced you to spend money like a drunken sailor on that precious bag of grub?

Before you become paralyzed with indecision, keep in mind that dog nutritionists have done most of the work for you, and that as long as your food passes some basic guidelines it will be adequate to sustain your dog's life. It may not make him bloom with condition, however. For that, you do need to do a little investigating.

Food for Thought

Some people assume dogs should eat only meat. But dogs are actually omnivorous, meaning their nutritional needs can best be met by a diet derived from both animals and plants. Most dogs do love meat, but a balanced meal should combine both meat and plant-based nutrients.

"Ever consider what they must think of us? I mean, here we come back from a grocery store with the most amazing haul — chicken, pork, half a cow. They must think we're the greatest hunters on earth!" —Anne Tyler

Dry food (containing about 10 percent moisture) is the most popular, economical, and healthy form of dog food. It's also the least enticing. Semi-moist foods (with about 30 percent moisture) contain high levels of sugar — used as a preservative. They are tasty, convenient, and very handy for traveling, but are not an optimal nutritional choice as a regular diet. Canned food has a high moisture content (about 75 percent), which helps to make it tasty, but the high moisture content also makes canned food comparatively expensive, because you are, in essence, paying for water as well as nutrients. Most Pit Bull owners feed a combination of dry and canned food, supplemented with dog biscuits as treats.

The Association of American Feed Control Officials (AAFCO) has recommended minimal nutrient levels for dogs based upon controlled feeding studies. Unless you are a nutritionist, the chance of your cooking up a homemade diet that meets these exacting standards is remote. So the first rule is to select a food that states on the label not only that it meets the requirements set by the AAFCO, but also that it has been tested in feeding trials.

Feed a high quality food from a name-brand company. Avoid food that's been sitting on the shelf for long periods or that has holes in the bag or grease on the bag. Use your common sense and skip over the dog food that's covered with webs or tiny moths.

Always strive to buy and use only the freshest food available. Dry food loses nutrients as it sits, and the fat can become rancid.

Good taste counts! Mealtime is a highlight of most dogs' days, so it only seems fair to try and offer Fido a yummy meal as well as a nutritious one (see Figure 10-1). But beware of one phenomenon that I've been burned by too many times: Dogs often seem to love a new food when it's first offered to them. You go to the store, buy a huge bag, and the dog suddenly seems to lose interest — the novelty's worn off! Another reason (freshness is the first) to not buy the largest bags of dog food that you can find.

"Dogs don't like variety in what they eat." Most dogs, unless they've been raised on only one food, prefer a varied menu.

Although you shouldn't devise your own home-cooked diets, you can prepare nutritious meals at home for your dog if you do some research first. Many balanced diets are available that you can use as guides; just be sure to examine the credentials of the diet's creator.

Figure 10-1:
Give your
dog food
that's
nutritious
and tasty
too.

Avoid feeding the following:

- Chicken, pork, lamb, or fish bones. These can be swallowed and their sharp ends can pierce the stomach or intestinal walls.

- Any bone that could be swallowed whole. Swallowing a bone could cause choking or intestinal blockage.

- Any cooked bone. Cooked bones tend to break and splinter.

- Mineral supplements (unless advised to do so by your veterinarian).

- Chocolate. It contains theobromine, which is poisonous to dogs.

- Onions. Onions can cause red blood cells to break down, sometimes causing serious illness in dogs that eat them.

- Alcohol.

Avoiding bloat

Bloat is a life-threatening emergency in which gas and fluid become trapped in the stomach. It is most common in large, deep-chested breeds. In the most thorough study of bloat to date, several factors affecting bloat emerged. Dogs who are fearful, eat fast, and eat only one meal a day are more likely to bloat. Stress seems to precipitate a bloating episode. Dogs with stable temperaments and dogs who eat some canned food and table scraps are less likely to bloat.

To be on the safe side, you should

✔ Feed several small meals instead of one large meal

✔ Include some canned food or table scraps

✔ Not allow the dog to gulp food

✔ Not allow your dog to be stressed around his mealtime

✔ Restrict water for an hour after eating

✔ Discourage your dog from running or jumping for an hour after eating

✔ Pre-moisten food, especially foods that expand when moistened

What about BARF?

Bones and Raw Food (BARF) diets have gained a lot of attention and many supporters. These diets advocate feeding dogs whole raw animal carcasses, particularly chicken, in order to simulate the foods that dogs have been eating for thousands of years. Feeding basically consists of throwing a carcass on the floor, which the dog then eats, bones and all.

Proponents claim good health, clean teeth, and economical food bills follow in the wake of BARF. But keep in mind that controlled studies on the safety and efficacy of the BARF diet have yet to be published.

Detractors point out that, even though the BARF diet is similar to the diet that wolves have, dogs are no longer wolves and haven't had to live off the land for thousands of generations. They worry that these diets may have safety problems because of the possibility of salmonella and *E. coli* associated with meat processing. (Dogs can get salmonella and *E. coli* poisoning, but they are more resistant to them than are humans.) If you decide to go ahead and follow the BARF route, avoid feeding raw meat to dogs with compromised immune systems and try to find meat that is fresh and locally processed.

"Large dogs should be given calcium supplements to help their bones grow." Don't fall for this one — it could be detrimental to your dog's health. High calcium intake results in an imbalance of other minerals and has been associated with cartilage problems and lameness.

Boning Up on Nutrition

A good rule to follow is that three or four of the first six ingredients of a dog food should be animal derived. These tend to be tastier and more highly digestible than plant-based ingredients; more highly digestible foods generally mean less stool volume and less gas problems.

When comparing food labels, keep in mind that differences in moisture content make it difficult to make direct comparisons, unless you first do some calculations to equate the percentage of dry matter food. The components that vary most from one brand to another are protein and fat.

Protein provides the necessary building blocks for the growth and maintenance of bones, muscle, and coat, and for the production of infection-fighting antibodies. The quality of protein is as important as the quantity of protein. Meat-derived protein is more highly digestible than plant-derived protein. Most Pit Bulls do fine on regular adult foods having protein levels of about 20 percent (in a dry food).

Fat is the calorie-rich component of foods, and most dogs prefer the taste of foods with higher fat content. Fat is necessary to good health, aiding in the transport of important vitamins and providing energy. Dogs who don't consume enough fat often have sparse, dry coats.

"The food with the most protein is always the best." Wrong again. Protein is an important component of dog foods, but most dogs don't need high protein foods unless they're under a great amount of physical stress.

Choose a food that has a protein and fat content best suited for your dog's life stage, adjusting for any weight or health problems. Remember that prescription diets formulated for specific health problems are available.

- Puppies, as well as pregnant and nursing mothers, need particularly high protein and somewhat higher fat levels in their diets — such as the levels found in puppy foods.
- Stressed, highly active, or underweight dogs should be fed food with a high protein level or even puppy food.
- Obese dogs or dogs with heart problems should be fed a low fat food.
- Older dogs, especially those with kidney problems, should be fed moderate levels of food with very high-quality protein. High protein diets do not cause kidney failure in older dogs; but a high protein diet will do a lot of harm to a dog who's already suffering from kidney stress. So decrease the overall level of protein, but increase the quality of the protein that you offer him.

Introduce new foods gradually, mixing in more and more of the new food with the old, each day for several days.

One of the great mysteries of life is why the dog, a species renown for his lead stomach and tendency to eat out of garbage cans, can develop a violently upset stomach from changing from one high-quality dog food to another. But it happens.

Eschewing the fat

The Pit Bull is an athlete and should have an athlete's body: lean and muscular. A Pit Bull in proper weight should have a slightly hourglass figure, whether viewed from above or the side. The stomach should be slightly tucked-up. There should be no roll of fat over the withers or rump. The ribs should be easily felt through a layer of muscle.

Putting your Pit Bull on a diet is hard, but you may have no choice. Obesity predisposes dogs to joint injuries and heart problems and makes many pre-existing problems worse. An obese Pit Bull is hardly a Pit Bull at all! After all, she can't run, jump, and frolic with boundless energy.

Overweight Pit Bulls should be fed a high fiber, low fat, and medium protein diet dog food. Commercially available diet foods, which supply about 15 percent fewer calories per pound, are preferable to just feeding your Pit Bull less of a fattening food. Home prepared diets are available that are both tasty and less fattening — just remember to do very careful research and ask your vet before you cook for your dieting dog.

Many people find that one of the many pleasures of dog ownership is sharing a special treat with their pet. Rather than giving up this bonding activity, substitute a low calorie alternative such as rice cakes or carrots. Keep your dog out of the kitchen or dining area at food preparation or meal times. Schedule a walk immediately following your dinner to get your dog's mind off of your leftovers — going for a walk is good for both of you.

If your dog remains overweight, seek your veterinarian's opinion. Heart disease, some endocrine disorders, such as hypothyroidism or Cushing's disease, or the early stages of diabetes can cause the appearance of obesity. A dog in whom only the stomach is enlarged, without fat around the shoulders or rump, is especially suspect and should be examined by a veterinarian. However, most fat Pit Bulls are simply fat!

Skin and bones

It's more unusual to see a skinny Pit Bull than to see an obese one. A dog that loses weight rapidly or steadily for no apparent reason should be taken to the veterinarian. A few dogs just don't gain weight well, and some are just picky eaters.

Sometimes picky eaters are created when their owners begin to spice up their food with especially tasty treats. The dog then refuses to eat unless the preferred treat is offered, and finally learns that if he refuses even that proffered treat, another even tastier enticement will be offered. Try a couple of dog food brands, but if your Pit Bull still won't eat then you may have to employ some tough love. Give your dog a good, tasty meal, but don't succumb to Pit Bull blackmail or you may be a slave to your dog's gastronomical whims for years to come.

One exception does exist: A sick or recuperating dog may have to be coaxed into eating. Cat food or a baby food with meat in it are relished by dogs and may entice a dog without an appetite to eat. You may also try cooking chicken breasts or other meat and offering that to your dog, but ask your veterinarian first.

Underweight Pit Bulls may gain weight if you feed them puppy food; add water, milk, bouillon, ground beef, or canned food and heat slightly to increase aroma and palatability. Be cautious if you add milk, as it causes many dogs to have diarrhea. Try only a little bit at first to see how your dog reacts. Of course, once you start this gourmet treatment, you know that you're making your picky eater even pickier.

Impress your friends with this bit of dog food trivia: Dogs have most of the same taste receptors that we do, including similar sugar receptors (which explains why many have a sweet tooth). But their perception of artificial sweeteners isn't like ours — artificial sweeteners taste bitter to them. Research has shown that dogs, in general, prefer meat (not exactly earth-shaking news), and though there are many individual differences, the average dog prefers beef, pork, lamb, chicken, and horsemeat, in that order.

Feeding Time

Some people let the dog decide when to eat by making food available at all times. If you choose to let the dog self-feed, monitor her weight to be sure she's not overindulging. Leave only dry food available. Canned food spoils rapidly and becomes both unsavory and unhealthy. If your dog starts to pack on the pounds, you'll have to intervene before you have a roly-poly Pit Bull on your hands. One other drawback to letting your dog self-feed: You don't get a sense of how her appetite is fluctuating. Dramatic appetite swings may signal illness.

Feeding your dog on a schedule is normally in her best interest. Adult dogs can be fed once a day, but smaller meals twice a day are better. Very young puppies should be fed three or four times a day, on a regular schedule. Feed them as much as they care to eat in 15 minutes. When pups get a little older, from the age of three to six months, they should be fed three times daily (see Figure 10-2).

Figure 10-2:
It's best to feed your Pit Bull pup on a schedule.

Terrier Perrier: Water for Your Dog

Water is essential for your Pit Bull's health and comfort. Don't just keep your dog's water bowl full by topping it up every day. Such a habit allows algae to form along the sides of the bowl and gives bacteria a chance to multiply. Empty, scrub, and refill the water bowl daily.

If the water bowl runs dry, your dog may turn to the toilet bowl as an alternative source. In fact, you should make it a practice to keep the lid down, because many dogs view the toilet bowl as an especially deluxe watering hole! It should go without saying that drinking from the toilet is not a healthy practice — and definitely not conducive to dog kisses!

Chapter 11

Primping Your Pit Bull

In This Chapter

▶ Bathing your Pit Bull the easy way

▶ Trimming your dog's nails

▶ Keeping your dog's ears and eyes healthy

▶ Brushing your dog's teeth

Pit Bulls don't need much primping to look their best. But good grooming isn't just important for the sake of beauty — it can also help prevent serious health problems. Grooming your Pit Bull involves more than an occasional brushing. Keeping the nails, teeth, eyes, and ears well groomed is probably more important than keeping your dog's coat in top condition. The well-groomed Pit Bull not only looks good, she feels good.

Taking Your Pit to the Cleaners

The Pit Bull beauty kit isn't very big. All you need is a natural bristle brush, which when used properly, distributes the natural oils, is easy on the skin, and feels good to the dog. But sometimes your Pit Bull will need more than brushing. Sometimes, she'll need that ultimate of Pit Bull torture devices: a bath!

"If they ever have a haunted house for dogs, I think a good display would be a bathtub full of soapy water." —Jack Handey

Don't wait until your Pit Bull is fully mature (and strong enough to give *you* a bath) before you introduce her to the wonders of soap and water. Start when she's little and still thinks that you have good ideas. Start your bath training with semi-baths. Use a tub of warm water, filled only to your dog's ankles. Wash only her feet during the first bath. The next bath, you might wash the rear legs. Bring some treats into the tub with you. Unless your dog has been sprayed by a skunk or has a skin disease, there's little to be gained by deep cleaning. The trick is to make baths short and sweet.

A few things to keep in mind before you commence with full-scale bathing:

- ✔ If you use your own tub, place a nonskid mat in the bottom of it and help your dog in and out so that she doesn't slip.

- ✔ A hand-held sprayer is essential for indoor bathing.

- ✔ The temperature of the water should never be too hot or too cold — it should be set so that you would be comfortable if you were taking a shower.

- ✔ Make sure a fractious pup can't accidentally hit a knob and turn the hot water up. Keeping one hand under the spray so that you can monitor the water temperature is a good idea.

Start by wetting the dog to the skin, leaving the head for last. You can try plugging the ears with cotton, but even then you should avoid spraying water into the ears, as the cotton gets soggy easily. Beware: Your dog will want to make sure that you, too, enjoy the benefits of the bath by shaking water all over you. Once wet (the dog, not you), apply the shampoo, again leaving the head for last. The shampoo will go a lot farther and be easier to work with if you mix it with water first. Once you've worked up a lather, start rinsing. Rinse from the head first and work your way back and down. Rinsing is a crucial step; shampoo remaining in the coat can cause dryness and itchiness. Most Pit Bulls don't require a crème rinse, but you can add a small amount if you like. It makes the hair a little softer and smoother.

To keep your dog from shaking, keep one hand clenched around the base of one ear. When you let go, stand back!

If your dog has healthy skin, any shampoo, or even liquid dishwashing detergent, works. But dog shampoo is the best. Dog skin has a pH of 7.5, while human skin has a pH of 5.5; bathing in a shampoo formulated for the pH of human skin can lead to scaling and irritation. Most shampoos (even people shampoos) kill fleas, but none (including flea shampoos) have any residual killing action on fleas.

No dog owner should be without one of the dog shampoos that requires no water or rinsing. These are wonderful for puppies, spot-baths, emergencies, and bathing when time does not permit a full-scale bath.

If your dog's skin isn't healthy, try a therapeutic shampoo. They are available for various skin problems:

- ✔ Itchy skin: oatmeal based anti-pruritic shampoos

- ✔ Dry scaly skin: moisturizing shampoos

- ✔ Excessive scale and dandruff: anti-seborrheic shampoos

- ✔ Damaged skin: antimicrobial shampoos

After the bath, let her shake off the excess water and then cover her with a towel. Rub her vigorously. Don't let your dog outside on a chilly day if she's still wet from a bath. You've removed the oils from the coat and saturated her down to the skin, so she's far wetter than she would ever get by going swimming, and thus more likely to become chilled.

On hot summer days, an outdoor hose is fine. Don't bathe your dog outside on chilly days and don't bathe her outside until she's used to getting a bath.

Smelling Like a Rose

Pit Bulls tend to have little doggy odor, but many of them help things along by rolling in popular canine perfumes, such as eau de cowpie or essence of carrion. When they smell like they've rolled in something but really haven't, your dog may have a problem. Infection is a common cause of bad odor; check the mouth, ears, feet, anus, and genitals. Impacted anal sacs or other medical problems can contribute to a bad odor. Generalized bad odor can indicate a skin problem, such as seborrhea. Don't exile the dog or hold your breath; find the source and take care of the problem!

Even dogs don't like smelling like skunks. If you live in an area where your dog could come face to rear with a skunk, be prepared with the following recipe: Mix one pint of 3 percent hydrogen peroxide, ⅔ cup baking soda, and one teaspoon of liquid soap or citrus-based dog shampoo with one gallon of water. Use immediately. Wear gloves and sponge the mixture onto the dog. Leave it on the dog about five minutes, rinse, and repeat if needed. ***Note:*** This solution may slightly bleach dark coats (but who cares?). Vinegar douche is also reported to work well.

Debugging Your Dog

No matter how often you plead with them, some Pit Bulls are always picking up hitchhikers and bringing them home for dinner. You need to make sure that your dog isn't providing free room and board for fleas, ticks, and mites.

Making fleas flee

How do you tell if you have a flea-bitten dog? The easiest way is to spot a flea scurrying around under the dog's coat, but that relies on chance. A better way is to use a flea comb, which has extremely fine teeth. Use it to comb your dog all over. Pay special attention to the areas around the rump, neck, and back, because these areas are deluxe flea resorts. Look for fleas caught in the comb or for flea dirt, which is a black, gritty material that is actually flea feces or digested blood. If you have any doubt as to whether you're looking at flea dirt, put some on a white paper towel and add water; flea dirt will create a reddish liquid.

Fleas crawl, bite, and suck, making your dog scratch and chew herself. They can also cause secondary problems, such as tapeworms, skin problems, and flea allergy dermatitis.

Flea control used to be a never-ending battle, and one that the fleas usually won. Recent advances in flea and tick control have finally put dog owners on the winning side. In any but the mildest of infestations, these new and more effective products are well worth their higher purchase price. Remember that putting an expensive product on your dog once every month is more cost-effective than reapplying a cheap product every day.

Some of the chemicals that work wonders, and the products that contain them, include

- **Imidacloprid (Advantage)** is a liquid applied once a month on the animal's back. It gradually distributes itself over the entire skin surface. It kills at least 98 percent of the fleas on the animal within 24 hours, and continues to kill fleas for a month. It can withstand some amount of water, but not repeated swimming or bathing.

- **Fipronil (Frontline)** comes as either a spray that you must apply all over the dog's body or as a self-distributing liquid applied only on the dog's back. After it's applied, fipronil collects in the hair follicles and then wicks out over time. Thus, it is resistant to being washed off and can kill fleas for up to three months on dogs. It is also effective on ticks, although for a shorter period.

- **Selamectin (Revolution)** is applied once a month on the dog's back. Some of it enters the bloodstream, some enters the digestive tract, and some redistributes to the skin's sebaceous glands. This wide distribution helps it to be effective against fleas, some ticks, ear mites, sarcoptic mange mites, and heartworms. In addition, it's somewhat effective against hookworms, roundworms, and whipworms.

- **Lufenuron (Program)** is given as a pill once a month. Fleas that bite the dog and ingest the lufenuron in the dog's system are rendered sterile. It is extremely safe. However, all the animals in your Pit Bull's environment must be treated in order for the regime to be effective.

Traditional flea control products are either less effective or less safe than these newer products. The permethrins and pyrethrins are safe, but have virtually no residual action. The large family of cholinesterase inhibitors (Dursban, Diazinon, malathion, Sevin, Carbaryl, Pro-Spot, Spotton) last a little longer, but have been known to kill dogs when overused, used in combination with cholinesterase-inhibiting yard products, or with cholinesterase-inhibiting dewormers.

"Ultrasonic flea repelling collars are great!" Nope! They have been shown to be both ineffective on fleas and irritating to dogs.

"Feeding dogs brewer's yeast or garlic will get rid of fleas." Another myth bites the dust. Scientific studies have shown that both are ineffective against fleas. However, many owners swear they work, and they don't seem to do any harm.

Ticking off ticks

Ticks are more difficult to keep off your dog than fleas are. Tick prevention collars are available that cause the ticks to die, eventually. Fipronil flea and tick spray or liquid can also help kill the ticks after awhile. Your best tool, however, is your sense of touch. Feel your dog all over for suspicious lumps; your dog will enjoy it! Ticks can be found anywhere on the dog, but most often burrow around the ears, neck, chest, and between the toes.

To remove a tick, use a tissue or tweezers. Be careful, as some tick-borne diseases can be transmitted to humans. First, soak the tick in rubbing alcohol so that it will loosen its grip. Grasp the tick as close to its head as possible, and pull slowly and steadily without twisting, trying not to leave the head in the dog. Don't squeeze the tick, as this can inject its contents into the dog. Clean the site with alcohol. Often, a bump will remain after the tick is removed, even if you got the head. It will go away with time.

Ticks can carry Rocky Mountain spotted fever, tick paralysis, Lyme disease, babesiosis, and, most commonly, tick fever (erlichiosis) — all very serious diseases.

Managing mange

Mange refers to skin problems caused by mites, which are microscopic parasites that live on or in the skin. These mites can cause two types of mange, both of which can make your dog miserable or unsightly. Sarcoptic mange, also called *canine scabies,* causes intense itching, often characterized by scaling of the ear tips, or by small yellow or red bumps where the mites are living. The mites prefer areas with little hair, such as the ear tips, underside of the body, the elbows, and forelegs. Note that sarcoptic mange is highly contagious and spread by direct contact, even having a temporary effect on people. Take precautions when dealing with an infested dog.

Treatment requires repeated shampoos or dips of not only the affected dog, but also other household pets that are in contact with her. Your veterinarian can administer injections that can help cure the problem faster than if you rely on just the shampoos and dips.

Demodectic mange, also called *red mange* or *demodicosis,* is not usually itchy. The demodex canis mite responsible for the condition lives in the hair follicles. This same mite can be found in the follicles of most dogs; nobody knows why it begins to multiply out of control and cause disease in only some dogs. Affected dogs are often related, however, and the condition seems to be especially prone to being passed from dams to offspring. It is more common in certain breeds. Pit Bulls are not especially predisposed to the condition, but can be affected by it. If your Pit Bull develops generalized demodectic mange, she should not be bred.

Demodectic mange is characterized by a moth-eaten appearance, most often around the eyes and lips. Most cases of demodectic mange appear in puppies, and most consist of only a few patches that often go away by themselves. But in those cases that continue to spread, or in adult-onset demodectic mange, aggressive treatment using an amitraz insecticidal dip is needed. Your veterinarian will need to perform a skin scraping to confirm the diagnosis before prescribing treatment. In particularly resistant cases, injections or heavy administration of some monthly heartworm preventives can provide an effective cure. Demodectic mange affecting the feet is also common, and can be extremely resistant to treatment. Left untreated, secondary infections can develop and the dog can become quite sick.

Cheyletialla mites live on the skin surface. Unlike other mites, they are large enough to be seen with the naked eye (although a magnifying glass is still helpful). They look like small, moving, white specks in the dog's hair near the skin, giving rise to their nickname: walking dandruff. They cause a varied degree of itchiness in their host. Many flea insecticides also kill these mites, but they are better treated by using special shampoos or dips, which must be readministered at least four times on a regular schedule. Your veterinarian can also give your dog an injection that can help kill the mites.

Another mite that can make your dog miserable is the ear mite, which is discussed later in this chapter.

Losing those lousy lice

Lice are not terribly common on dogs, but they can be present and cause problems. They cause itching and an unhealthy coat; some types of lice can suck so much blood that the dog can become anemic and even die. You can see lice with a magnifying glass under bright light. Treatment is with an insecticidal shampoo, repeated every few weeks.

Saving Your Dog's Skin

Skin problems make up most of the sick-dog cases a veterinarian sees. Problems can result from parasites, allergies, bacteria, fungus, endocrine disorders, or a long list of other possible causes.

Scratching the surface of allergic itching

Like people, many dogs can have allergic reactions to pollens or other inhaled allergens. Unlike people, they don't manifest these allergies by sneezing or wheezing. Instead, they itch. They itch around their feet, ears, eyes, and bellies. The most common sign of allergies is chewing and licking the paws, often causing the paws to be stained pink from saliva. Allergies usually first appear in young dogs and get progressively worse.

New blood tests for antibodies are much easier and less expensive (though less comprehensive) than the traditional intradermal skin testing. Adding omega-3 and omega-6 fatty acids to the diet can help some dogs. Antihistamines can provide temporary relief. Allergy shots provide the best long-term therapy, but results may not be noticeable for several months.

Some dogs itch from food allergies. Food allergies can be difficult to distinguish from inhalant allergies. Some food allergies manifest as recurrent ear infections. They may not occur until a dog has been eating a particular ingredient for months or years. Blood tests for food allergies are not very accurate. If you suspect that your Pit Bull has food allergies, the best way to investigate is through dietary trials in which the dog is fed only certain ingredients at a time.

Flea allergy dermatitis (FAD) is the most common of all skin problems. Itchy, crusted bumps with hair loss in the region around the rump, especially at the base of the tail, result from a fleabite (actually, the flea's saliva) anywhere on the dog's body. The dog chews at herself as though nibbling on a corncob, and scratches at her neck and sides. She can damage her skin to the point that it becomes infected. Yet she may have only a single flea on her — or none, since the bite may have occurred over a day before the allergic reaction began. For such dogs, products that require a flea to bite the dog before killing or sterilizing the flea may not be optimal, since even one flea bite can elicit an allergic reaction. Talk to your vet if your dog has ever had FAD about how best to prevent any further allergic reactions.

Pyoderma and impetigo

Pyoderma, characterized by pus-filled bumps and crusting, is another common skin disease. Impetigo is characterized by such bumps and crusting also, most often in the groin area of puppies. Both are treated with antibiotics and antibacterial shampoos.

Cooling down hot spots

A reddened, moist, itchy spot that suddenly appears is most likely a hot spot (pyotraumatic dermatitis), which arise from an itch-scratch-chew cycle that most often is caused by fleas or flea allergy. Wash the area with an oatmeal-based shampoo and prevent the dog from further chewing. Use an Elizabethan collar (available from your veterinarian, or you can fashion one from a plastic pail) or an anti-chew preparation such as Bitter Apple (available from most pet stores). Your veterinarian can also prescribe anti-inflammatory medication. As a temporary measure, you can give an allergy pill (Benadryl — ask your veterinarian about dosage). It alleviates some itching and causes drowsiness, both of which should decrease chewing.

Hair loss can also be caused by mange, autoimmune problems, or endocrine problems. Hair may be lost in a bilaterally symmetric pattern, without itching, as a result of hypothyroidism, Cushing's syndrome, or testicular tumors.

Nailing Down Nail Care

Pit Bulls do not catch fish or climb trees with their long claws. Despite this amazing bit of animal information, many pet owners seem determined to get their dog in the record book for having the world's longest toenails.

Canine nails evolved to withstand traveling 20 miles or so a day. Unless your dog is a marathon runner, you're going to need to help out a little. When you can hear the pitter-patter of clicking nails, with every step the nails are hitting the floor. When nails hit the floor, the bones of the foot spread, causing discomfort and, eventually, splayed feet and lameness. If dewclaws (the rudimentary "thumbs" on the wrists) are left untrimmed, they can get caught on things more easily and be ripped out, or actually loop around and grow into the dog's leg. In other words, you must trim your dog's nails every week or two to keep her healthy!

Dogs who have no experience with nail cutting assume that you're cutting off their toes and react as you might expect. You need to convince dogs from the time they're puppies that a nail trim won't hurt a bit. Begin by handling the feet and nails daily. Then start cutting the very tips of your puppy's nails every week, taking special care not to cut the quick, which is the central core of blood vessels and nerve endings (see Figure 11-1). After every cut, give your dog a tiny treat. Some dogs are calmer if you hold the foot backwards, much as a horse's hoof is held when being shod. This way, your Pit Bull can't see what's going on and you can see the bottom of the nail. You should see a solid core culminating in a hollow nail. Cut the tip up to the core, but not beyond. On occasion, you will slip up and cause the nail to bleed. Apply styptic powder to the nail to stop the bleeding. If you don't have any styptic powder available, dip the nail in flour or hold it to a wet tea bag. And be more careful next time!

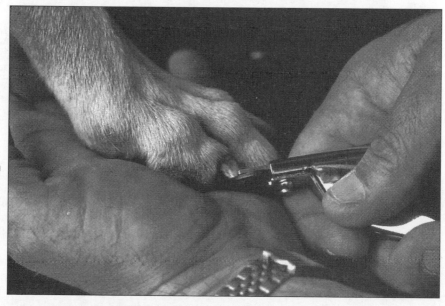

Figure 11-1:
Cutting your dog's nails: Be sure not to cut too much off the ends.

Going in One Ear and Cleaning Out the Other

Many people glance in their dogs' ears and assume that everything's fine if the ears aren't clogged with debris. You need to examine them more closely (see Figure 11-2). Dog ears aren't like people ears, though. Besides the obvious difference in the pinna (ear flap) shape, the dog's ear canal doesn't travel in a straight line toward the eardrum. Instead, it travels downward and then makes a sharp turn inward. Not only can you not see what's going on beyond the bend, but all sorts of ear infections can flourish in this sheltered environment. The fecund climate inside the ear canal isn't as big a problem in Pit Bulls as it is in other breeds because the ear flap, whether cropped or not, still allows plenty of ventilation to reach the canal.

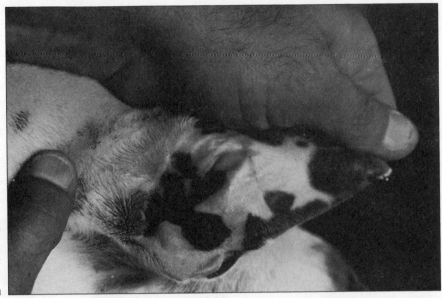

Figure 11-2:
Examining
an ear.

Signs of ear problems include inflammation, discharge, debris, foul odor, pain, scratching, shaking, tilting of the head, or circling to one side. Extreme pain may indicate a ruptured eardrum. Ear problems can be difficult to cure once they have become established, so early veterinary attention is crucial. Bacterial and yeast infections, ear mites or ticks, foreign bodies, inhalant allergies, seborrhea, or hypothyroidism are possible underlying problems.

Don't stick cotton swabs down in the ear canal, as they can irritate the skin and pack debris into the horizontal canal. Never use powders in the ear, which can cake, or hydrogen peroxide, which leaves the ear moist. The best recipe for disaster is to stick some ear powder in, follow with a little liquid, pack it all down with a cotton swab, allow it all to dry into a solid plug, and then just wait for a full-fledged problem to explode.

If your dog has a build up of debris but no signs of pain, you can clean the debris out using one of the many products made for that purpose and sold in pet supply catalogs or veterinary clinics. You can also make your own with a mixture of one part alcohol to two parts white vinegar. Armed with this potion, take your dog outside. Hold the ear near its base and quickly squeeze in the ear cleaner (the more slowly you let it drip in, the more it will tickle). Now gently massage the liquid downward and squish it all around. When your dog can't stand it anymore (usually after about 15 seconds), jump back and let your dog shake it all out. You'll be glad to be outside, because dissolved earwax is not a great thing to have on your walls. You may have to repeat this step a few times. If the ear is so black with gunk that repeated rinses don't clean it right up, you have a problem that will need veterinary attention. If the ear is red, swollen, or painful do not attempt to clean it yourself. Your dog may need to be sedated for cleaning and may have a serious problem. Cleaning solutions will flush debris but will not kill mites or cure infections.

If your dog is shaking her head, scratching at her ears, and perhaps carrying her head sideways, she may be suffering from ear mites. The ear mite's signature is a dark, dry, waxy buildup resembling coffee grounds in the ear canal, usually of both ears. This material is actually dried blood mixed with earwax. If you place some of this wax on a piece of dark paper, and have very good eyes or use a magnifying glass, you may be able to see the tiny moving culprits. Many people automatically assume any ear problem is due to ear mites, but unless you actually see mites, don't treat the dog for them. You could make another problem worse.

Over-the-counter ear mite preparations can cause worse irritation, so ear mites are best treated by your veterinarian. If you must treat your dog yourself, get a pyrethrin and mineral oil ear product. First flush the ear with an ear cleaning solution. Then apply the ear mite drops daily for at least a week, and possibly a month. Because these mites are also found in the dog's fur all over her body, you should also bathe the pet weekly with a pyrethrin-based shampoo, or apply a pyrethrin flea dip, powder, or spray. Separate a dog with ear mites from other pets and wash your hands after handling her ears. Ideally, every pet in a household should be treated.

Keeping an Eye on the Bull's Eye

Unlike many breeds that are plagued with lid and retinal problems, Pit Bulls have healthy eyes. Like all dogs, however, they can have some eye problems. If these problems are ignored, they can rob your dog of her vision. So check out your dog's eyes once in a while (see Figure 11-3).

Notice if your Pit Bull is squinting, avoiding light, or pawing at her eye. Squinting or tearing can be due to an irritated cornea or foreign body. Examine under the lids and flood the eye with saline solution, or use a moist cotton swab to remove any debris. If no improvement occurs after a day, have your veterinarian examine your Pit Bull.

You also need to be aware of the risk posed by glaucoma. Although avoiding light or pawing at the eyes is behavior most likely caused by a foreign body, it could also indicate glaucoma. Glaucoma is extremely painful and is an emergency situation. An acute attack of glaucoma can lead to blindness almost overnight.

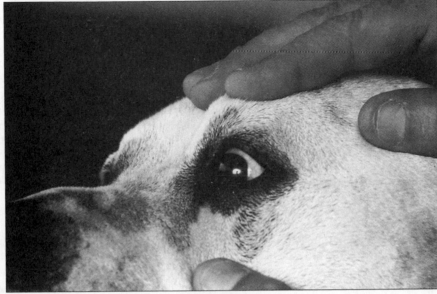

Figure 11-3:
Giving the
eyes a
once-over.

Notice if your Pit Bull's pupils react to light. In a dim room, flash a light in each eye and make sure each pupil responds. If a dog has glaucoma or brain damage, the pupils may not respond. This is another reason for a trip to the emergency vet.

Check to see if your Pit Bull has any discharge from her eyes. A watery discharge without squinting can be a symptom of allergies or a tear drainage problem. A clogged tear drainage duct can cause the tears to drain onto the face rather than the normal drainage through the nose. Your veterinarian can diagnose a drainage problem with a simple test. A gooey mucus discharge indicates an infection. Prescription eyedrops are normally needed to cure it.

Notice if your dog's lenses are clear. Do this by looking through her pupils. They should look black. If they are whitish, grayish, or bluish your dog may have cataracts. Some Pit Bulls have juvenile cataracts, in which the lens develops opacities at a young age — usually before the age of six years. In some Pits, the cataracts are present at birth, but aren't visible until dog is a couple of months old. If the cataracts become too severe, they can be removed by a veterinary ophthalmologist.

When in doubt, get eye problems checked out!

For contact with eye irritants, flush the eye for five minutes with water or saline solution. For injuries, cover the eye with clean gauze soaked in water or saline solution. In both cases, get immediate veterinary advice.

Keeping Your Dog Armed to the Teeth

The notion of brushing a dog's teeth is fairly new to most people. Bear in mind that the notion of people brushing their own teeth was fairly radical until recent times. Now you wouldn't dream of letting your teeth turn brown. Why should you let your dog's teeth get that way? Tooth plaque and tartar are not only unsightly, but contribute to bad breath and health problems. So keep an eye on your dog's teeth (see Figure 11-4).

Plaque attracts bacteria and minerals, which harden into tartar, which can, in turn, cause an infection to form along the gum line. The infection can gradually work its way down the sides of the tooth until the entire root is undermined. The tissues and bone around the tooth erode and the tooth finally falls out. Meanwhile, the bacteria may have entered the bloodstream and traveled throughout the body, causing infection in the kidneys and heart valves. Neglecting your dog's teeth can do more harm than causing bad breath; neglect could possibly kill your dog.

Some people feed their dogs hard dog biscuits as a means of keeping their dog's teeth clean. Dry food and hard dog biscuits, carrots, rawhide, and Nylabone chewies are helpful, but they can't do the whole job. If they did, don't you think we'd have people biscuits for our teeth?

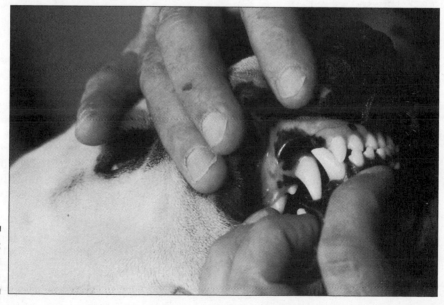

Figure 11-4:
Inspecting
the teeth.

Brushing your Pit Bull's teeth once or twice weekly (optimally daily) with a child or dog toothbrush and doggy toothpaste is the only really effective way to remove plaque. If you can't brush your Pit's teeth, your veterinarian can supply a cleansing solution that helps to kill plaque-forming bacteria. You may also have to ask your veterinarian to clean your dog's teeth under anesthesia as often as once a year.

Pit Bulls have tougher jaws than most dogs, but they don't have tougher teeth. Their dogged determination to hang tight to tree limbs, ropes, and toys, and to tackle objects they would be better off leaving alone tends to be bad news for their teeth. Examine your dog's teeth regularly to check for cracks and breaks. If the root is exposed, your dog may need a root canal to spare her a good deal of pain. Sometimes immediate capping can spare the tooth's root after a break or crack.

Puppy Pit Bulls require special tooth monitoring. You should check to make sure your puppy is developing correct occlusion. In a correct Pit Bull bite, the top incisors should fit snugly in front of the bottom incisors. Too large a gap between the upper and lower incisors could cause eating difficulties or result in the tongue lolling out of the mouth. In some cases, the lower canine teeth are situated too far toward the middle of the mouth, so the tooth pierces the upper palate or gum line when the mouth is closed. The offending baby teeth must be pulled for the pup's comfort. In fact, pulling some teeth can help occlusion develop properly, so ask a veterinarian's advice if your pup's bite doesn't seem right.

Between four and seven months of age, Pit Bull puppies will begin to shed their baby teeth and show off new permanent teeth. Often deciduous (baby) teeth, especially the canines (fangs), are not shed, so that the permanent tooth grows in beside the baby tooth. If this condition persists for over a week, consult your veterinarian. Retained baby teeth can cause misalignment of adult teeth.

Bite is the canine term for occlusion, the way the teeth and jaws mesh when the mouth is closed. The correct Pit Bull bite is a scissors bite, in which the incisors (the small front teeth) of the upper jaw just slightly overlap in front of those of the lower jaw. In an overshot bite, the top incisors are so far in front of the lower that a gap exists between them. In an undershot bite, the upper incisors are behind the lower incisors.

You've bathed her, brushed her, debugged her, cleaned her eyes and ears, and polished her pearly whites. Now it's time to put on her best collar and leash, fix yourself up, and strut her through the neighborhood for all to admire.

Chapter 12

A Clean Bull of Health

In This Chapter

▶ Recognizing signs of illness

▶ What you need in your medicine cabinet

▶ The vaccinations your dog must have

▶ The wonderful world of worms

*Y*our Pit Bull can't tell you where she hurts or, sometimes, even if she hurts at all. To be a responsible dog owner (without financing your vet's retirement) you have to educate yourself about Pit Bull health. I don't mean learning how to perform Pit Bull brain surgery in your kitchen, but you do need to learn the signs of both a well dog and a sick one, and to practice good preventive medicine. *Preventive medicine* encompasses accident prevention, vaccinations, and parasite control, as well as good hygiene and grooming.

Examining Your Pit Bull

Performing a quick health check takes only about five minutes — the most important five minutes you spend with your dog each week. You get to know how your dog looks when she's healthy, you get a head start on any problems, and your dog thinks that you just can't resist petting her all over.

Check these areas, and use Figure 12-1 if you don't know where they are:

- ✔ The mouth for loose teeth, ulcers of the tongue or gums, bad breath, or red, bleeding, swollen, or pale gums
- ✔ The eyes for discharge, cloudiness, or discolored whites
- ✔ The ears for foul odor, redness, discharge, or crusted tips
- ✔ The nose for thickened or colored discharge
- ✔ The skin for parasites, hair loss, crusts, red spots, or lumps
- ✔ The feet for cuts, abrasions, split nails, bumps, or misaligned toes
- ✔ The anal region for redness, swelling, or discharge

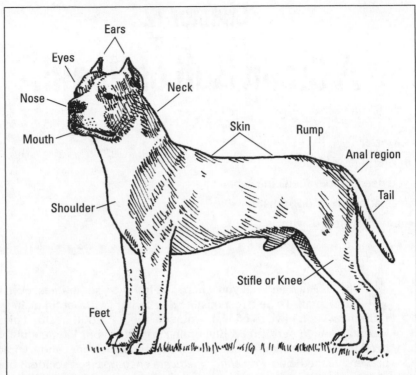

Figure 12-1:
Pit Bull
anatomy.

To check your dog's hydration, pick up the skin on the back just above the shoulders. It should make a slight tent above the body. The skin should "pop" back into place almost immediately. If it remains tented and separated from the body, your dog is dehydrated.

Watch your dog for signs of lameness or a lack of coordination, a sore neck, circling, loss of muscle, or any behavioral change. Run your hands over the muscles and bones and check that they are symmetrical from one side to the other. Weigh your dog and observe whether she's putting on fat or wasting away. Check for any growths or swellings, which could indicate cancer or a number of less serious problems. A sore that does not heal, or any pigmented lump that begins to grow or bleed, should be checked by a veterinarian immediately. Look out for mammary masses, changes in testicle size, discharge from the vulva or penis, increased or decreased urination, foul smelling or strangely colored urine, incontinence, swollen abdomen, black or bloody stool, change in appetite or water consumption, difficulty breathing, lethargy, coughing, gagging, or loss of balance.

Pit Bulls are amazingly stoical, even when you're certain that they must be in pain. Because a dog may not be able (or willing) to express that she's in pain, you must be alert to changes in your Pit Bull's demeanor. A stiff gait, low head carriage, reluctance to get up, irritability, dilated pupils, whining, or limping are all indications that your pet is in pain.

In the pink: Checking gums

The simplest — yet most overlooked — checkpoint is your dog's gums. The gums are the one place you can actually see your dog's blood without extracting it. The color of a dog's blood says a lot about the health of the animal. Have you ever noticed how a vet looks at your dog's gums before doing anything else?

Get used to looking at your dog's gums — a window to her blood.

- ✔ Normal gum color is a good deep pink.
- ✔ Pale gum color can indicate anemia or poor circulation.
- ✔ White or tan gum color can indicate shock, severe anemia, or very poor circulation.
- ✔ Bluish gum or tongue color indicates a life-threatening lack of oxygen.
- ✔ Bright red gum color can indicate carbon monoxide poisoning.
- ✔ Yellowish color can indicate jaundice.
- ✔ Little tiny red splotches (called *petechia*) can indicate a blood clotting problem.

Don't confuse a red line around the gum line with healthy gums. A dog with dirty teeth can have gum disease, giving a rosy glow to the gums, especially at the margins around the teeth.

Capillary refill time, which is a measure of blood circulation, can be estimated by pressing on the gum with your finger and lifting your finger off. The gum where you pressed will be momentarily white, but will quickly repink as the blood moves back into the area. If the gums take longer than a couple of seconds to repink, circulation is poor.

Checking body temperature

Your dog's body temperature is another clue about what's going on inside. You can't put your hand on your Pit Bull's forehead and get an idea, and you can't have your dog hold a thermometer under her tongue. You can get a very rough idea by feeling your dog's ears, but for an accurate reading you need to take your dog's temperature rectally. Your dog will appreciate it if you lubricate the thermometer first. As in humans, body temperature is slightly lower in the morning and higher in the evening. Normal temperature for a Pit Bull is about 100 degrees to 102 degrees F. If the temperature is

- ✔ 103 degrees or above, call the vet and ask for advice.
- ✔ 105 degrees or above, go to the emergency vet. A temperature of 106 degrees and above is dangerous.
- ✔ 98 degrees or below, call the vet.
- ✔ 96 degrees or below, go to the emergency vet.

"You can tell if a dog is well by whether she has a wet nose." Wrong! Sick dogs can have wet noses and well dogs can have dry noses.

Checking pulse, heartbeat, and breathing rate

The easiest way to check your dog's pulse is to feel the pulse through the femoral artery. If your dog is standing, cup your hand around the top of her leg and feel around the inside of it, almost where it joins with the torso. If your dog is on her back, you can sometimes even see the pulse in this area. Normal pulse rate for a Pit Bull at rest is about 60 to 120 beats per minute.

You can feel your dog's heartbeat by placing your hand on her lower ribcage just behind her elbow. Don't be alarmed if it seems irregular; the heartbeat of many dogs is irregular compared to a human's heartbeat. Have your vet check the heartbeat out, then get used to how it feels when it is normal.

Normal respiration rate for a Pit Bull at rest is about 10 to 30 breaths per minute.

The Good Doctor

No matter how diligent you are, eventually your Pit Bull will need professional medical attention. A good veterinarian is also needed to monitor your dog's internal signs by way of blood tests and other procedures. When choosing your veterinarian, consider availability, emergency arrangements, costs, facilities, and how well you communicate.

Some veterinarians include fairly sophisticated tests as part of their regular checkups. Such tests, while desirable, add to the cost of a visit. Unless money is no object, don't be embarrassed to ask about fees and reach an understanding about procedures before having them performed. Veterinarians know that clients want the best for their pets — but don't have bottomless pockets.

You and your veterinarian should form a team that works together to protect your Pit Bull's health, so your rapport with your dog's veterinarian is very important. The veterinarian should listen to your observations and should explain to you exactly what is happening with your dog.

The clinic should be clean and have safe, sanitary overnight accommodations. Trained veterinary technicians are a valuable asset to any clinic, but not all clinics have them. A clinic staffed by several veterinarians is usually better than a clinic with only one vet, because the vets can confer about tough cases and at least one of them is likely to be available for emergencies. Remember that your veterinarian should be reachable in cases of extreme emergency, even if your vet's clinic normally refers customers to an emergency clinic for after-hours crises.

Most veterinarians are general practitioners. Their days are filled with routine cases: checkups, vaccinations, skin allergies, spaying and neutering, and some of the more common illnesses. A good veterinarian will not hesitate to utter the phrases, "I don't know" and, "Perhaps you would like to be referred to a specialist." If your dog has a serious disease, you should ask if a specialist's opinion would be helpful.

Most specialists are at university veterinary teaching hospitals, although some can be found in private practices in larger cities. As with human doctors, expect to pay more for a specialist's opinion. Sometimes, even a specialist can do nothing for your Pit Bull, but many owners find peace in knowing that they did everything they could and left no stone unturned while trying to find a cure for their beloved Pit.

Veterinarians aren't always right. Don't hesitate to question your veterinarian's diagnosis or treatment or seek a second opinion. Be informed about Pit Bull health issues so that you can take part in conversations with a vet, instead of just nodding your head and automatically trusting the veterinarian's judgement.

Blood Tests

Your Pit Bull's blood can provide valuable clues about her health. In fact, it's a good idea to have blood values for your Pit Bull when she's well so that you have a benchmark against which to compare later results. You should insist on blood tests before your pet undergoes surgery, to ensure that she is healthy enough for the procedure. The time to find out that your dog has a clotting problem isn't when she's on the operating table, bleeding.

The most common tests are the Complete Blood Count (CBC) and the Blood Chemistry Test (also known as *Chem panel*). Many other specialized tests are also fairly common.

The CBC reports:

- Red blood cells — the cells responsible for carrying oxygen throughout the body
- White blood cells — infection fighting cells
- Platelets — components responsible for clotting blood to stop bleeding

A Blood Chemistry Test reports:

- Albumin (ALB) — reduced levels are suggestive of liver or kidney disease or parasites
- Alanine aminotransferase (ALT) — elevated levels suggest liver disease
- Alkaline phosphatase (ALKP) — elevated levels can indicate liver disease or Cushing's syndrome
- Amylase (AMYL) — elevated levels suggest pancreatic or kidney disease
- Blood urea nitrogen (BUN) — elevated levels suggest kidney disease
- Calcium (CA) — elevated levels suggest kidney or parathyroid disease or some types of tumors
- Cholesterol (CHOL) — elevated levels suggest liver or kidney disease or several other disorders
- Creatinine (CREA) — elevated levels suggest kidney disease or urinary obstruction
- Blood Glucose (GLU) — low levels can suggest liver disease
- Phosphorous (PHOS) — elevated levels can suggest kidney disease
- Total bilirubin (TBIL) — level can indicate problems in the bile ducts
- Total protein (TP) — level can indicate problems of the liver, kidney, or gastrointestinal tract

Medicine at Home

Your Pit will often have to take medicine at home. Most dogs have no problems with pills. Just open your dog's mouth and place the pill well to the back and in the middle of the tongue. Close the mouth and gently stroke the throat until your dog swallows. Prewetting capsules or covering them with cream cheese or some other food helps prevent the capsules from sticking to the tongue or roof of the mouth.

For liquid medicine, tilt the head back, keep the dog's mouth almost (but not tightly) closed, and place the liquid in the pouch of the cheek. The medicine is easier to give if you put it in a syringe (without the needle!). Hold the mouth almost closed until the dog swallows.

For eye medications, first clean any goop out of your dog's eye — the goop can prevent the medication from contacting the eye. Do your best to pry the eye partially open. Place the drops or ointment in the inner corner of the eye. Because dogs have an extra eyelid and an extra muscle that pulls the eye back into the eye socket, they can do a good job of appearing to be eyeless and of making your job as difficult as possible.

For ear medication, first clean any heavy debris from the ear, if possible. Place the medicine as deep into the canal as you can. The ear canal goes down vertically and then turns abruptly toward the center of the dog's head — this means that you should hold the head vertically at first, so that the medicine can drop down to the curve, and then try to turn the dog's head so that the ear you're medicating is turned upward. Since most dogs aren't cooperative as you turn their head this way and that, you may have to massage the base of the ear, hoping to squish the medicine inward. Medicating ears outside of the house is a good idea, because as soon as you let go your Pit will shake her head and medicine will fly in every direction.

Always give the full course of medications prescribed by your veterinarian. If a medicine is worth giving, it's worth giving a full course of. Don't give human medications unless you've been directed to do so by your veterinarian. Some medications for humans have no effect upon dogs and some can have a very detrimental effect.

Aspirin or prescription medications may alleviate some of the discomfort of injuries, but never give them if your dog is on her way to surgery. If you administer pain medication, you must confine your dog; a lack of pain could encourage her to use an injured limb, for example, ultimately resulting in further injury.

Keep these items in your doggie medicine chest at home:

- Anti-diarrhea medication
- Antiseptic skin ointment
- Clean sponge
- First aid instructions
- Hydrogen peroxide
- Instant cold compress
- Ophthalmic ointment
- Pen light
- Poison control center number
- Rectal thermometer
- Scissors
- Self-adhesive bandage (such as Vet-Wrap)

- ✔ Soap
- ✔ Sterile gauze dressings
- ✔ Stethoscope (optional)
- ✔ Syringe
- ✔ Towel
- ✔ Tweezers
- ✔ Veterinarian and emergency clinic numbers

A Shot in the Bark: Vaccinations

Vaccinations save lives. Although some disagreement exists over whether too many vaccinations can have detrimental effects in some dogs, the fact that they are absolutely essential to your Pit's health is beyond dispute. Because some questions exist about vaccinations, you need to be informed. By understanding vaccinations, you can make the best choice about your dog's vaccination schedule.

Puppy vaccinations

Puppy vaccinations are the most vital, but most confusing, of all the vaccinations that your Pit will receive. Puppies receive their dam's immunity from *colostrum,* the special type of milk the dam produces in the first days of life. Colostrum is why it's important that the dam is properly immunized long before breeding, and that her pups are able to nurse from her. The immunity gained from the dam wears off after several weeks, however, and then the pup is susceptible to disease unless you provide immunity through vaccinations. The problem is that there's no way to know exactly when the second-hand immunity gained from colostrum will wear off, and vaccinations given before that time are ineffective. You must revaccinate over a period of weeks so that your pup will not be unprotected and will receive effective immunity — which is why puppies get a series of shots instead of just one or two.

Your pup's breeder should have given the first vaccinations to your pup before she was old enough to go home with you. Bring all the information you have about your pup's vaccination history to your veterinarian on your first visit, so that the pup's vaccination schedule can be maintained. Meanwhile, not letting your pup mingle with strange dogs is a good idea — wait until you know that her immune system is a-okay.

Vaccinations are available for several diseases. Some vaccinations are mandatory from a legal standpoint, some are mandatory from a good sense standpoint, and some are optional.

Proof of current vaccination is often needed to transport your dog by air, cross international lines with your Pit, attend obedience classes with your Pit, board your Pit at a kennel, or have your Pit work as a therapy dog. (Intrigued by the idea of having your tough guy warm hearts as a therapy dog? See Chapter 17 for more information.)

Rabies

Rabies is inevitably fatal once symptoms have appeared, and unvaccinated dogs remain the principal host for the disease in undeveloped countries. It's passed mostly through the saliva of carnivores and bats. Because of its deadly consequences (to humans as well as dogs), state laws mandate that all dogs must be vaccinated. The initial rabies vaccination should be given at around three to four months of age, again one year from the first vaccination, and then every three years (although to comply with local law, you may have to give a booster every year).

Distemper

Distemper has killed dogs, broken hearts, and ravaged kennels for centuries. The production of a vaccine was one of the greatest developments in the progress of canine health. Today, distemper is seen almost exclusively in unvaccinated puppies. Initial symptoms are upper respiratory problems and fever, followed by vomiting, diarrhea, and neurological signs. It's not always fatal, but curing distemper is definitely a lot more expensive than getting a simple vaccination! Very young puppies (about 6 weeks old) usually get a distemper/measles vaccination, because the measles fraction can give temporary immunity even in the presence of maternal antibodies. Subsequent distemper inoculations are given every 3 to 4 weeks until the pup is about 16 weeks old. Annual boosters are normally recommended.

Hepatitis

Infectious canine hepatitis type 1 is highly contagious and incurable. Often fatal, it is most often seen in puppies. It's caused by an adenovirus (called *CAV-1*) found mostly in foxes and dogs, but also in coyotes, wolves, skunks, and bears. Vaccination with CAV-2 (which works just as well but doesn't result in the "blue-eye" reaction that CAV-1 caused when it was used years ago) is usually done along with distemper vaccination.

Leptospirosis

Leptospirosis is a bacterial disease that causes serious liver, kidney, and blood abnormalities. It is thought to be more prevalent in rural areas. Vaccination for lepto is not particularly satisfying, because a vaccination only protects for about 3 to 6 months, and does not protect against all strains of leptospirosis. In addition, a small percentage of puppies have a transient adverse reaction to the vaccination. Thus, some people prefer not to include lepto in their vaccination regime, although most veterinarians include it as part of a combination vaccine.

Parvovirus

In the late 1970s a worldwide virus broke out that caused often fatal intestinal bleeding. Parvovirus was an entirely new virus thought to have arisen through mutation. The advent of a vaccination was a major triumph, although breeders still fear parvo. It is extremely contagious and can remain in the environment for years. Vaccination for parvo is often interfered with by maternal antibodies; for this reason, three vaccinations by the age of 16 weeks are recommended, with an optional fourth vaccination at around 18 to 20 weeks. Annual boosters are normally recommended.

Coronavirus

Coronavirus causes extreme diarrhea, in rare cases resulting in death. Younger dogs are most adversely affected. A vaccination is available, but is considered optional.

Tracheobronchitis (kennel cough)

Kennel cough is highly contagious and tends to spread when dogs share closed spaces. Its name comes from its tendency to occur in dogs about a week after they've been in a kennel. However, kennel cough can also be acquired at dog shows or even in a vet's waiting room. Kennel cough is characterized by a dry, honking cough that can last for weeks. Vaccinations are available, but are imperfect because kennel cough can be caused by many different infectious agents. The vaccines protect against only the most common causes of kennel cough (CPIV, CAV-2, and *Bordetella*). The vaccines' effects also do not last for very long. For these reasons, and because kennel cough is not fatal, some people prefer not to vaccinate for it. Nonetheless, kennel cough vaccination can be a good idea for dogs who are boarded or shown. The vaccine should be given a week before exposure or administered through annual boosters.

Calling the shots

Recent studies have implicated repeated vaccinations with combinations of vaccines with some *autoimmune* problems (meaning the body's immune system turns against other parts of the body). Some veterinarians thus recommend staggering different types of vaccines and discourage over-vaccination. They also discourage vaccination in any dog who is under stress or not feeling well. Don't take your sick dog to the vet and decide to get her vaccinations just because you happen to be there. Don't take your dog in to be spayed or neutered (or have any surgery) and decide to get your dog's vaccinations because it's convenient to get them then. Many dogs seem to feel under the weather for a day or so after getting their vaccinations, so don't schedule your appointment the day before boarding, a trip, or a big doggy event. Get your dog's vaccinations according to a schedule.

But what schedule? Several respected veterinary teaching hospitals have recently revised their vaccination protocols to include fewer booster shots. One such protocol suggests giving a three-shot series for puppies, each shot containing parvovirus, adenovirus 2 (CAV-2), parainfluenza (CPIV), and distemper, with one rabies vaccination at 16 weeks. Following this regimen, a booster is given one year later, and then subsequent boosters are given every three years. Other respected epidemiologists disagree and prefer the traditional vaccination schedule. The great vaccination debate is far from over, so confer with your veterinarian about current thinking on the matter. One thing is for sure: No matter what their possible side effects, vaccinations are a good thing. All dogs must be vaccinated, for their health as well as the health of others.

Lyme disease

Lyme disease is known to cause severe problems in humans, but its effects on dogs are less clear. A vaccination is available, but it's not universally considered necessary. Only dogs living in endemic areas should be considered candidates for Lyme disease vaccination. Consult with your veterinarian about the prevalence of Lyme disease in your area of the country.

Global Worming

Hookworms, whipworms, ascarids, threadworms, and lungworms can infect dogs of all ages, but have the most devastating effect on puppies. Left untreated, worms can cause vomiting, diarrhea, dull coat, listlessness, anemia, and death. Have your puppy tested for internal parasites regularly. Some heartworm preventives also prevent most types of intestinal worms (but not tapeworms).

The classic wormy puppy has a dull coat, skinny body, and distended belly, but many pups with worms don't show all these symptoms. Because you can buy worming medication over the counter, many people figure this is their chance to save a little money and skip a trip to the vet. Others have been taught that in order to be good dog owners, they should "worm" their dog once a month. But over-the-counter wormers are largely ineffective, and are often more dangerous than those available through your veterinarian. Further, no dog should be wormed unless she actually has worms. When you take your dog to be vaccinated, bring along a stool specimen so that your veterinarian can check for these parasites.

Don't think that only puppies from bad homes have worms. Most puppies do have worms at some point, even pups from the most fastidious breeders. This is because some types of larval worms become encysted in the dam's body long before she ever becomes pregnant — perhaps even when she herself was a pup. They lie dormant and immune from worming, until hormonal changes caused by her pregnancy activate them. Then they infect her fetuses or her newborns through her milk.

"Feeding a dog sweets will give it worms." And Pit Bulls are a lot like Chihuahuas. You've got plenty of good reasons not to feed a dog sweets, but worms have nothing to do with it.

Ascarids

Toxocara canis (more commonly known as *ascarids*) are found in virtually every puppy. Most puppies are infested with the larvae before birth, and eggs can be found in the pups' feces by the time they are three weeks old. Adult worms can sometimes be seen in vomit or feces. *Toxocara* can also be spread by ingesting the eggs — and they can be spread to people as well as dogs. Infected puppies can become quite ill, with heavy infestations leading to convulsions or death. Most mortalities occur around two to three weeks of age. Children playing in sandboxes or playgrounds can contract *Toxocara* and can become very dangerously ill from it if *Toxocara*-infested feces are on the premises.

Programs that control *Toxocara* in puppies come from the Centers for Disease Control and were developed for the purpose of controlling *Toxocara* in humans. Puppies should be wormed at least twice for *Toxocara*, and many protocols advocate more frequent worming, with worming at age 2, 4, 6, and 8 weeks of age. Further control the threat by picking up feces regularly and not allowing dogs to defecate where children play (both of which are good ideas for other reasons, come to think of it).

Hookworms

Hookworms are especially prevalent in warm, humid climates. They can be acquired before birth, through penetration of the larvae through the skin, or by eating the larva. Puppies with heavy infestations can become anemic and have bloody, black, or tarry diarrhea. Without prompt treatment, these puppies usually die.

Treatment consists of deworming, blood transfusions, and follow-up prevention. After the intestinal tract has been cleared of worms, larva in the muscle tissue migrate to the intestines and repopulate them, so another deworming treatment is needed two weeks following the first. Adult dogs usually build up an immunity to hookworms, although some dogs have chronic hookworm disease. Chronic cases occur most often in dogs with compromised immune systems or dogs who live in the midst of feces. Removing feces from the backyard (or whatever are your dog uses) at least twice a week is the most cost-effective means of hookworm control.

Whipworms

Whipworms inhabit the large intestine, where they puncture blood vessels and have a feast at your dog's expense. A heavy infestation can cause diarrhea, anemia, and weight loss. Dogs get whipworms by ingesting the eggs. Eggs can live in the environment for up to five years, especially in cold climates. Unlike some other types of internal parasites, dogs do not develop an immunity to whipworms. Treatment consists of repeated deworming, often every other month for a year. Properly disposing of feces is an essential part of controlling whipworms.

"Dogs should be wormed every month or so." Nope! Dogs should be wormed when, and only when, they have been diagnosed with worms. No worm medication is completely without risk, so using them unnecessarily is foolish.

Tapeworms

Tapeworms plague some Pits throughout the dog's entire life. Several species exist, by far the most common being *Dipylidium caninum*. No preventive exists, except to diligently rid your Pit Bull of fleas, because fleas transmit this kind of tapeworm to dogs. Some other types of tapeworms are obtained by eating raw rabbits or fish.

Tapeworms look like moving, white, flat worms on fresh stools, or may dry up and look like rice grains around the dog's anus. Tapeworms are one of the least debilitating of all the worms, but their segments can be irritating to the dog's anal region and are certainly unsightly.

Tapeworms are in the cestode family, and do not respond to the same dewormers as those in the nematode family. This means that the heartworm preventives that also prevent several nematodes will not affect tapeworms.

"A dog who scoots her rear on the ground must have worms." That's a lot of Bull! Although scooting may be a sign of tapeworms, a dog who repeatedly scoots more likely has impacted anal sacs.

More worms

Two more types of nematodes that occasionally infect dogs are threadworms and lungworms. Neither is particularly common. Threadworms live in the small intestine and can cause bloody diarrhea and coughing. They are more common in warm weather, and are treated with high doses of deworming medicine.

Lungworms are found in the respiratory tract, lung tissue, and blood vessels. They can cause large, wart-like nodules on the bronchi of the lungs, leading to bronchitis, coughing, and lack of appetite. The condition is difficult to treat and has a high mortality rate in puppies.

Another uncommon worm is actually carried by earthworms. *Capillaria* is a type of lungworm that lives in the nasal passages, trachea, and bronchi. Heavy infestations can cause sneezing and coughing. The worms themselves resemble whipworms and are often misdiagnosed as them. The worms are susceptible to regular deworming medication. Dogs get *Capillaria* from eating earthworms (yet another reason not to eat worms!).

Even more rare and exotic worms can be found on the insides of dogs. The giant kidney worm, for example, must be removed surgically. Dogs get them from eating earthworms or by eating fish or frogs that have eaten an infected worm. In southern climates, *Spirocerca lupi* causes thickened nodules in the esophagus or stomach and causes narrowing of the aorta or trachea. Dogs get them from eating dung beetles or from eating something that ate an infected dung beetle. Treatment is with deworming medication. *Physaloptera* are found in the stomach or small intestine and can cause anemia, gastritis, and vomiting. Dogs get this parasite by eating infected beetles, crickets, cockroaches, or animals that ate infected beetles, crickets, or cockroaches. Seems like nothing's safe to eat anymore!

Gut Feelings

Puppies and dogs also suffer from protozoan intestinal parasites, such as coccidia and, especially, *Giardia*. Your veterinarian can prescribe appropriate medication.

Coccidia

Coccidia are often associated with diarrhea, but many infected dogs show no apparent symptoms. Thus, the dangers of coccidia infection in dogs are still being debated. A stool sample is needed for diagnosis. Affected dogs respond well to supportive treatment and drugs. The most important preventive measure is removal of feces.

Giardia

Giardia, also called *beaver fever,* is found fairly commonly in puppies and dogs. It can cause chronic or intermittent diarrhea, but may also have no symptoms. It can be diagnosed with a stool sample, and is more likely to be found in loose or light-colored stool. Many dogs carry *Giardia* and have no symptoms, so the presence of *Giardia* in the stool may not necessarily account for any illness a dog may be showing. *Giardia* is treated with drug therapy.

Heartworming Relationships

Heartworms are deadly parasites carried by mosquitoes. Wherever mosquitoes are present, dogs should be on heartworm prevention. Several effective types of heartworm preventive are available, and some also prevent many other types of worms. Some require daily administration and others require only monthly administration. The latter type is more popular and actually has a wider margin of safety and protection. The preventive that's administered monthly doesn't stay in the dog's system for a month, but instead acts on a particular stage in the heartworm's development. Giving the drug each month prevents any heartworms from maturing. In warm areas, your dog may need to be on a preventive year-round, but in milder climates your dog may only need to use a preventive during the warmer months. Your veterinarian can advise you about when your puppy should start and if year-round prevention is necessary in your area.

If you forget to give the preventive as prescribed by a vet, your Pit Bull may get heartworms. If you think that your dog has heartworms, do not give her a daily preventive. A fatal reaction could occur.

The most common way of checking for heartworms is to check the blood for circulating microfilarae (the immature form of heartworms), but this method may fail to detect the presence of adult heartworms in as many as 20 percent of all tested dogs. An *occult* heartworm test, though slightly more expensive, tests for the presence of antigens to heartworms in the blood and is more accurate. With either test, the presence of heartworms will not be detectable until nearly seven months after infection. Heartworms are treatable in their early stages, but the treatment is expensive and is not without risks — although a treatment that's less risky than prior ones has recently become available. If untreated, heartworms can kill your Pit Bull.

Chapter 13

Sick as a Dog

- -

In This Chapter

▶ Looking out for behaviors that could indicate disease

▶ Stopping vomiting and diarrhea

▶ Taking care of a lame dog

- -

Maybe you think that your Pit Bull's just not quite right — he seems a little down, his habits have changed, or you just have a feeling. Or maybe your dog is definitely sick — he's losing hair, for example. But what could the problem be? You have to be part detective and part veterinarian to try to get to the bottom of the matter. By knowing what to look for, you can give your veterinarian a head start in diagnosing your dog's problem and, hopefully, give your Pit Bull a head start on the road to recovery.

Just Not Himself

We all have mood swings. So do Pit Bulls. We (and our dogs) change behavior as we mature and age. So sometimes knowing if a change in behavior is a symptom of a problem is hard. Maybe your dog's just behaving differently because he's a bit older. Maybe he's just acting a bit differently for no reason at all.

Some behavioral changes are natural consequences of hormonal states. Sexually intact males may become more excited and unmanageable if they are around females in estrus (heat). Females in estrus may be aggressive toward males making unwanted advances.

Dogs tend to calm down as they age. They can also get tired from stress and exercise. But being calm or tired isn't the same thing as being lethargic. A lethargic dog tends to show little interest in his surroundings. He could be sick, and the possible causes include

- ✔ Anemia (check gum color)
- ✔ Cancer
- ✔ Circulatory problems (check gum color and pulse)

- Infection (check for fever)

- Metabolic diseases

- Pain (check limbs, neck, and vertebrae for signs of discomfort upon movement; check mouth, ears, and eyes for signs of pain; check abdomen for pain — pain in the abdomen often causes dogs to stand in a hunched position)

- Poisoning (check gum color and pupillary reaction; look for signs of vomiting or abdominal pain)

- Sudden loss of vision

Extreme lethargy, lethargy that lasts for more than one day or is accompanied by a fever, pain, vomiting, diarrhea, or signs of circulatory problems all probably mean that a trip to the vet is a good idea.

Aggressive behavior is usually not a sign of disease unless it's totally unprecedented. It can be a sign of pain, an endocrine problem, or a brain problem. Cases of sudden aggression toward people mean that your Pit Bull is dangerous; do not excuse the incidents as part of the breed's baggage. Aggressive Pit Bulls need professional help. They should see a neurologist or a veterinarian specializing in behavior.

In general, unprecedented behavior of any kind means that you should take your Pit to the veterinarian's. Be particularly alert to persistent circling or pacing, disorientation, loss of balance, head-pressing, hiding, tremors, seizures, lack of bowel or urine control, and dramatic changes in appetite (see Figure 13-1).

Diarrhea

Dogs get diarrhea — it's almost unavoidable. You may not realize that your dog is sick unless your dog gets locked inside and is forced to have diarrhea in the house. Being on the look out for diarrhea is one reason you need to keep an eye on your dog's bowel movements when he answers the call of nature.

Diarrhea can result from excitement, nervousness, a change in diet or water, sensitivity to certain foods, overeating, intestinal parasites, viral or bacterial infections, or ingestion of toxic substances. The appearance of the diarrhea can provide important information to your vet, so even though your neighbors will think you're a bit strange, take a good look at your dog's diarrhea. What is the consistency? Does it contain blood or mucous? If so, how much? Can you identify foreign objects or parasites? What color is it? These are all clues to the severity and possible causes of your dog's problem.

Figure 13-1:
If you pay
attention to
your Pit
Bull's
disposition,
you're more
likely to
notice
health
problems.

Bloody diarrhea, diarrhea with vomiting, fever, or other signs of toxicity, or a diarrhea that lasts for more than a day should not be allowed to continue without veterinary advice. Some of these could be symptomatic of potentially fatal disorders.

You can treat mild diarrhea by withholding or severely restricting food and water for 24 hours. Ice cubes can be given to satisfy thirst. Administer human diarrhea medication in the same weight dosage as recommended for humans. A bland diet consisting of rice, tapioca, or cooked macaroni, along with cottage cheese or tofu for protein, should be given for several days. Feed nothing else. Your Pit Bull may not be delighted when you present him with a block of tofu and some macaroni for dinner, but his intestinal tract needs time off in order to heal. ***Note:*** Dogs with some other illness in addition to diarrhea may not be candidates for food or water restriction.

Vomiting

In addition to the occasional bout of diarrhea, dogs vomit fairly often. A typical vomit episode begins with retching, followed by vomiting on your best rug, and then, within a minute, another bout of retching and vomiting (hopefully, by now not on your best rug). Following the episode the dog usually appears to be just fine.

When people vomit, it usually means they feel sick. When dogs vomit, it's hard to tell how they feel. Some dogs almost seem to like to vomit, and will eat grass to ensure that they have the opportunity to puke. Vomiting after eating grass is common and is usually of no great concern. If the vomiting continues, it's not typical "recreational" vomiting and is cause for concern.

- ✔ Overeating is a common cause of occasional vomiting in puppies, especially if they follow eating with playing. This problem is easily solved by feeding your Pit smaller meals more frequently.

- ✔ Vomiting immediately after meals could indicate an obstruction of the esophagus.

- ✔ Repeated vomiting could indicate that the dog has eaten spoiled food, indigestible objects, or may have a stomach illness.

- ✔ Sporadic vomiting with poor appetite and generally poor overall condition could indicate internal parasites or a more serious internal disease.

Consult your veterinarian immediately if your dog vomits a foul substance resembling fecal matter (indicating a blockage in the intestinal tract), blood (partially digested blood resembles coffee grounds), or if there is projectile or repeated vomiting. Repeated vomiting can result in dehydration, so if your dog can't hold anything down for a prolonged period, he may have to get intravenous fluids.

Coughing

You know how miserable you feel when you have a cough; having a cough makes your Pit Bull feel just as miserable. An occasional cough is one thing, but a persistent cough should be checked by your veterinarian. Allergies, foreign bodies, pneumonia, parasites, tracheal collapse, tumors, and especially kennel cough and heart disease, can cause coughing.

Kennel cough (canine infectious tracheobronchitis) is a highly communicable air-borne disease caused by several different infectious agents. It's characterized by a gagging cough arising about a week after exposure. After a few days, the cough takes on a honking sound. Inoculations are available and are an especially good idea if you plan to have your dog around other dogs at training classes or while being boarded. Treatment consists of resting the dog and avoiding situations that may lead to coughing. Cough suppressants may break the coughing cycle. Left untreated, coughing can irritate a dog's throat and eventually cause more serious problems. Antibiotics may be needed if secondary infections arise from prolonged irritation.

Heart disease commonly results in coughing, most often following exercise or in the evening. Affected dogs will often lie down with their front legs spread and point their nose in the air in order to breathe better. Veterinary treatment is essential. A low sodium diet and drug therapy can help alleviate the symptoms.

One of the most common of all congenital heart defects in dogs is patent ductus arteriosis. It is seen occasionally in Pit Bulls. During fetal life, the lungs are not functional, so a vessel (the ductus arteriosis) allows blood to bypass the lungs. This vessel normally closes shortly after birth. In some dogs, however, it remains open, allowing blood to leak through it and placing a strain on the heart. Affected dogs have a heart murmur, and can be diagnosed with an ultrasound. Surgical correction is necessary to cure the condition. Left untreated, heart failure can result.

Urinary Problems

Dogs can have a variety of urinary problems. Too often, the symptoms go unnoticed until the dog starts urinating in the house. Even then, many owners don't understand the cause and ban the dog from the house rather than get him the medical treatment he needs.

Increased urination can be an early sign of kidney disease. Although the excessive urination may cause problems in keeping your house clean or your night's sleep intact, never try to restrict the water intake of a dog with kidney disease. A low protein and low sodium diet can slow the progression of the disease.

Increased urination can also be a sign of diabetes or a urinary tract infection. Your veterinarian can discover the cause with some simple tests. These conditions can be treated.

If your dog has difficulty or pain in urination, urinates suddenly and often but in small amounts, or passes cloudy or bloody urine, he may be suffering from a problem of the bladder, urethra, or prostate. Bladder infections must be treated promptly to prevent the infection from reaching the kidneys.

Dribbling of urine during sleep can indicate a hormonal problem; it is not uncommon in spayed females. In males, infections of the prostate gland can lead to repeated urinary tract infections, often with blood or pus in the urine, as well as possible painful defecation. Castration and long-term antibiotic therapy is required for improvement.

Blockage of urine can result in death. Inability to urinate requires immediate emergency veterinary attention.

Endocrine Disorders

The most widespread hormone-related disorders in dogs are diabetes, hypothyroidism, and Cushing's syndrome. The most common of these is hypothyroidism.

Hypothyroidism

Hypothyroidism is one of the most commonly diagnosed conditions in pure-bred dogs. Symptoms may include weight gain, lethargy, and coat problems such as oiliness, dullness, symmetrical hair loss, and hair that is easily pulled out. Hypothyroidism has been implicated in everything from behavioral problems to infertility to a lack of energy. Diagnosis is with a blood test; ask your veterinarian about the more sophisticated and accurate tests that are now available. Treatment is with daily thyroid replacement drugs.

Cushing's syndrome

Cushing's syndrome (hyperadrenocorticism) is seen mostly in older dogs and is characterized by increased drinking and urination, pot-bellied appearance, symmetrical hair loss, darkened skin, and susceptibility to infections. Diagnosis is with a blood test. Treatment is with drug therapy.

Immunological Problems

The immune system is your dog's defense against microscopic intruders. Autoimmune diseases occur when the body's immune system turns against parts of itself. Specific types of autoimmunity include autoimmune hemolytic anemia, autoimmune thrombocytopenia, systemic lupus erythematosus, and discoid lupus erythematosus, as well as many others. Treatment is with drugs that suppress the immune system.

In autoimmune hemolytic anemia, the body destroys its own red blood cells, leading to severe anemia. Affected dogs may be feverish, lethargic, and have whitish gums. In autoimmune thrombocytopenia, the body destroys its own platelets, leading to spontaneous bleeding. Signs may include petechia (small red spots on the surface of the gums and skin and also within the eye). Autoimmune hemolytic anemia and thrombocytopenia often occur together. Symptoms can be confused for several other problems, including pyometra (infection of the uterus) and tick-borne diseases such as erlichiosis.

In systemic lupus erythematosus, many organ systems are affected. Symptoms may include a recurring fever, as well as arthritis in several joints, small ulcers of the skin on the face or toes, and some other less common symptoms.

In discoid lupus erythematosus, ulcers arise on the nose and face. They are aggravated by exposure to ultraviolet light.

Blood Parasites

Blood parasites? The name doesn't sound pleasant, and neither are the conditions that can affect your dog.

Erlichiosis

Erlichiosis (also called *tick fever* or *tropical canine pancytopenia*) is an under-diagnosed yet serious disease spread by ticks. Symptoms are varied, and may include lack of energy, dullness of coat, occasional vomiting, and occasional loss of appetite. But aside from a fever in the initial phases of the disease, no strong signs of disease are present. Owners may complain that the dog just doesn't seem as playful or is just not quite right. Other less common symptoms may include coughing, arthritis, muscle wasting, seizures, spontaneous bleeding, anemia, and a host of others. No one or two symptoms, of themselves, suggest erlichiosis. Definitive diagnosis requires getting a blood titer. Erlichiosis wreaks its havoc by parasitizing the white blood cells, crippling the immune system. If diagnosed early, it can be treated effectively. If not, it can be fatal.

Babesia

Potentially fatal parasites, protozoa of the genus *Babesia* are transmitted by ticks and parasitize the red blood cells. This causes the dog to become anemic and may also precipitate an autoimmune response in which the dog's immune system begins to destroy its own red blood cells. Platelets may also be destroyed. Symptoms include a fever, lethargy, loss of appetite, and, in severe cases, darkened urine. Affected dogs can die within a week of the first appearance of these symptoms. Diagnosis is with blood tests.

The symptoms of a *Babesia* infestation are similar to those of autoimmune hemolytic anemia. If your dog is diagnosed with either of these conditions, make sure that your veterinarian tests to rule out the other condition.

Cancers

Cancers occur relatively frequently in all breeds of dogs. Among the more common cancers are

- **Mammary gland tumors.** These tumors occur mostly in females who weren't spayed early in life. Approximately half of all mammary tumors are malignant. Therapy may include surgical excision and chemotherapy. *Note:* Spaying after the age of two years doesn't impart the protection from mammary cancer that earlier spaying does.

- **Lymphosarcoma.** This cancer affects the blood and lymph systems. Symptoms may include swelling of the lymph nodes, especially those of lower neck area and behind the knees. Chemotherapy extends the life of many affected dogs.

- **Osteosarcoma (bone cancer).** This cancer occurs more frequently in large breeds. It normally develops on a long bone of a leg and can sometimes be seen as a lump. More often, though, owners first become aware that something's wrong when the dog starts to limp — osteosarcoma is very painful. Owners face the terrible decision of amputation that must be made quickly, as time is of the essence to prevent the spread to other parts of the body. Most dogs adjust to the loss of a limb fairly easily, but factors such as age, weight, arthritis, and the presence of other joint problems all can slow down, or even prevent, a dog's transition to having only three legs. Even with the best of therapy, survival time for dogs with osteosarcoma is usually only a few months.

Lame but Game

Pit Bulls play hard and they have a high pain threshold. This combination can lead them to keep right on playing even after they've hurt themselves — often creating a major injury out of a minor one. Even mild lameness requires complete rest. If the lameness persists after three days, your dog will need to be examined by her veterinarian.

Sometimes, Pit Bulls mysteriously become gimpy. You come home from work, and your pet is dragging a paw. But if you're lucky enough to be present when your dog hurts himself, immediately applying an ice pack can reduce the amount of swelling.

If a dog is lame and also exhibits swelling or deformation in the affected leg, extreme pain, or the leg makes grinding or popping sounds, the dog could have a break or another serious problem. It's imperative that the fractured area not be further traumatized by attempts to immobilize it. Immediate veterinary attention is required.

If a toe is swollen, does not match its fellow on the opposite foot in shape and position, or makes a grinding sound when moved, the toe should be immobilized and checked by your veterinarian. Meanwhile, minimize swelling by applying cold packs or placing the foot in a bucket of cold water.

Complete rest and total inactivity are the best way to care for lameness without a trip to the vet. Rest your dog until he quits limping. Then rest him some more.

An arm and a leg

Puppies are especially susceptible to bone and joint injuries. They should never be allowed to jump from high places or run until exhausted. Persistent limping in puppies may result from one of several developmental bone problems and should be checked by the veterinarian. Discourage both puppies and adult dogs from romping on slippery floors, where they could lose their footing.

Knee injuries, especially of the cruciate ligaments, are common in dogs. Overweight dogs are particularly at risk. Knee injuries can also arise if the dog is pushed sideways while running, jumps straight up and lands at a funny angle, or even when he pushes off at a dead run. Ruptured cruciate ligaments can be hard to diagnose in a Pit Bull because their dense muscle mass stabilizes the knee despite the rupture. Because most cruciate tears don't get well on their own, they usually require surgery. However, cruciate surgery requires a commitment to careful post-surgery nursing and should not be undertaken casually.

Older dogs or dogs with a previous injury often limp as a result of osteoarthritis. Arthritis can be treated with buffered aspirin, but only under veterinary supervision. Your veterinarian can also prescribe other drugs that may be more effective. If a young or middle-aged dog ever shows signs of arthritis, especially in a joint that has not been previously injured, the vet should be consulted.

Examine the feet of a lame dog for burs, cuts, peeled pads, misaligned toes, or damage to the nails. Split or broken nails can be treated by cutting the nail as short as possible and soaking it in warm salt water. Apply an antibiotic and then a human fingernail mender, followed by a bandage.

Cuts and peeled pads should be carefully flushed with warm water, and an antibacterial ointment applied. Cover the area with gauze, then wrap the foot with Vet-Wrap (a stretchable bandage that clings to itself.) You can also add padding. Change the dressing twice daily (or anytime it gets wet) and restrict exercise until the wound heals. Peeled pads are very painful. A local anesthetic such as hemorrhoid cream or a topical toothache salve can help ease some of the discomfort.

If you need a quick fix for a minor injury, you can fashion a makeshift pad by adhering a thin piece of rubber or leather to the bottom of the pad with Super-Glue, or you can apply a coat of Nu-Skin (available at drug stores) if the injury is not too extensive.

If your dog has deep cuts or extensive peeling, your veterinarian should check for foreign objects or tendon damage.

From the hip

Hip dysplasia (HD) occurs frequently among Pit Bulls. Nineteen percent of American Pit Bull Terrier radiographs submitted to the Orthopedic Foundation for Animals are judged dysplastic. Yet, few Pit Bulls exhibit the crippling effects that the severity of the damage shown in the X-rays predicts. Perhaps their dense muscle mass stabilizes the hip joint and compensates somewhat, or perhaps the Pit Bull's high pain tolerance and stoical nature enables Pits to simply ignore the pain. However, some unlucky Pits have ultimately been in such pain that euthanasia was the only alternative to chronic discomfort.

HD occurs when the ball of the femur (thigh) bone does not fit properly in the acetabulum (socket) of the pelvic bone. The fit is affected both by the depth and shape of the socket and the laxity of the joint. With pressure on the joint, even the amount of pressure that occurs when the dog walks or runs, the combination of laxity and a shallow socket allows the ball of the femur to pop in and out of the socket. This movement further deteriorates the rim of the socket, making the condition get worse, which is why early diagnosis and treatment is important.

Hip radiographs can diagnose dysplasia before outward signs of the disorder are perceivable. In the United States, radiographs are most often rated by either the Orthopedic Foundation for Animals (OFA) or the Pennsylvania Hip Improvement Program (PennHIP).

The OFA certification is the most common. During the process, a panel of specialists subjectively rates radiographs, based upon a number of specific joint characteristics. A dog with normal hips (which receive ratings of excellent, good, and fair) receives an OFA number. Borderline normal ratings indicate that a dog should be rechecked in another 6 to 8 months. Dysplastic hips receive ratings of mild, moderate, and severe. (Ratings are not given until dogs are two years old, but preliminary ratings can be obtained before then.)

A dog with normal hips receives an OFA number, such as PBT133G24MT.

- PBT stands for Pit Bull Terrier.
- 133 means this dog is the 133rd APBT to receive an OFA number.
- G stands for good.

> ✔ 24 stands for the dog's age, in months, when X-rayed.
>
> ✔ M stands for male.
>
> ✔ T stands for tattooed (M stands for microchipped).

PennHip evaluations are based upon objectively measured degrees of joint laxity, reported as a Distraction Index (DI), with lower numbers reflecting tighter (better) hips. The X-rays must be taken, using special procedures, by veterinarians approved to do them by PennHip.

Breeders disagree about which method is better; many breeders thus elect to have two radiographs taken at the same time, submitting one to each registry. Both registries are good; the only bad choice is to have no certification at all.

Hip dysplasia becomes progressively more crippling and painful, even for a stoical Pit Bull. The good news is that even dogs who have **severe cases** of HD can live full lives if given timely surgery. If the condition is detected in a young dog before secondary changes (osteoarthrosis) have occurred, a procedure called a *triple pelvic osteotomy* (TPO) can be performed. In a TPO, the orientation of the dog's hip socket is surgically changed, allowing the femur head to better fit into the socket.

Older dogs or dogs with more advanced dysplasia are candidates for a total hip replacement. The procedure is similar to the one performed on humans. The ball of the femur is replaced with a metallic ball and the socket is replaced with a plastic cup.

Another procedure, which is less effective in large dogs, is to simply remove the head of the femur. It may be a reasonable choice, for financial reasons, if you have an older dog who only needs to be comfortable while walking around the house.

Doctoring Your Dog

Most veterinarians adhere to traditional western medicine, based upon rigorous scientific experimentation, testing, and clinical trials in animals and humans. In most cases, the therapy available at a typical vet's is the best care that you can give your dog. Nonetheless, alternative medicines are sometimes a reasonable adjunct to traditional medicine. Some forms of alternative medicine, in particular, have more promise and more evidence favoring their efficacy. When your dog is suffering from a serious illness, trying anything that may help is tempting. As long as you remember to be an intelligent consumer, you should certainly explore alternative treatments. Do not do so at the expense of traditional therapies, however. The best option may be to find a veterinarian who is well versed in both traditional and alternative medicine.

Holistic medicine

Holistic medicine focuses on the entire dog, rather than the single problem area. As such, it emphasizes nutritional, emotional, and social health, as well as overt physical health. This is an approach that makes intuitive good sense. Many traditional veterinarians are adapting elements of holistic medicine.

Homeopathic medicine

Homeopathic medicine is a system of treatment in which minute amounts of a chemical are given to treat various ailments. The chemical that's given would produce the same symptoms as the disease it's supposed to be curing if that chemical were given in a larger amount. This approach sounds sort of like a vaccination, except that homeopathic remedies are for symptoms only, and only after the symptoms appear. Little, if any, scientific evidence exists to support the efficacy of these treatments. They probably do no harm — unless they're given at the expense of proven therapies.

Herbology

Many of the drugs used in western medicine are derived from herbs and other plants or from chemical compositions that mimic the active agents found in nature. In fact, herbs are an ancient form of medicinal therapy. Many people prefer them because they consider herbs safer than chemicals, but of course they contain just as many chemicals as any other drug. They can also be just as deadly. Most herbs have not been scientifically tested to determine their safety or efficacy in animals. In addition, the dosage may vary from one batch to another because they are unregulated. Consistently finding a dose that works without creating the risk of an overdose is difficult.

Chiropractic medicine

Chiropractic medicine is popular with humans and is becoming more common with dogs. By manipulating the spine, and sometimes the limbs, minor misalignments that may result in pain can be corrected. Chiropractic manipulation is most helpful to dogs who have problems of the neck, lower back, pelvis, and knees. You must have a cooperative Pit Bull who will relax enough to allow a stranger to manipulate him before you can consider taking your dog in for a session of bending, twisting, and rearranging. Yet another reason to be certain that your dog is well socialized and well trained. Some risks exist, so be sure that you use a veterinarian certified by the American Veterinary Chiropractic Association.

Acupuncture

Acupuncture involves the placement of needles in specific locations in the skin, where they may be left for up to ten minutes. Dogs tend to tolerate it quite well. It is most commonly used in veterinary practice to relieve pain; many people swear their dogs show great improvement after treatment, but considerable controversy still exists about its efficacy. Nonetheless, acupuncture will do no harm and is worth a try if your dog is in pain.

Home Remedies

In general, if your dog is sick enough to need treatment, he's sick enough to go to the doctor. But don't you ever find yourself avoiding human doctors unless you're really sick, and trying to come up with ways to heal yourself if you're just a bit under the weather? For those of you who may want to tinker with your Pit's health, be warned: The consequences could be dire. But if you're careful about when you use them and are ready to take your dog to the vet should things worsen, some household remedies can take care of a lot of Pit problems. But before using any of these remedies, at least talk to your vet and get her opinion.

- ✔ To decrease swelling from injuries, use an icepack or ice cubes wrapped in a towel.
- ✔ To drain abscesses and infections, use a towel soaked in hot water (and wrung out) as a moist compress.
- ✔ To clean superficial cuts, use a providone-iodine solution.
- ✔ To treat superficial cuts, use a human antibiotic ointment.
- ✔ To reduce allergic reactions, use a human antihistamine pill such as Benadryl (diphenhydramine).
- ✔ To control diarrhea, use a human medicine such as Pepto-Bismol or Immodium, but for a short time only.
- ✔ To decrease pain and inflammation, use aspirin, but for a short time only.
- ✔ To induce vomiting: use hydrogen peroxide, table salt, or mustard.
- ✔ To absorb ingested toxins, use activated charcoal.
- ✔ To control coughing: use a human pediatric cough suppressant, but for a short time only.
- ✔ To treat constipation, use mineral oil.

Chapter 14

Pit Bull First Aid

● ●

In This Chapter

▶ Being ready for an emergency

▶ Understanding artificial respiration and CPR

▶ Handling specific emergencies

● ●

*E*ven experienced Pit Bull owners have a difficult time deciding what consti-
tutes a true canine emergency. When in doubt, err on the side of caution
and call the emergency clinic or your veterinarian for a professional opinion.

Consider it an emergency if your Pit Bull is . . .

✔ Hit by a car

✔ Suffering severe trauma

✔ Bleeding profusely

✔ Bleeding from the nose, mouth, ears, eyes, rectum, or has blood in the
urine or stools

✔ Collapsing

✔ Extremely lethargic

✔ Breathing with difficulty

✔ Drowning

✔ Suffering heat stroke

✔ Showing a temperature over 104 degrees

✔ Exhibiting signs of hypothermia or frostbite

✔ Vomiting repeatedly

✔ Vomiting material that contains blood or that looks like coffee grounds
or feces

✔ Attempting to vomit but unable to do so, especially if the stomach is
swollen

- Restless, if the stomach is swollen
- Experiencing frequent, watery diarrhea
- Bitten by a poisonous snake or spider
- Stung multiple times by insects
- Possibly poisoned, especially if you think she drank antifreeze
- Suffering from clusters of seizures or a prolonged seizure
- Paralyzed
- Showing pupils that are unresponsive or unequal
- Squinting, with red eyes and aversion to light
- Suffering from electric shock
- Dehydrated

One of the best gifts that you can give your dog is to take a first aid course. Some courses are available specifically for pets, but even a human first aid course is invaluable. Because no paramedics exist for dogs, you must be ready to assume that role. By the way, there aren't any ambulance drivers for dogs, either — be ready for that role, too. It sounds daunting, but the prep work will keep your dog and your family happy and healthy (see Figure 14-1).

Figure 14-1:
Knowing first aid for your pets is a family requirement.

Prepare now, while your Pit is healthy. Study the emergency procedures described in this chapter and keep this book handy. Misplaced instructions can result in a critical loss of time. Know the phone number and location of the emergency veterinarian in your area. Keep the number next to the phone; don't rely on your memory, which may fail you during a crisis. Another thing to keep in mind: Always have enough fuel in your car to make it to the emergency clinic (stopping for gas is the last thing you want to do if your Pit is bleeding in the back seat).

In general:

✔ Make sure that you and your dog are in a safe location.

✔ A dog in pain may bite. Make an emergency muzzle by looping a cloth around the muzzle and then tying it behind the ears.

✔ Move the dog as little and as gently as possible.

✔ Use a piece of plywood or a blanket to transport the dog.

ABCs of First Aid

In an emergency, check to see if the dog is responsive by calling her name or tapping on her head. If she doesn't respond, quickly use the ABCs of first aid:

A: Airway

B: Breathing

C: Circulation

✔ **Airway:** Make sure the airway is open. Extend the head and neck, open the mouth, and pull the tongue forward.

✔ **Breathing:** Make sure the dog is breathing. Is the chest rising and falling? Can you feel exhaled air against your cheek? If not, give two rapid breaths through the nose before checking circulation.

✔ **Circulation:** Check gum color, capillary refill time, and pulse. Gum color should be pink. When you press your thumb on the gum, it should regain its color within two seconds. Check the pulse by feeling either the heart beat (on the left side of the rib cage, a couple of inches behind the elbow) or feeling the pulse (on the inside of the thigh, near the groin).

If your dog has a pulse, but she's not breathing, administer artificial respiration. If your dog does not have a pulse, administer cardio-pulmonary resuscitation (CPR). I explain both life-saving techniques in the sections that follow.

Artificial respiration

You may need to perform some vital, preliminary first aid before you perform artificial respiration. If an object is obstructing the airway, wrap your hands around your dog's abdomen, behind the rib cage, and compress briskly. Repeat if needed. If the dog loses consciousness, extend the head and neck forward, pull the tongue out fully, and explore the throat for any foreign objects.

If the dog is in danger of drowning, turn the dog upside down, hold her around her waist, and sway back and forth so that water can run out of her mouth. Now you're ready to perform artificial respiration:

1. **Open the dog's mouth, and clear the passage of secretions and foreign bodies.**

2. **Pull the dog's tongue forward.**

3. **Seal your mouth over the dog's nose and mouth. Blow into the dog's nose for two seconds, and then release.**

4. **You should see your dog's chest expand; if not, try blowing with greater force, making a tighter seal around the lips, or checking for an obstruction.**

5. **Repeat at a rate of one breath every four seconds.**

6. **Stop every minute to monitor breathing and pulse.**

7. **If air collects in the stomach, push down just behind the ribcage every few minutes.**

8. **Continue until the dog breathes on her own.**

CPR

To perform CPR on a dog:

1. **Place your hands, one on top of the other, on the left side of the chest, about 2 inches up from and behind the point of the elbow.**

2. **Press down quickly and release.**

3. **Compress at a rate of about 100 times per minute.**

4. **After every 15 compressions, give two breaths through the nose. If you have a partner, the partner can give breaths every two or three compressions.**

Vital statistics for your Pit Bull

Respiration: 10 to 30 breaths per minute at rest

Pulse: 60 to 120 beats per minute at rest

Temperature: 101.5 to102.5 degrees F

Capillary refill time: Less than 2 seconds (checked by pressing on the gums)

Gum color: Pink (not white, red, bluish, yellowish, or pink with tiny red spots)

Hydration: Skin should pop back into position within 3 seconds of being lifted

---

Specific Emergencies

Most other types of emergencies give you a little more time to act — but not much. For the following situations, administer first aid and seek veterinary attention.

Poisoning

Signs of poisoning vary, depending on the type of poison, but commonly include vomiting, convulsions, staggering, and collapse. If in doubt about whether your Pit ingested poison, call the veterinarian anyway. If possible, bring the suspected poison and its container with you to the veterinarian. If the dog vomits, put the vomit in a plastic bag and bring it with you to the vet.

This list contains items you may have around the house that could poison your dog. The poisonous compound is given in parenthesis.

- **Acetaminophen,** such as is found in Tylenol: A toxic dose for dogs is over 75 mg/lb.

- **Antifreeze** (ethylene glycol): Causes kidney failure; prognosis is poor once symptoms have begun. Veterinary treatment must be obtained within two to four hours of ingestion of even tiny amounts if the dog's life is to be saved. You can reduce the risk of antifreeze poisoning by using a brand that does not contain ethylene glycol.

- **Chocolate** (theobromine): Causes vomiting, diarrhea, restlessness, fever, seizures, coma, and death; toxic dose for dogs is 50 mg/lb. Dark chocolate contains over 400 milligrams of theobromine per ounce, so a five ounce candy bar can be life threatening to a 40 pound dog.

✔ **Flea and tick poison and dewormers** (organophosphates): Overdose can cause vomiting, muscle tremors, pupil constriction, diarrhea, excitability, difficulty breathing, and death. Prognosis for recovery varies — it can be poor, depending on a variety of factors.

✔ **Fleet enema** (hypertonic sodium phosphate): Can cause sleepiness, muscle rigidity, unsteadiness, seizures, vomiting, shock, and death. Toxic dosage for a Pit Bull is four ounces. Prognosis depends on the amount ingested and how quickly treatment begins.

✔ **Ibuprofen:** Can cause vomiting, stomach ulcers, and kidney failure. Kidney failure can result from dosages of 150 mg/lb.

✔ **Insect poison, weed killer, and wood preservatives** (arsenic): Cause vomiting, diarrhea, weakness, and eventually kidney failure, coma, and death; prognosis is poor if symptoms have already started.

✔ **Lead:** Causes abnormal behavior, unsteadiness, seizures, loss of appetite, vomiting, diarrhea, and blindness. Lead can be found in paint, golf ball coatings, linoleum, and even newsprint. Prognosis is usually good.

✔ **Rodent poison** (warfarin compounds): Contains anticoagulants that cause uncontrolled internal bleeding; prognosis ranges from good (if caught soon after ingestion) to poor (if several days have elapsed).

✔ **Rodent poison** (cholecalciferol): Deposits calcium in the blood vessels, causing kidney failure and other problems; prognosis is poor, even if your Pit only ate small amounts.

✔ **Rose fertilizer** (iron): Can cause kidney and liver failure; toxic dose is one teaspoon of 5 percent concentration per 20 pounds. Prognosis is varied, depending upon the amount ingested and the delay in treatment.

✔ **Snail and slug poison** (metaldehyde): Causes anxiety, unsteadiness, tremors, coma, and death; prognosis is fair.

✔ **Squirrel and bird poison** (strychnine): Can cause seizures, hyper-reactivity to noise, and rigid muscles. This poison is usually ingested by way of birdseed with a blue coating of strychnine. Prognosis is poor.

✔ **Tricyclic antidepressants:** Overdose can cause seizures and fatal heart rhythm abnormalities; prognosis varies.

✔ **Zinc:** Causes breakdown of red blood cells. Symptoms include decreased appetite, vomiting, diarrhea, depression, pale gums, and brown urine. Zinc can be found in pennies, zinc oxide skin cream, calamine lotion, fertilizers, and shampoos. Prognosis varies.

Call the veterinarian or a poison control hotline and give as much information as possible. Induce vomiting (except in the cases outlined below) by giving either hydrogen peroxide (mixed 1:1 with water), salt water, or dry mustard and water. Treat for shock and get your Pit Bull to the veterinarian at once. Be prepared for convulsions or respiratory distress.

Do not induce vomiting if the poison was an acid, alkali, petroleum product, solvent, cleaner, tranquilizer, or if a sharp object was swallowed; also do not induce vomiting if the dog is severely depressed, convulsing, comatose, or if over two hours have passed since ingestion. If the dog is neither convulsing nor unconscious, dilute the poison by giving milk, vegetable oil, or egg whites. Activated charcoal can absorb many toxins. Baking soda or milk of magnesia can be given for ingested acids, and vinegar or lemon juice for ingested alkalis.

The National Animal Poison Control Center can be reached at 1-800-426-4435 or 1-900-680-0000. A charge of $30 applies.

Seizures

A dog undergoing a seizure may drool, become stiff, or have uncontrollable muscle spasms.

- ✔ Remove other dogs from the area (they may attack the convulsing dog).
- ✔ Wrap the dog securely in a blanket, to prevent her from injuring herself on furniture or stairs.
- ✔ Never put your hands (or anything else) in a convulsing dog's mouth.
- ✔ Most convulsions are over in a few minutes. (If they continue for more than 10 minutes, you must get the dog to the emergency clinic).
- ✔ After the seizure, treat the dog for shock.
- ✔ Call your veterinarian for advice, as some seizures can result from poisoning, high fever, or other conditions that must be treated immediately. Taking careful note of all the characteristics of the seizure and the sequence of seizure activity can help your vet diagnose the cause.

Heat stroke

Early signs of heat stroke include rapid, loud breathing; abundant, thick saliva; bright red mucous membranes; and high rectal temperature. Later signs include unsteadiness, diarrhea, and coma.

Wet the dog and place her in front of a fan. If doing so is not possible, immerse the dog in cool water. *Do not plunge the dog in ice water;* the resulting constriction of peripheral blood vessels can make the situation worse. Offer small amounts of water for drinking.

You must lower your dog's body temperature quickly, but you don't want it to go below 100 degrees F. Stop cooling the dog when the rectal temperature reaches 103 degrees F, because it will continue to fall without your help.

Hypothermia

Shivering and sluggishness are signs of a dog who has become excessively chilled. Later signs include a very low (under 95 degrees F) body temperature, slow pulse and breathing rates, and coma.

Warm the dog gradually. Wrap her in a blanket (preferably one that has been warmed in the dryer). Place plastic bottles filled with hot water outside the blankets (not touching the dog). You can also place a plastic tarp over the blanket, making sure the dog's head is not covered. Monitor the dog's temperature. Stop warming when the temperature reaches 101 degrees F.

Bleeding

Consider wounds to be an emergency if your dog is bleeding profusely, if the wounds are extremely deep, or if they open to the chest cavity, abdominal cavity, or head.

- ✔ Do not remove impaled objects; seek veterinary attention.
- ✔ Control massive bleeding.
- ✔ Cover the wound with clean dressing and apply pressure.
- ✔ Don't remove blood-soaked bandages; apply more dressings over them until bleeding stops.
- ✔ If possible, elevate the wound and apply a cold pack to it.
- ✔ If the wound is on an extremity, apply pressure to the closest pressure point.

Apply pressure to stop the bleeding from an extremity. For a front leg, press inside of the leg, just above the elbow; for a rear leg, press inside of the thigh, where the femoral artery crosses the thigh bone; for the tail, press the underside of the tail, close to where it joins the body.

- ✔ Use a tourniquet only in life threatening situations and only when all other attempts to reduce bleeding have failed. Check for signs of shock.
- ✔ For sucking chest wounds, place a sheet of plastic or other nonporous material over the hole and apply a bandage to make as airtight a seal as possible. It probably still won't work very well, but it may help.
- ✔ For abdominal wounds, place a warm, wet, sterile dressing over any protruding internal organs and cover with a bandage or towel. Do not attempt to push organs back into the dog.
- ✔ For head wounds, apply gentle pressure to control bleeding. Monitor for loss of consciousness or shock and treat accordingly.

✔ For animal bites, allow some bleeding, then clean the area thoroughly and apply antibiotic ointment. A course of oral antibiotics will probably be necessary. It's best not to suture most animal bites, but a large one (over one half inch in diameter) or one on the face or other prominent position may need to be sutured.

Limb fractures

In most cases of limb fracture, you should simply transport the dog to the veterinarian as gently as possible, taking great care to prevent the affected limb from hitting anything. You risk doing more damage than good if you try to splint the leg. If you must try to splint, use lots and lots of padding and tape the splint outside of the padding. If the bone is exposed, place a sterile covering over it. Don't try to push the bone back in.

Bloat (gastric torsion, gastric dilatation-volvulus)

Bloat is a life-threatening emergency in which gas and fluid become trapped in the stomach. It is most common in large, deep-chested breeds. Symptoms include distention of the abdomen, unproductive attempts to vomit, excessive salivation, and restlessness. A dog with these symptoms needs to go to the emergency clinic right now — not tomorrow, not even an hour from now.

The veterinarian will try to pass a tube into the stomach so gases can escape. Often, the stomach has twisted and rotated on its axis, so the tube can't get into the stomach. Dogs with rotated stomachs require emergency surgery in order to save their lives. The rotation of the stomach cuts off the blood supply to the stomach wall, which will die, and subsequently kill the dog, if surgery isn't performed quickly. Other organs may also be compromised. During surgery, the veterinarian should tack the stomach in place to prevent future rotation. Dogs who bloat once will often continue to do so.

Insect stings and allergic reactions

Insects often sting dogs on the face or feet. Remove any visible stingers as quickly as possible by brushing them with a credit card or stiff paper; grasping a stinger often injects more venom into the dog. Administer a paste of baking soda and water to bee stings and vinegar to wasp stings. Clean the area and apply antibacterial ointment. Keep an eye on the dog in case she has an allergic reaction, including swelling that could interfere with breathing, or any change in consciousness.

Call your veterinarian immediately if you think that the dog may be having a severe reaction. Insect stings are the most common cause of extreme allergic reactions. Swelling around the nose and throat can block the airway. Other possible reactions include restlessness, vomiting, diarrhea, seizures, and collapse. If any of these symptoms occur, immediate veterinary attention is probably necessary.

Snakebite

Poisonous snakebites are characterized by swelling, discoloration, pain, fang marks, restlessness, nausea, and weakness. Most bites are to the head and are difficult to treat with first aid.

Restrain the dog and keep her quiet. Be able to describe the snake. If (and only if) you can't get to the veterinarian immediately, apply a pressure bandage (not a tourniquet, but a firm bandage) between the bite and the heart. If the bite is on a leg, keep it lower than the rest of the body.

In North America, copperheads are the most likely to bite, but are the least venomous. Coral snakes are least likely to bite, but are the most venomous. Rattlesnakes and water moccasins usually try to avoid biting and can have deadly bites.

Burns

Deep burns, characterized by charred or pearly white skin, with deeper layers of tissue exposed, are serious threats to your dog's health.

Cool burned areas with towels soaked in cool water or by immersing them in cold water. If over 50 percent of the dog is burned, do not immerse the dog in water as doing so increases the likelihood of shock. Cover the area with a clean bandage or towel to avoid contamination. Do not apply pressure; do not apply ointments. Monitor for shock.

Electrical shock

A dog who chews an electrical cord may collapse and have burns inside her mouth. Before touching the dog, disconnect the plug or cut the power; if that cannot be done immediately, use a wooden stick to knock the cord away from the dog. Keep the dog warm and treat for shock. Monitor breathing and heartbeat.

Chapter 15

Staying Well Up in Years

· ·

In This Chapter

▶ Feeding and exercising the older Pit Bull

▶ Coping with special health concerns

▶ Saying goodbye

▶ Coping with loss of a true friend

· ·

Pit Bulls are the Peter Pans (well, maybe if Peter Pan were a wrestler) of the dog world, eternally young at heart. They remain young of body as well — up to a point. While your Pit Bull may be active and healthy for a long time, one day you will look at your youngster and be shocked to discover that his face has silvered and his gait has stiffened. He sleeps longer and more soundly than he did as a youngster, and he's slower to get going. He may be less eager to play and more content to lie in the sun. Feeling a bit sad is natural, but getting your dog to a healthy old age is a worthy accomplishment.

Few things are as adorable as a mischievous Pit Bull pup discovering the world, or as magnificent as an adult Pit Bull exuding self-confidence, but other Pit Bulls pale in comparison to the wise and stately Pit Bull elder.

Older Pit Bulls can enjoy full and active lives, as long as you know what extra measures to take.

Average life expectancy for a Pit Bull is about 11 to 13 years, although many have reached ripe old ages of 15 or 16.

Eat and Run

Many Pit Bull owners have the idea that their macho little dog won't ever slow down with age. But staying in a state of denial about your dog's increasing age or decreasing abilities is not doing him any favors.

Older Pit Bulls, who may have had minor joint problems when young, really begin to suffer from them. Keeping your older Pit Bull relatively active, without putting too much stress on his joints, is critical to his health (see Figure 15-1). If your dog is sore the day after you exercise, you've probably asked too much. You may have to walk with your dog and do your marathon running by yourself. Swimming is an excellent low-impact exercise, as long as the dog doesn't get chilled and is never put in a dangerous situation. Remember that exercise is *essential* to keeping your dog healthy and happy.

Figure 15-1:
Older Pit Bulls still need an active lifestyle to stay healthy.

Older dogs should be fed several small meals instead of one large meal, and should be fed on time (see Figure 15-2). Moistening dry food or feeding canned food can help a dog with dental problems enjoy his meal. He may also enjoy eating while lying down or eating off of a raised platform.

Older dogs engage in less physical activity and have lower metabolic rates, so they require fewer calories than they used to. Older dogs who are fed the same amount of food as when they were young can become obese; obese dogs have a greater risk of cardiovascular and joint problems.

Some Pit Bulls lose weight with age, which can be as unhealthy as gaining weight. Your dog needs a little bit of fat, so that he has something to fall back on if he gets sick. Consuming high quality (not quantity) protein is especially important for older dogs. The good news is that most older dogs do not require a special diet unless they have a particular medical need for it.

Figure 15-2:
Feed your older Pit Bull several small meals per day.

Act Your Age

Older dogs tend to like a simple life. Although they're still up for adventure, that adventure may have to be toned down a bit. Long trips can be grueling for an older dog, and boarding in a kennel may be extremely upsetting. Consider getting a house sitter whom your dog knows if you want to go on vacation.

Some older dogs become cranky and impatient, especially when dealing with puppies or boisterous children. But don't excuse behavioral changes, especially if they're sudden, as entirely due to aging. They could be symptoms of pain or disease.

The slight haziness that appears in an older dog's pupils is normal and has minimal effect upon vision, but some dogs, especially those with diabetes, may develop cataracts. Cataracts can be seen through the dog's pupils as a densely clouded area. The lens can be removed by a veterinary ophthalmologist if the cataract is severe. Older dogs may experience hearing or visual loss. Be careful not to startle a dog with impaired senses, as a startled dog could snap in self-defense.

Dogs with gradual vision loss can cope well, as long as they are kept in familiar surroundings and extra safety precautions are followed. For example, don't move furniture, and place sound or scent beacons throughout the house or yard to help the dog locate specific landmarks. Also lay pathways in the yard, such as gravel or block walkways, and even in the house, using carpet runners. Block open stairways or pools. Dogs with hearing loss can learn hand gestures and also respond to vibrations.

The immune system may be less effective in older dogs. As a result, shielding your dog from infectious disease, chilling, overheating, and any other stressful condition is important. A bit of good news: An older dog who's never exposed to other dogs may not need to be vaccinated as often or for as many diseases as a younger dog. Discuss this with your veterinarian.

Vomiting and diarrhea can signal that an older dog may have various problems; keep in mind that an older dog cannot tolerate the dehydration that results from continued vomiting or diarrhea. You should not let it continue unchecked.

An older Pit Bull should see the veterinarian at least twice a year. Blood tests can detect early stages of diseases, and your vet may be able to spot developing problems without any tests whatsoever.

Older dogs are somewhat more at risk when they undergo anesthesia. Most of the increased risk can be negated, however, by carefully screening dogs to determine if they're healthy enough to undergo the procedure. Many older dogs need tooth cleaning under anesthesia — this is generally safe, as long as your dog is healthy.

Older dogs tend to have a stronger body odor. Don't just ignore increased odors, though. They could indicate specific problems, such as periodontal disease, impacted anal sacs, seborrhea, ear infections, or even kidney disease. Any strong odor should be checked by your veterinarian.

Like people, dogs lose skin moisture as they age. Although dogs don't have to worry about wrinkles, their skin can become dry and itchy. Regular brushing can help to stimulate oil production.

Although Pit Bulls of any age enjoy a soft, warm bed, such a bed is an absolute necessity for older Pit Bulls. Arthritis is a common cause of intermittent stiffness and lameness, and it can be helped with heat, a soft bed, moderate exercise, and possibly drug therapy. New arthritis medications have made a huge difference in the quality of life for many older Pit Bulls, but not every dog can use them. Ask your veterinarian to evaluate your dog's ability to take some of the new medicines, if your Pit has arthritis.

In general, any ailment that an older dog has is magnified in severity on account of age. Some of the more common symptoms of illness that an older Pit Bull may display, and the possible causes of the symptoms, include

- **Diarrhea:** kidney or liver disease; pancreatitis
- **Coughing:** heart disease; tracheal collapse; lung cancer
- **Difficulty eating:** periodontal disease; oral tumors

> ✔ **Decreased appetite:** kidney, liver, or heart disease; pancreatitis; cancer
>
> ✔ **Increased appetite:** diabetes; Cushing's syndrome
>
> ✔ **Weight loss:** heart, liver or kidney disease; diabetes; cancer
>
> ✔ **Abdominal distention:** heart or kidney disease; Cushing's syndrome; tumor
>
> ✔ **Increased urination:** diabetes; kidney or liver disease; cystitis; Cushing's syndrome
>
> ✔ **Limping:** arthritis; hip or elbow dysplasia; degenerative myelopathy
>
> ✔ **Nasal discharge:** tumor; periodontal disease

If you're lucky enough to have an older Pit Bull, you must accept that an end will come. Heart disease, kidney failure, and cancer eventually claim most of these senior citizens. Early detection can help delay the effects of these diseases, but, unfortunately, can seldom defeat them.

When You've Done Everything

Despite the best of care, a time will come when neither you nor your veterinarian can prevent your dear friend from succumbing to old age or an incurable illness. It seems hard to believe that you will have to bid farewell to an animal who has been such a focal point of your life — in truth, a real member of your family. That dogs live such a short time compared to humans is a cruel fact, but one that you must ultimately face.

You should realize that both of you have been fortunate to share so many good times. You must also make sure that your Pit Bull's remaining time is still pleasurable. Many terminal illnesses make your dog feel very ill, and there comes a point when your desire to keep your friend with you for as long as possible may be cruel to both of you. If your dog no longer eats his dinner or treats, he's giving you a sign that he doesn't feel well and you must face the prospect of doing what's best for your beloved friend. Every Pit Bull owner has to determine when they feel the point has come, using whatever criteria they feel is right. In my opinion, many people put off making the difficult choice for longer than they should and for longer than is kind to the dog. They don't want to act in haste and be haunted by thoughts that, just maybe, the most recent dip into lethargy and illness was a temporary setback. And of course, they put it off because they can't stand the thought.

Euthanasia is a difficult and personal decision that no one wishes to make, and no one can make it for you. Ask your veterinarian if there is a reasonable chance of your dog getting better and if your dog is likely suffering. Ask yourself if your dog is getting pleasure out of life, and if he enjoys most of his days. Financial considerations can be a factor too, if you'd have to go into debt to keep your dog alive for just a bit longer. Your own emotional state must also be considered.

We all wish that, if our dog has to go, he could just fall asleep and never wake up. This, unfortunately, almost never happens. Even when it does, you're left with the regret that you never got to say goodbye. The best way you can simulate a natural death is with euthanasia. Euthanasia is painless and involves giving an overdose of an anesthetic. The dog falls asleep and dies almost instantly. In a very sick dog, because the circulation is compromised, it may take slightly longer for the anesthetic to go into effect.

If you do decide that euthanasia is the kindest thing you can do for your beloved friend, discuss with your veterinarian what will happen. You may ask about giving your dog a tranquilizer beforehand, if he's afraid of the vet's office. You may feel better having the doctor meet you at home or if the vet comes out to your car. Although it won't be easy, try to remain with your dog so that his last moments will be filled with your love; otherwise, have a friend whom your dog knows stay with him. Try to recall the wonderful times you've shared, and realize that, however painful losing such a once-in-a-lifetime dog is, it's better than never having had such a partner at all.

Eternally in Your Heart

After losing such a cherished friend, many people say that they will never get another dog. True, no dog will ever take the place of your dog. But you'll find that another dog is a welcome diversion and will help keep you from dwelling on the loss of your first pet, as long as you don't keep comparing the new dog to the old. It's true that by getting another dog you're sentencing yourself to the same grief in the future, but wouldn't you rather have that than miss out on a second once-in-a-lifetime dog?

The loss of your companion may mark the end of an era for you, a time when you and your Pit Bull grew up or grew old together. But one could scarcely ask for a better life partner than a special Pit Bull. As long as you hold your memories close, your relationship with your dog will last forever.

What better tribute to your Pit Bull could you make than to give your love to another Pit Bull and your efforts to ensuring that Pit Bulls will one day be lifted from the shadow of suspicion under which they have labored? Your Pit Bull taught you what a magnificent breed this is; don't let his lessons go unheeded. No breed of dog has given so much — it's time to give back.

Part V
The Part of Tens

The 5th Wave   By Rich Tennant

"We try to pay personal attention to the dog's grooming but it's time consuming and lately Agnes has been hacking up hair balls."

In this part . . .

*E*very *For Dummies* book ends with top ten lists, and this one is no exception. I give you many more than ten Pit Bull resources, and I offer ten ways to help improve the Pit Bull's reputation.

Chapter 16

More Than Ten Pit Bull Resources

In This Chapter

▶ Organizations and activities

▶ Periodicals, books, and Web sites

All-Breed Organizations

American Kennel Club (AKC)
5580 Centerview Dr., Raleigh, NC 27606-3390
919-233-9767
e-mail: info@akc.org
www.akc.org

United Kennel Club (UKC)
100 East Kilgore Rd., Kalamazoo, MI 49001-5593
616-343-9020
www.ukcdogs.com

Pit Bull–Only Organizations

American Dog Breeders Association (ADBA)
P.O. Box 1771, Salt Lake City, UT 84110
members.aol.com/bstofshw

APBT Rescue Network
e-mail: mbur@nyx.net
www.nyx.net/~mbur/apbtfaqrescue.html

Activities

Agility Association of Canada (AAC)
R.R. #2, Lucan, Ontario N0N 2J0
519-657-7636

International Weight Pull Association
56 Rising Sun Circle, Kalispell, MT 59901
e-mail: samoyed@eskimo.com
www.eskimo.com/~samoyed/iwpa/

Therapy Dogs International
88 Bartley Rd., Flanders, NJ 07836
973-252-9800
e-mail: tdi@gti.net
www.tdi-dog.org

United Kennel Club
(Conformation, obedience, agility)
100 East Kilgore Rd., Kalamazoo, MI 49001-5593
616-343-9020

United Schutzhund Clubs of America (USA)
3810 Paule Ave., St. Louis, MO 63125-1718
314-638-9686
e-mail: USA Schutzhund@worldnet.att.net
www.germanshepherddog.com/

United States Dog Agility Association (USDAA)
P.O. Box 850995, Richardson, TX 75085-0955
972-231-9700
e-mail: info@usdaa.com
www.usdaa.com/

Organizations to Help You Monitor Legislation

American Dog Owners Association
1654 Columbia Turnpike, Castleton, NY 12033
518-477-8469
e-mail: adoa@global2000.net
www.adoa.org

American Kennel Club Legislation Department
www.akc.org

United Kennel Club State Canine Awareness Network
www.ukcdogs.com

Books and Periodicals

Coile, D. Caroline. *Show Me!* Hauppauge, NY: Barron's Educational Series, Inc., 1997.

Colby, Louis B. *Colby's Book of the American Pit Bull Terrier.* Neptune City, NJ: TFH Publications, 1997.

Fraser, Jacqueline. *The American Pit Bull Terrier: An Owner's Guide to a Happy Healthy Pet.* New York, NY: Howell Book House, 1995.

Hearne, Vicki. *Bandit: Dossier of a Dangerous Dog.* New York, NY: HarperCollins, 1991.

Hoban, Mike. *A Complete History of Fighting Dogs.* New York, NY: Howell Book House, 1999.

Semencic, Carl. *Pit Bulls and Tenacious Guard Dogs.* Neptune City, NJ: TFH Publications, 1991.

Stevens, Bob. *Dogs of Velvet and Steel.* (2200 Lynette Dr., Greensboro, NC 27403) Privately published, 1981.

American Pit Bull Terrier Gazette
Available through the ADBA

Bloodlines
Available through the UKC (organization)

Dog Fancy Magazine
3 Burroughs, Irvine, CA 92618-2804
www.dogfancy.com

Dog Sports (covers Schutzhund, search and rescue, and others)
231 Orin Way, Douglas, WY 82633-9232
307-358-3487
e-mail: DSM@coffey.com
www.cyberpet.com/cyberdog/products/pubmag/dgsptmag.htm

Dog World Magazine
P.O. Box 56240, Boulder, CO 80322-6240
800-361-8506
www.dogworldmag.com

Pit Bull Reporter
667 Bailey Rd., Austin, AR 72007
www.pitbulls.com

Purebred Dogs/AKC Gazette
Available through the AKC (organization)

Schutzhund USA
Available through United Schutzhund Clubs of America

Web Sites (Pit Bull–Specific and All-Breed)

FAQs about the American Pit Bull Terrier
www.nyx.net/~mbur/apbtfaqtoc.html

A site dedicated to the American Pit Bull Terrier
www.geocities.com/Heartland/Prairie/5672

A site dedicated to AmStaffs and APBTs
www.geocities.com/Heartland/Pointe/8959/
AmStaff_and_Pit_Bull_page.html

Everything you ever wanted to know about the sport of agility
www.dogpatch.org/agility

Links about the sport of obedience
www.basset.net/heather/obedience.html

UKC obedience e-mail list
www.onelist.com/subscribe.cgi/ukcobedience

To find a dog trainer
www.apdt.com
(Association of Pet Dog Trainers)

A site dedicated to the sport of tracking
personal.cfw.com/~dtratnac

National Association for Search and Rescue (NASAR) home page
www.nasar.org

Lots of information and links on dog training
http://www.uwsp.edu/psych/dog/dog.htm

A collection of veterinary science–related links
netvet.wustl.edu/vetmed.htm

An online encyclopedia of dog terms
www.vetinfo.com/dencyclopedia/deindex.html

Rainbow Bridge tribute page for deceased pets
rainbowbridge.tierranet.com/bridge.htm

In Case of Poisoning

National Animal Poison Control Center
1-800-548-2423
1-888-4ANIHELP (1-888-426-4435) $30 per case — charged to a credit card
1-900-680-0000 $30 per case — charged to your phone bill
www.napcc.aspca.org

Chapter 17

Ten Ways to Help the Pit Bull's Reputation

. . . .

In This Chapter

▶ Ways to enlighten folks on Pit Bulls
▶ Pit Bull causes

. . . .

As the owner of a breed subject to so much discrimination, you have a special obligation to make sure your Pit Bull is a walking example of why this breed can be so great. More than most dogs, Pit Bulls attract attention wherever they go. That means you have a ready-made audience. Make the most of your time in the spotlight by showing the Pit Bull in a good light.

Putting Temperament to the Test

Many people think Pit Bulls are just plain mean and not to be trusted. What better way to prove them wrong than to have your dog pass an official temperament test? The American Temperament Test Association (ATTS) offers a ten-part test that evaluates aspects of a dog's temperament, such as stability, shyness, aggressiveness, and friendliness. The test simulates an everyday walk — except it's a very exciting everyday walk. No special training beyond proper socialization is needed. Those dogs who pass earn the TT (Temperament Tested) title after their names. The ATTS keeps records of how many dogs in each breed pass or fail. Pit Bulls score among the best of breeds, a fact that can only help the breed's image. Can your dog add to the score?

Contact the ATTS at P.O. Box 397, Fenton, MO 63026; 314-225-5346; e-mail info@atts.org; Web site www.atts.org.

Earning a Citizenship

Not everybody wants to go all out training his or her dog to be the seventh wonder of the world. Even so, your Pit Bull must act with good manners, both for his own good and for the breed's reputation.

In order to formally recognize dogs who behave in public, the AKC offers the Canine Good Citizen (CGC) certificate. The CGC certificate may be of use in convincing landlords or insurance agents that your dog is a proper canine citizen. Your Pit Bull doesn't have to be AKC registered or even purebred to participate. The test is a low-pressure evaluation of your dog's ability to accept strangers, remain calm, sit politely, walk politely on a loose lead, and more.

Heeling and Healing

Some people are surprised to find Pit Bulls acting as therapy dogs. Yet, more and more Pit Bulls are bringing entertainment, affection, and unconditional love to people in nursing homes, mental health facilities, prisons, and other places that dogs cannot usually inhabit. Therapy dogs need to be well trained, friendly, and most of all, stable.

Your Pit Bull will need to complete a short course in order to be certified as a Therapy Dog. Contact Therapy Dogs International at 88 Bartley Road, Flanders, NJ; 973-252-9800; e-mail tdi@gti.net; Web site www.tdi-dog.org.

Coming to the Rescue

No machine has been developed that can outperform a dog's nose in olfactory detection or that can outperform a dog when it comes to finding buried, lost, or even dead people. Not every dog is up to the challenge, however. To be a Search and Rescue dog (SAR), not only must a dog have a good nose, but he must also be courageous, strong, nimble, obedient, intelligent, enthusiastic, and tough. This sounds like a job for a Pit Bull!

Contact the American Rescue Dog Association for more information about training for SAR: The American Rescue Dog Association; P.O. Box 151; Chester, New York 10918; Web site: www.ardainc.org.

Sniffing Out Trouble

Dogs are the best detectors of illicit drugs, foods, animals, and explosives ever created. Several breeds are employed as sniffer dogs by police departments, customs agencies, agricultural inspection stations, and private companies. Although not the most popular breed for this job, Pit Bulls have demonstrated that they can sniff out contraband with the best of them. They have good noses, they're agile, athletic, and they have a strong desire to both please and play — all essential attributes for a dog who must give total concentration to a job where people's lives may be on the line. Not only do the dogs work to help humans, but they also help the Pit Bull's image by doing so.

Competing with the Best of Them

Many people think all Pit Bulls can do is fight. They couldn't be more wrong. Pit Bulls can compete in conformation shows, weight pulling competitions, obedience, tracking, and agility trials, and even in herding and Schutzhund competitions. Every time a Pit Bull passes an obedience trail with flying colors, gives her all in a weight pulling contest in exchange for her handler's praise, jumps with joy around the agility ring, or even calls off the attack the instant her handler commands in Schutzhund, it furthers the breed's reputation as an obedient, loving, and trustworthy companion. Who knows, the person you beat may decide if you can't beat 'em, join 'em, and become a Pit Bull owner.

Organizing a Local Pit Bull Group

Sometimes it's difficult to lead your own private crusade, but there's strength in numbers — and few things are stronger than a group of determined Pit Bull owners. Your group can organize competitions and perhaps even hold sanctioned events under the auspices of the ADBA, UKC, or AKC; you may also conduct Canine Good Citizen tests or Temperament Tests.

Setting an Example

Some people look for things to complain about, and Pit Bulls are easy targets. Don't give them a chance. Don't let your Pit Bull roam the neighborhood. When you're in public, obey all leash laws. Have her heel or sit at your side when in crowds. Don't let your Pit Bull scare people, challenge other dogs, chase cats, bark uncontrollably, or act aggressive in any way. Always treat your Pit Bull with love and tenderness; believe it or not, some people assume you just have her for fighting and don't regard her as a true pet. Be a model dog owner. Pick up after her and dispose of the waste properly. Show the world that Pit Bulls and their owners are the good guys!

Spreading the Word

All your good deeds will be undone if uneducated or uncaring Pit Bull owners let their dogs run amuck. It's difficult to be a one-person crusade, but you may have to show these people the light in order to make the world a better place for Pit Bulls in general and your dog in particular. Perhaps you could write a dog care column for your local paper. Publicize cases of Pit Bull hero-ism and good deeds. You could volunteer at the local Humane Society and take special care to educate Pit Bull adopters. You could call up classifieds in the paper advertising Pit Bulls and make yourself available to these people or to their puppy buyers for advice. You could pass out Pit Bull information at dog events. Make yourself known in your community as a dedicated and responsible dog owner and lover. Make it difficult for community leaders to say anything bad about Pit Bull owners, because they will think of you first. Remember that your Pit Bull is the best ambassador for the breed you have, but you have to be his PR agent.

Supporting the Cause

Perhaps being in the public spotlight just isn't for you. You can still do your part by joining a national or international group that fights for dog rights. You can contribute your time, money, or expertise to fight dog fighting, animal abuse, breed-specific legislation, or unjust laws. Dog fighting gives the Pit Bull a bad public image; many other ways exist to test this breed's gameness that don't involve cruel practices or illegal venues. Animal abuse occurs every-where. It's just as bad if it happens to a mixed breed as to a Pit Bull. Become involved in stopping it not only because it's the humane thing to do, but because as a Pit Bull owner you have the chance to show that Pit Bull owners care about humane animal care. Fight unjust laws no matter where they are or if they affect you or not. Every unfair law that goes unchallenged in another community helps your community leaders to justify passing the same laws where you live. Help people in other communities fight their battles, and they will be there for you. The following organizations may be of help:

✔ The American Dog Owner's Association, 1654 Columbia Turnpike, Castleton, NY 12033; phone 518-477-8469; fax 518-477-4034; e-mail adoa@global2000.net; Web site www.adoa.org.

✔ The American Kennel Club Legislation Department, 5580 Centerview Drive, Raleigh, NC 27606-3390; phone 919-233-3720; fax 919-854-0168; e-mail doglaw@akc.org; Web site www.akc.org

✔ The United Kennel Club State Canine Awareness Network, 100 East Kilgore Road, Kalamazoo, MI 49002-5598; phone 616-343-9020; Web site www.ukcdogs.com/scan.html

✔ Dogwatch: www.dogwatch.net/index.html

Index

● ●

● A ●

ABCs of first aid, 181
accident prevention
  activity level and, 34
  housetraining, 68–69
Ace title, 118
activities of breed
  organizations for, 197–198
  overview of, 15, 33–34
activity level, 35–36, 53
acupuncture, 177
ad for puppy, 42–43
ADBA. *See* American Dog Breeders
  Association (ADBA)
adult dog, selecting, 49
Advantage (imidacloprid), 138
aggressiveness. *See also* biting
  attacks, 15, 39, 124
  castration and, 95
  communicating, 71–72, 92
  gameness compared to, 37
  sudden onset of, 166
  toward cats, 87–88
  toward family member, 93–95
  toward other dog in household, 88–90
  toward strange dog, 90–91
  toward stranger, 95–96
agility competition, 44, 121–122
airway, 181, 182
AKC. *See* American Kennel Club (AKC)
allergic itching, 141
allergic reaction, 187–188
alone training, 73–74
alternative medicine, 175–177
American Boarding Kennel Association, 83
American Dog Breeders Association
  (ADBA)
  American Pit Bull Terrier, 12
  contact information, 197
  recognition of AKC and UKC stock, 46

registration, 46, 48
standards, 19–23
weight pulling competition, 117–118, 119
American Dog Owner's Association
  (ADOA), 14, 205
American Herding Breed Association, 124
American Kennel Club (AKC)
  agility competition, 122
  Canine Good Citizen certificate, 202
  conformation shows, 30–31
  contact information, 197
  description of, 10
  Indefinite Listing Privilege, 47
  Legislation Department, 205
  obedience trials, 121
  registration, 46, 47–48
  standards, 25–27
  tracking trials, 123
  UKC shows compared to, 29–30
American Pit Bull Terrier (APBT)
  ADBA and, 12
  conformation shows, 28–30
  registration, 46
  standards, 19–23
  UKC and, 11
American Rescue Dog Association, 202
American Staffordshire Bull Terrier, 46
American Staffordshire Terrier (AmStaff)
  APBT compared to, 12
  conformation shows, 30–31
  registration, 47–48
  standards, 25–27
American Temperament Test Association,
  201
American Veterinary Chiropractic
  Association, 176
AmStaff. *See* American Staffordshire
  Terrier (AmStaff)
anal sacs, 162
anemia, 170
anesthesia, 192

angular process, 22
animal fighting, history of, 8
animal shelter, 45
anxiety, 70
APBT. *See* American Pit Bull Terrier (APBT)
APBT Rescue Network, 197
appearance, 22, 48. *See also* standards
arthritis, 173, 192
artificial respiration, 182
ascarids, 160
Association of American Feed Control
    Officials (AAFCO), 128
attacks
  Pit Bulls blamed for, 15
  Schutzhund training and, 124
  study on, 39
autoimmune problems, 159, 170–171

• *B* •

Babesia, 171
baby, introducing dog to, 75–77
baby gate, 54, 59
back, 24, 26
back end, 20–21
backyard breeder, 43
balconies, 54
balls for play, 59
barking, 98
bathing, 135–137
bed
  crate, 57–58
  need for, 56
  older dog, 192
  own, 57
  sleeping with owner, 57
behavior. *See also* aggressiveness; training
  barking, 98
  biting, 92–93, 95, 96
  changes in, 165–166
  chewing, 67–68
  digging, 98
  neutering and, 48, 89, 90
  in public, 203–204
  soiling in house, 69–70
  training bad by accident, 102
  when in pain, 150–151

Bennett, Chauncy, 11
biceps femoris, 21
bite, treating, 187
bite (occlusion), 148
biting
  distinguishing playful from aggressive,
    92–93
  fatal, 39
  fear and, 95, 96
biting pressure, 23
Bitter Apple, 142
bladder infection, 69, 169
bleeding, 186–187
bloat, 130, 187
Blood Chemistry Test, 153–154
blood parasites, 171
blood sport, 8
blood tests, 153–154
boarding at kennel, 83
body temperature, checking, 151–152
bone cancer, 172
bone injury, 173
bones
  as chewies, 62
  in food, 129
Bones and Raw Food diet, 130
books, recommended, 198–199
bowl for food and water, 62
breaking up fight, 89
breathing rate, checking, 152, 181, 183
breed characteristics, 17–18, 36–39, 90
breed-specific legislation, 39
breeder
  backyard type, 43
  dog fighting and, 41, 42, 43–44
  guarantee of, 49
  hobby type, 43–44
  radiograph, 175
  registration by, 45, 46–47
  temperament of dog, 48
  tips to avoid bad, 41–42
  vaccinations, 156
breeds, 7–10
brush, 65, 135, 192
brushing teeth, 65, 147–148
buckle collar, 62–63, 105
Bull and Terrier, 8, 12

bull-baiting, 8, 9
Bulldog (ADBA term), 19
Bulldog strain, 8–9, 12
Bullenbeisser, 8, 9
burns, 188
Buster Cube, 60

● *C* ●

cage anxiety, 70
calcium, 130
campground, staying in, 81
cancers, 172
canine scabies, 139–140
canned food, 128
Capillaria, 162
capillary refill time, 151, 183
car
  exiting, 109
  leaving dog in, 80
  riding in, 81
cardio-pulmonary resuscitation, 182
carpet, cleaning after accident, 68, 69
castration, aggression and, 95
cataracts, 146, 191
"Catch" command, 113
cats, 87–88
chain leash, 64
characteristics of breed, 17–18, 36–39, 90
chest, 21, 24, 26
chewies, 61–62
cheyletialla mites, 140
children
  attacks on, 39
  introducing dog to, 75–77
chiropractic medicine, 176
chocolate, 129, 183
choke collar, 63, 105–106
cholinesterase inhibitors, 138
circulation, checking, 181
citizenship, 202
cleaning ears, 144–145
click sound for training, 101
coat, 22, 24, 26, 131
coccidia, 163
cold tolerance, 56
collar, 62–64

color
  of dog, 24, 26
  of nose, 25
color vision, 71
colostrum, 156
"Come" command, 106–108
command
  "Come," 106–108
  "Down," 109, 111
  "Heel," 110, 111–112
  parts of, 101–102
  raised surface for training, 109
  "Sit," 108–109
  "Stay," 109–110
  for tricks, 113
  "Watch me," 106
commitment to dog, 33–35
communication
  aggressiveness vs. playfulness, 92
  behavior changes and, 165–166
  overview of, 70–71, 72
  pain, 150–151
competition
  agility, 44, 121–122
  conformation, 10, 12, 15, 27–31, 44
  herding, 124
  obedience, 44, 105, 119–121
  participating in, 203
  Schutzhund, 124
  tracking trials, 123
  weight pulling, 44, 63–64, 115–119
Complete Blood Count (CBC), 153–154
conditioning
  for agility competition, 122
  equipment for, 43
  for weight pulling, 117
conformation competition
  AKC, 12, 30–31
  description of, 10
  overview of, 15, 27–28
  selecting dog for, 44
  UKC, 28–30
consistency in training, 103
convulsions, 185
cord, electrical, 54
coronavirus vaccination, 158
coronoid process, 22

cost
  of puppy, 41, 44
  veterinarian bills, 34
coughing, 168–169
CPR, 182
crate
  alone training, 73–74
  attaching to car, 80, 81
  uses of, 57–58
Cushing's syndrome, 170

• *D* •

death of dog, 193–194
decks, 54
dehydration, 168
demodectic mange, 140
deodorant, 65
destruction
  activity level and, 35–36
  preventing, 91–92
  toys and, 61
diarrhea, 82, 166–167, 192
Dibo bred, 19
diet. *See also* food
  Bones and Raw Food, 130
  for obese dog, 132
  for older dog, 190
  overview of, 127–129
  protein and fat in, 131–132
digging, 98
Dipylidium caninum, 161–162
discharge from eye, 146
discoid lupus erythematosus, 171
discussion list, 44
distemper vaccination, 157
DNA samples, 47
Dog Fancy magazine, 44, 199
dog fighting
  ADBA and, 12
  AKC and, 10
  breeder and, 41, 42, 43–44
  characteristics for, 17–18
  history of, 8, 9
  legislation against, 14–15
  rules of, 11
dog/human relationship, 7

Dog USA magazine, 44
Dog World magazine, 44, 199
doggy door, 68, 69
doghouse, 56
dogmen, 14
dominance, establishing over dog, 94–95
dominant dog, behavior toward, 90
doors, 54, 109
"Down" command, 109, 111
dry food, 128
drying after bathing, 137
Dudley nose, 27

• *E* •

E. coli bacteria, 130
ear-fighter, 19
ear medication, 155
ear mites, 140, 145
ears, 25, 143–145
earthworms, 162
educating public, 204
electrical cords and outlets, 54
electrical shock, 188
elimination, 68–70
emergency
  ABCs of first aid, 181
  allergic reaction, 187–188
  artificial respiration, 182
  bleeding, 186–187
  bloat, 187
  burns, 188
  CPR, 182
  diagnosing, 179–180
  electrical shock, 188
  heat stroke, 185
  hypothermia, 186
  insect sting, 187–188
  limb fracture, 187
  poisoning, 183–185
  preparing for, 180–181
  seizures, 185
  snakebite, 188
end of life issues, 193–194
endocrine disorders, 170
English Bulldog, 9
erlichiosis, 171

escape, 35, 97
estrus, 48, 89, 165
euthanasia, 193–194
examining
  dog, 149–151
  eyes, 145–146
  gums, 151, 183
exercise. *See also* walking dog
  conditioning equipment, 43
  jogging, 79
  on leash, 77–78
  need for, 33–34
  off-leash, 77
  older dog, 190
  pen for, 59, 81
  swimming, 79–80, 190
exposure to new experiences, 73–74
eye medication, 155
eyes
  cataracts, 146, 191
  examining, 145–146
  standards, 22, 24, 25
  vision, 71, 191

• *F* •

fanging, 11, 19
fangs, 22
fat in diet, 131–132
fatal dog bite, 39
faults, 26–27
fear biting, 95, 96
fearfulness, 73, 96–97
female dog
  estrus, 48, 89, 165
  spaying, 89, 95
fenced-in yard, 35, 54–56, 97
fipronil (Frontline), 138
first aid
  ABCs of, 181
  allergic reaction, 187–188
  artificial respiration, 182
  bleeding, 186–187
  bloat, 187
  burns, 188
  class for, 180
  CPR, 182

  electrical shock, 188
  heat stroke, 185
  hypothermia, 186
  insect sting, 187–188
  limb fracture, 187
  poisoning, 183, 185
  seizures, 185
  snakebite, 188
flea allergy dermatitis, 141
fleas, 137–139
fleece toy, 60
flooding, 96
food
  allergy to, 141
  amount per month, 34
  to avoid, 129
  bowl for, 62
  freshness of, 128
  label on, 131–132
  older dog, 190
  overview of, 127
  picky eater, 133
  as reward, 100–101
  schedule for, 134
  self-feeding, 133–134
  toy for, 60
  types of, 128
  weight pulling training and, 117
foot injury, 173–174
force, using, 103
fracture of limb, 187
friend, visiting, 81
front end, 21
Frontline (fipronil), 138
full drop ears, 25

• *G* •

gameness or game dog, 8, 11, 37, 88, 115
Giardia, 163
gladiator, 8, 9
glaucoma, 145–146
gluteal muscle, 20–21
grooming supplies, 65, 135
group, organizing local, 203
guarantee from breeder, 49
guard duty, 34
gums, checking, 151, 183

• H •

hair loss, 142
half prick ears, 25
handmade toy, 60, 61
harness, 63–64, 116, 118
head, 21–22, 23, 25
head collar or halter, 63–64, 105
health check, weekly
  body temperature, 151–152
  gums, 151
  overview of, 149–151
  pulse, heartbeat, breathing rate, 152
health concerns. *See also* medicine;
    vaccinations; veterinarian
  bloat, 130, 187
  blood parasites, 171
  cancer, 172
  coughing, 168–169
  diarrhea, 166–167
  endocrine disorders, 170
  fleas, 137–139
  hip dysplasia, 42, 48–49, 174–175
  immunological problems, 170–171
  kidney problems, 131, 169
  lethargy, 165–166, 170
  lice, 140
  mange, 139–140
  obesity, 132
  odor, 137
  older dog, 191–193
  parasites, 163–164
  permission to treat, 83
  skin problems, 141–142
  ticks, 139
  underweight dog, 133
  urinary problems, 169
  vaccinations, 73, 156–159
  vomiting, 167–168
  worms, 159–162
heart disease and cough, 168–169
heartbeat, checking, 152
heartworms, 163–164
heat, female dog in, 48, 89, 165
heat stroke, 185
heat tolerance, 56, 79
"Heel" command, 110, 111–112

height to weight ratio, 20
hepatitis vaccination, 157
herbology, 176
herding, 124
hip, 20
hip dysplasia, 42, 48–49, 174–175
history of breed, 7–10
hobby breeder, 43–44
hock, 20
hog catching, 78
holistic medicine, 176
home remedies, 177
homeopathic medicine, 176
hookworms, 161
hooves as chewies, 62
hot spots, 142
house
  carpet, cleaning after accident, 68, 69
  multiple dogs in, 89
  preparing for puppy, 53–54
  preventing destruction of, 91–92
  soiling in, 69–70
house rules, 67–68
housetraining, 68–70
human, aggression toward. *See also* biting
  family member, 93–95
  stranger, 95–96
human/dog relationship, 7
hydration, checking for, 150, 183
hypothermia, 186
hypothyroidism, 170

• I •

identification tags, 84
imidacloprid (Advantage), 138
immunological problems, 170–171
impetigo, 142
inbred (UKC), 47
Indefinite Listing Privilege (AKC), 47
injury
  to bone and joint, 173–174
  lameness, 172–173
insect sting, 187–188
inside, living, 56
intelligence, 36, 37

International Weight Pull Association (IWPA)
  competition, 118–119
  contact information, 116, 197
Internet listserv, 44
introducing
  another dog, 89–90
  children, 75–77
invisible fencing, 55
irresponsible owner, 2, 39

• *J* •

jaw, 22, 23
jogging with dog, 79
joint injury, 173

• *K* •

kennel, boarding at, 83
kennel breeder, 43–44
kennel cough, 158, 168
kidney disease, 131, 169
knee injury, 173
Kong, 60

• *L* •

label on food, reading, 131–132
lameness
  bone and joint injury, 173–174
  hip dysplasia, 174–175
  overview of, 172–173
latch on crate, 58
laws
  breed-specific legislation, 39
  dog fighting, 14, 15
  organizations to help monitor, 198, 204–205
  unjust, 204
lead. *See* leash
leash. *See also* walking dog
  training and, 105
  types of, 64
  using, 77–78
legs, 26

leptospirosis vaccination, 158
lethargy, 165–166, 170
lice, 140
life expectancy, 189
lifestyle and commitment to dog, 33–35
limb fracture, 187
Limited Privilege Listing (UKC), 47
Limited Registration (AKC), 47
lippy, 22
liquid medicine, giving, 154
listserv, 44
Little Rascals, The, 13
loin, 21
lost dog, searching for, 83–84
lufenuron (Program), 138
lungworms, 162
Lupine harness, 64
Lyme disease, 159
lymphosarcoma, 172

• *M* •

magazines, 44, 199
male dog
  hormonal states, 165
  marking territory, 48, 69
  neutering and behavior problems, 48, 89, 90
mammary gland tumors, 172
mange, 139–140
marking territory, 48, 69
martingale collar, 63
Mastiff family of dogs, 8
match show, 28
media, 15
medicine
  allergic itching, 141
  alternative medicine, 175–177
  arthritis, 192
  diarrhea, 167
  for fleas, 138
  giving at home, 154–155
  home remedies, 177
  hot spots, 142
  mange, 140
  preventive medicine, 149
  supply chest, 155–156

metatarsal bones, 21
microchip identification, 84
mites, 139–140
Molossian, 8, 9
mosquitoes and heartworms, 163–164
motel, staying in, 81
multiple dogs in household, 89
musculature, 23
muzzle, 24, 25

• N •

nail care, 142–143
nail clippers, 65
name of dog and registration, 48
names of breed, 12
National American Pit Bull Terrier
    Association, 29, 47
National Animal Poison Control Center,
    185, 200
neck, 24, 26
nervousness, communicating, 70–71
neutering
    aggression and, 89, 90, 95
    behavior problems and, 48
    competition and, 47
newspaper ad for puppy, 42–43
night vision, 71
noise phobia, 97
nose, 24, 25
nose-fighter, 19
Novice exercises (UKC), 120
nursing dog, diet for, 131

• O •

obedience classes, 104–105
obedience competition
    breeder experience with, 44
    classes in, 120–121
    overview of, 119–120
    preparing for, 105
obese dog, 132
occlusion, 148
odor, 137, 192
off-leash, allowing dog to be, 77

older dog
    diet for, 131, 190
    exercise for, 190
    health of, 191–193
    signs of, 189
omnivorous, definition of, 127
onions, 129
Open exercises (UKC), 120
Orthopedic Foundation for Animals,
    42, 48–49, 174–175
osteoarthritis, 173
osteosarcoma, 172
Our Gang, 13
outlet, electrical, 54
outside. *See also* yard
    bathing, 137
    living, 56

• P •

packing to travel, 82
parasites, 163–164
parvovirus vaccination, 158
patent ductus arteriosus, 169
patience, need for, 70, 104
pen, 55–56, 59
Pennsylvania Hip Improvement Program
    (PennHIP), 42, 174, 175
people lover and people pleaser
    characteristics, 38, 90
performance competition, 10
Performance Pedigree (UKC), 47
personality of breed, 36–39, 48. *See also*
    temperament
pet sitter, 82–83
Petey, 13
pet, aggression toward other in household,
    87–90
phobias, 96–97
Physaloptera, 162
physique
    ADBA standards, 19–23
    AKC standards, 25–27
    overview of, 17–18
    UKC standards, 23–24
picky eater, 133

pig ears as chewies, 62
pill, giving, 154
plaque on teeth, 147
plastic crate, 58
play-bow position, 72, 92
"Play dead" command, 113
playfulness
  communicating, 71, 72, 92
  gameness and, 37
point of hip, 20
point of shoulder, 20
poisons, 54, 183–185
pole lure, 61
police dog, 203
pools, 54, 56
poop scoop, 65, 79
popularity of breed, 13–14
praise, 100
pregnant dog, diet for, 131
preparing
  for emergency, 180–181
  for puppy, 53–54
present, living in, 102
pressure, applying to stop bleeding,
    186–187
preventing
  destructive behavior, 91
  heartworms, 163–164
  shaking when wet, 136
preventive medicine, 149
prey drive, 87
privacy fence, 55
profile, 19–20
Program (lufenuron), 138
protein in diet, 131–132
publicity about breed, 204
pulse, checking, 152, 183
punishment
  for chewing, 67–68
  cruelty and, 103
  effectiveness of, 100
  living in present and, 102
puppy
  bone and joint injury, 173
  diet for, 131
  exposing to new experiences, 73–74

feeding, 134
holding bowels, expectations for, 68
jogging with, 79
kindergarten class for, 75
preparing home for, 53–54
requirements of, 49
shaking, 68
springpole, 61
teeth of, 148
training, 70, 106
tug toy, 59
vaccinations for, 156–157
vomiting, 168
walking, 78
worms and, 159–160
Purple Ribbon (UKC), 47
pyoderma, 142
pyotraumatic dermatitis, 142

• *R* •

rabies vaccination, 157
radiograph of hip dysplasia, 174
rawhide chewies, avoiding, 61–62
registration
  ADBA, 46, 48
  AKC, 47–48
  breeder and, 45, 46–47
  overview of, 45–46
  UKC, 46–47
reputation
  dog fighting and, 14–15
  improving, 201–205
  misconceptions about, 1, 2
  misconceptions about breed, 7
rescue group, 45, 197
resources, 198–199. *See also* Web pages
respiration, checking, 152, 183
retractable leash, 64, 78
Revolution (selamectin), 138
rewards
  for bad behavior, 102
  click sound, 101
  food, 100–101
  intermittent, 103
  praise, 100
rib cage, 21, 24, 26

rinsing after bathing, 136
roach back, 20
"Roll over" command, 113
rose ears, 25

• S •

salmonella, 130
schedule
  feeding, 134, 190
  vaccinations, 159
Schutzhund training, 123–124
scolding, 108
scooting behavior, 162
"scratch," 11
Search and Rescue dog, 202
searching for lost dog, 83–84
seatbelt, 81
seizures, 185
selamectin (Revolution), 138
selecting dog
  from ad, 42–43
  adult vs. puppy, 49
  from animal shelter, 45
  appearance, 48
  from breeder, 41–42
  health issues, 48–49
  from rescue group, 45
  temperament, 48
selecting veterinarian, 152–153
self-feeding, 134
semi-moist food, 128
sense of humor, 33–34, 37
sensitivity, 38
separation anxiety, 70, 73, 91–92
"Shake hands" command, 113
shaking puppy, 68
shaking when wet, preventing, 136
shampoo, 65, 136
shape, 19–20
shelter, 35
shoe, using as toy, 61
shoulders, 21, 24, 26
show pose, 30
shyness, 96–97
single register
  ADBA, 46
  UKC, 47

"Sit" command, 108–109
size
  of dog, 9–10, 26
  of head, 21–22
skin, 22, 192
skin problems, 141–142
skunk, removing odor of, 137
sleeping, bed for, 56–58
slip collar, 63, 105–106
snakebite, 188
sniffer dog, 203
socialization, 73–74, 75, 201–202
soiling, 68–70
spaying, 89, 95, 172
"Speak" command, 113
specialist veterinarian, 153
Spirocerca lupi, 162
springpole, 61
squeak toy, 59
Staffordshire Bull Terrier, 76
Staffordshire Terrier, 12
stairways, 54
standards
  ADBA, 19–23
  AKC, 25–27
  UKC, 23–24
staring at dog, 76, 77, 110
"Stay" command, 109–110
stick, playing with, 60
stifle, 20
stoicism, 38, 150
stop, 22
strains, 7–10
stress
  bloat and, 130
  diet and, 131
Stubby, 13
submission, communicating, 70, 71
submissive urination, 69
supplies
  grooming, 65, 135
  medicine chest, 155–156
  travel, 82
suspicion, 73
swimming, 79–80, 190
systemic lupus erythematosus, 171

• T •

tail, 22, 24, 26, 99–100
tapeworms, 161–162
tartar on teeth, 147
taste receptors, 133
tattoo, 84
teeth, 22, 147–148
temperament
 American Temperament Test Association, 201
 fearfulness, 73, 96–97
 overview of, 36–39
 puppy, selecting, 48
 sense of humor, 33–34, 37
 separation anxiety, 70, 73, 91–92
 shyness, 96–97
 stoicism, 38, 150
temperature, checking, 151–152, 183
terminal illness, 193
testing for heartworms, 164
therapeutic shampoo, 136
therapy dog, 202
thighbone, 20
threadworms, 162
thunder, fear of, 97
tick fever, 171
ticks, 139, 171
toilet, drinking from, 134
tooth brushing, 65
total hip replacement, 175
toxocara canis, 160
toys, 59–61
traces (weight pulling), 118
tracheobronchitis, 158, 168
tracking trials, 123
training. *See also* command
 bad behavior by accident, 102
 for bath, 135–136
 to be alone, 73–74
 click sound and, 101
 command, parts of, 101–102
 conditions for optimum, 103–104
 consistency, importance of, 103
 equipment for, 105–106
 force, using, 103

 fun and, 99–100
 importance of, 99
 introducing children, 75–77
 length of session
 for nail trimming, 142–143
 need for, 34
 new experiences, 73
 obedience classes, 104–105
 patience, need for, 70, 104
 punishment and, 102, 103
 puppy kindergarten, 75
 rewards for, 100–101
 temper during time of, 70, 104
 ten commandments of, 102–104
 tricks, 113
 for weight pulling, 116–117
travel
 crate for, 58
 with dog, 80–82
 older dog, 191
 pet sitter or kennel during, 82–83
trimming nails, 142–143
triple pelvic osteotomy, 175
truck, riding in back of, 81
tug toy, 59
"turn," 11

• U •

underweight dog, 133
United Kennel Club (UKC)
 agility competition, 122
 AKC shows compared to, 29–30
 conformation shows, 28–30
 contact information, 197
 founding of, 11
 Limited Privilege Listing, 47
 obedience titles, 120–121
 registration, 46–47, 48
 standards, 23–24
 State Canine Awareness Network, 205
 Temporary Listing, 29
untrustworthy dog, 89
urinary problems, 169
Utility exercises (UKC), 121

• V •

vaccinations
   coronavirus, 158
   distemper, 157
   hepatitis, 157
   leptospirosis, 158
   Lyme disease, 159
   for older dog, 192
   overview of, 156
   parvovirus, 158
   for puppy, 156–157
   rabies, 157
   schedule for, 159
   tracheobronchitis, 158, 168
veterinarian
   acupuncture, 177
   alternative medicine, 175
   cost of, 34
   chiropractic medicine, 176
   euthanasia, 193–194
   leaving permission to treat with, 83
   older dog and, 192
   selecting, 152–153
vision, 71
vision loss, 191
vital statistics, 183
vomiting
   causes of, 167–168, 192
   inducing, 184–185

• W •

wagging tail, 99–100
walking dog
   collar, 62–64
   "Come" command, 108
   distance, 78
   "Heel" command, 110, 111–112
   leash, 64
   poop scoop, 65
"Watch me" command, 106
water
   bowl for, 62
   in diet, 134
weather, 56

Web pages
   activity organizations, 197–198
   all-breed organizations, 197
   dog organizations, 199–200
   kennel breeders, 43
   legislation-monitoring organizations, 198
   National Animal Poison Control Center, 200
   Pit Bull-only organizations, 197
weight pulling competition
   ADBA, 117–118, 119
   harness and, 63–64, 118
   IWPA, 118–119
   overview of, 115
   selecting dog for, 44
   training for, 116–117
whipworms, 161
window, sticking head out of, 81
wire crate, 58
Working Dog title, 119
World War I, 13
worms
   ascarids, 160
   hookworms, 161
   lungworms, 162
   overview of, 159–160
   tapeworms, 161–162
   threadworms, 162
   whipworms, 161
wound, bleeding from, 186–187

• X •

X-pen, 59, 81

• Y •

yard
   digging in, 98
   escape-proofing, 97
   fence, 35, 54–56
   pathways in, 191–192

• Z •

zygomatic arch, 22

FOR

DUMMIES®

The easy way to get more done and have more fun

PERSONAL FINANCE

Personal Finance FOR DUMMIES

0-7645-5231-7

Investing FOR DUMMIES

0-7645-2431-3

Home Buying FOR DUMMIES

0-7645-5331-3

Also available:

Estate Planning For Dummies
(0-7645-5501-4)

401(k)s For Dummies
(0-7645-5468-9)

Frugal Living For Dummies
(0-7645-5403-4)

Microsoft Money "X" For Dummies
(0-7645-1689-2)

Mutual Funds For Dummies
(0-7645-5329-1)

Personal Bankruptcy For Dummies
(0-7645-5498-0)

Quicken "X" For Dummies
(0-7645-1666-3)

Stock Investing For Dummies
(0-7645-5411-5)

Taxes For Dummies 2003
(0-7645-5475-1)

BUSINESS & CAREERS

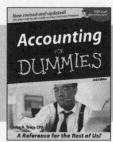

Accounting FOR DUMMIES

0-7645-5314-3

Grant Writing FOR DUMMIES

0-7645-5307-0

Resumes FOR DUMMIES

0-7645-5471-9

Also available:

Business Plans Kit For Dummies
(0-7645-5365-8)

Consulting For Dummies
(0-7645-5034-9)

Cool Careers For Dummies
(0-7645-5345-3)

Human Resources Kit For Dummies
(0-7645-5131-0)

Managing For Dummies
(1-5688-4858-7)

QuickBooks All-in-One Desk Reference For Dummies
(0-7645-1963-8)

Selling For Dummies
(0-7645-5363-1)

Small Business Kit For Dummies
(0-7645-5093-4)

Starting an eBay Business For Dummies
(0-7645-1547-0)

HEALTH, SPORTS & FITNESS

Fitness FOR DUMMIES

0-7645-5167-1

Golf FOR DUMMIES

0-7645-5146-9

Diabetes FOR DUMMIES

0-7645-5154-X

Also available:

Controlling Cholesterol For Dummies
(0-7645-5440-9)

Dieting For Dummies
(0-7645-5126-4)

High Blood Pressure For Dummies
(0-7645-5424-7)

Martial Arts For Dummies
(0-7645-5358-5)

Menopause For Dummies
(0-7645-5458-1)

Nutrition For Dummies
(0-7645-5180-9)

Power Yoga For Dummies
(0-7645-5342-9)

Thyroid For Dummies
(0-7645-5385-2)

Weight Training For Dummies
(0-7645-5168-X)

Yoga For Dummies
(0-7645-5117-5)

Available wherever books are sold.
Go to www.dummies.com or call 1-877-762-2974 to order direct.

FOR DUMMIES®

A world of resources to help you grow

HOME, GARDEN & HOBBIES

Feng Shui
0-7645-5295-3

Gardening
0-7645-5130-2

Guitar
0-7645-5106-X

Also available:

Auto Repair For Dummies
(0-7645-5089-6)

Chess For Dummies
(0-7645-5003-9)

Home Maintenance For Dummies
(0-7645-5215-5)

Organizing For Dummies
(0-7645-5300-3)

Piano For Dummies
(0-7645-5105-1)

Poker For Dummies
(0-7645-5232-5)

Quilting For Dummies
(0-7645-5118-3)

Rock Guitar For Dummies
(0-7645-5356-9)

Roses For Dummies
(0-7645-5202-3)

Sewing For Dummies
(0-7645-5137-X)

FOOD & WINE

Cooking
0-7645-5250-3

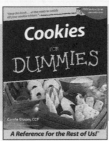
Cookies
0-7645-5390-9

Wine
0-7645-5114-0

Also available:

Bartending For Dummies
(0-7645-5051-9)

Chinese Cooking For Dummies
(0-7645-5247-3)

Christmas Cooking For Dummies
(0-7645-5407-7)

Diabetes Cookbook For Dummies
(0-7645-5230-9)

Grilling For Dummies
(0-7645-5076-4)

Low-Fat Cooking For Dummies
(0-7645-5035-7)

Slow Cookers For Dummies
(0-7645-5240-6)

TRAVEL

Italy
0-7645-5453-0

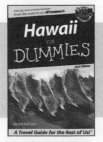
Hawaii
0-7645-5438-7

Las Vegas
0-7645-5448-4

Also available:

America's National Parks For Dummies
(0-7645-6204-5)

Caribbean For Dummies
(0-7645-5445-X)

Cruise Vacations For Dummies 2003
(0-7645-5459-X)

Europe For Dummies
(0-7645-5456-5)

Ireland For Dummies
(0-7645-6199-5)

France For Dummies
(0-7645-6292-4)

London For Dummies
(0-7645-5416-6)

Mexico's Beach Resorts For Dummies
(0-7645-6262-2)

Paris For Dummies
(0-7645-5494-8)

RV Vacations For Dummies
(0-7645-5443-3)

Walt Disney World & Orlando For Dummies
(0-7645-5444-1)

Available wherever books are sold. Go to www.dummies.com or call 1-877-762-2974 to order direct.

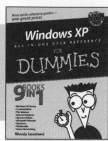

FOR DUMMIES®

Helping you expand your horizons and realize your potential

INTERNET

0-7645-0894-6

0-7645-1659-0

0-7645-1642-6

Also available:

America Online 7.0 For Dummies
(0-7645-1624-8)

Genealogy Online For Dummies
(0-7645-0807-5)

The Internet All-in-One Desk Reference For Dummies
(0-7645-1659-0)

Internet Explorer 6 For Dummies
(0-7645-1344-3)

The Internet For Dummies Quick Reference
(0-7645-1645-0)

Internet Privacy For Dummies
(0-7645-0846-6)

Researching Online For Dummies
(0-7645-0546-7)

Starting an Online Business For Dummies
(0-7645-1655-8)

DIGITAL MEDIA

0-7645-1664-7

0-7645-1675-2

0-7645-0806-7

Also available:

CD and DVD Recording For Dummies
(0-7645-1627-2)

Digital Photography All-in-One Desk Reference For Dummies
(0-7645-1800-3)

Digital Photography For Dummies Quick Reference
(0-7645-0750-8)

Home Recording for Musicians For Dummies
(0-7645-1634-5)

MP3 For Dummies
(0-7645-0858-X)

Paint Shop Pro "X" For Dummies
(0-7645-2440-2)

Photo Retouching & Restoration For Dummies
(0-7645-1662-0)

Scanners For Dummies
(0-7645-0783-4)

GRAPHICS

0-7645-0817-2

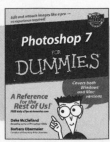

0-7645-1651-5

0-7645-0895-4

Also available:

Adobe Acrobat 5 PDF For Dummies
(0-7645-1652-3)

Fireworks 4 For Dummies
(0-7645-0804-0)

Illustrator 10 For Dummies
(0-7645-3636-2)

QuarkXPress 5 For Dummies
(0-7645-0643-9)

Visio 2000 For Dummies
(0-7645-0635-8)

FOR DUMMIES®

The advice and explanations you need to succeed

SELF-HELP, SPIRITUALITY & RELIGION

Sex FOR DUMMIES

0-7645-5302-X

Parenting FOR DUMMIES

0-7645-5418-2

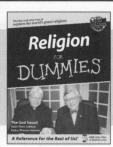

Religion FOR DUMMIES

0-7645-5264-3

Also available:

The Bible For Dummies
(0-7645-5296-1)

Buddhism For Dummies
(0-7645-5359-3)

Christian Prayer For Dummies
(0-7645-5500-6)

Dating For Dummies
(0-7645-5072-1)

Judaism For Dummies
(0-7645-5299-6)

Potty Training For Dummies
(0-7645-5417-4)

Pregnancy For Dummies
(0-7645-5074-8)

Rekindling Romance For Dummies
(0-7645-5303-8)

Spirituality For Dummies
(0-7645-5298-8)

Weddings For Dummies
(0-7645-5055-1)

PETS

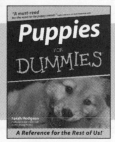

Puppies FOR DUMMIES

0-7645-5255-4

Dog Training FOR DUMMIES

0-7645-5286-4

Cats FOR DUMMIES

0-7645-5275-9

Also available:

Labrador Retrievers For Dummies
(0-7645-5281-3)

Aquariums For Dummies
(0-7645-5156-6)

Birds For Dummies
(0-7645-5139-6)

Dogs For Dummies
(0-7645-5274-0)

Ferrets For Dummies
(0-7645-5259-7)

German Shepherds For Dummies
(0-7645-5280-5)

Golden Retrievers For Dummies
(0-7645-5267-8)

Horses For Dummies
(0-7645-5138-8)

Jack Russell Terriers For Dummies
(0-7645-5268-6)

Puppies Raising & Training Diary For Dummies
(0-7645-0876-8)

EDUCATION & TEST PREPARATION

Spanish FOR DUMMIES

0-7645-5194-9

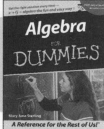

Algebra FOR DUMMIES

0-7645-5325-9

The ACT FOR DUMMIES

0-7645-5210-4

Also available:

Chemistry For Dummies
(0-7645-5430-1)

English Grammar For Dummies
(0-7645-5322-4)

French For Dummies
(0-7645-5193-0)

The GMAT For Dummies
(0-7645-5251-1)

Inglés Para Dummies
(0-7645-5427-1)

Italian For Dummies
(0-7645-5196-5)

Research Papers For Dummies
(0-7645-5426-3)

The SAT I For Dummies
(0-7645-5472-7)

U.S. History For Dummies
(0-7645-5249-X)

World History For Dummies
(0-7645-5242-2)

Available wherever books are sold. Go to www.dummies.com or call 1-877-762-2974 to order direct.